An Historical Guide
To
ARMS&ARMOR

An Historical Guide
To
Arms & Armor

STEPHEN BULL

EDITED BY
TONY NORTH

Facts On File
New York • Oxford

This edition published 1991 by Facts on File, Inc,
of 460 Park Avenue, South, New York, NY 10016, USA.

First published 1991 by Studio Editions Ltd.
Princess House, 50 Eastcastle Street,
London W1N 7AP, England.

Library of Congress Cataloging-in-Publication data is available
on request from Facts on File.

Facts on File books are available at special discounts when purchased
in bulk quantities for businesses, associations, institutions or sales
promotions. Please call our Special Sales Department in New York
at 212/683-2244 (dial 800/322-8755 except in NY, AK or HI).

Designed by T.K. Designs Ltd., Farnborough, Hants, UK.

ISBN 0-8160-2620-3

Printed and bound in Hong Kong.

8 7 6 9 4 3 2 1

CONTENTS

FOREWORD

From the earliest times, arms and armour have had a social significance beyond the needs of defence and offence. Prestige, wealth and power were all reflected in the armour that the warrior wore, and in the weapons that he carried. It is no coincidence that some of the earliest forms of trade-goods were weapons. The distinctive grey polished axes from a remote peak in the Langdale valley were as early as 3000 BC traded throughout Europe and are found in far-away graves.

In the Louvre there is a late pre-dynastic Egyptian flint knife from Gebal el-Araq dating from 3000 BC. Its fine, carefully shaped blade is set in an ivory handle carved with scenes of warriors and fighting vessels. Such a delicate handle and fine blade were never intended for hard use but were made as an item of luxury, suitable for a wealthy ruler. The Egyptian predynastic period also produced fine decorative mace-heads carved from a variety of stones like porphyry. These too were never intended for use but were used as symbols of command and rank; their descendants are the mace held by officers and the marshal's baton carried by commanders in our own day.

Precious metals such as gold and silver were also used in decorative weapons. Very luxurious weapons from the royal cemetery at Ur, dating from 2500 BC, have both the blade and the hilt made of gold, and axes from 1400 BC have blades pierced in a variety of openwork designs which would render them virtually useless in combat.

Armour was well-known to the Egyptians by 1500 BC. A wall-painting in a tomb dating from the reign of Amenhotep II (1436–1411 BC) clearly shows a defensive garment formed of overlapping bronze scales. These were sewn to a cloth backing. Resembling a long shirt with short sleeves and an opening for the neck, the resulting garment would have provided a good defence against missile weapons. Its portrayal on the wall-painting also shows what appear to be gilding and a series of narrow, coloured borders at the edges. Bronze scales from similar armours have survived, including a group from the Flinders Petrie collection in the University of London which appear to be among the earliest datable examples yet discovered. These scales are large, so these defensive coats must have been extremely heavy and can have been worn only for a comparatively short time.

Important sources for the arms and armour of the Assyrian world are the panels used to decorate the walls of palaces at Nimrud and Nineveh, dating from about 900–600 BC. Made from a soft gypsum, which could be easily worked, these panels show battle-scenes in the greatest detail, including particulars of horse-harness, costume and all manner of arms – even siege-engines and battering-rams.

The importance of archery is clear from these panels – many scenes show the short curved bow being used, often from a chariot. Lances have broad blades and are capable of being wielded in one hand. Swords are shown as long and straight, with a vestigial guard, hung from a baldric over the shoulder. An interesting decorative feature is the scabbard terminal, which is often in the form of animal heads. Some of the warriors in chariots also are shown with what appear to be saddle-axes, that is, small hatchets fitted into the side of quivers.

Defensive arms shown include round shields and a large shield with a rounded top, curved to fit the body. Their appearance suggests that they were made of some form of wickerwork, and they are usually shown being carried by

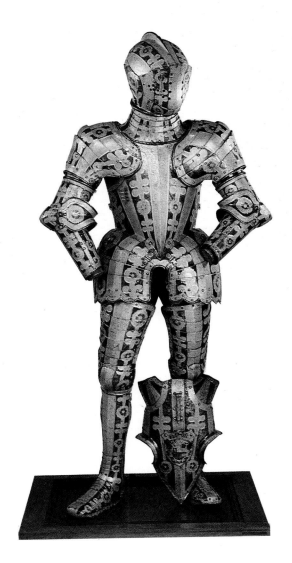

Detail (left) showing decoration on a breastplate for a youth; Italian (Milan), c.1585. (The Victoria and Albert Museum, London.)

Armour ordered by Henry, Prince of Wales for the Duke of Brunswick; English (Greenwich), c.1613. (Christie's, London.)

spearmen. Some of the figures are wearing what is clearly lamellar armour – small, rectangular scales arranged in parallel rows – a form of armour which was to last in the East until well into the sixteenth century AD.

These low-relief sculptures are of vital importance as a record of the military equipment used by Assyria and its various adversaries. Some bronze helmets, shields and arms have been excavated from military and civil sites, but so much of the more fragile equipment has been lost that these sculptures are virtually the only source for what an Assyrian warrior looked like during the period under discussion.

There is a much better survival record of actual weapons and defensive arms from the world of the Mycenaeans and the Greeks. Most students of arms and armour are familiar with the weapons found in the shaft graves of Mycenae. Dating from about 1600 BC, the best-known are a series of bronze daggers with short, tapering, double-edged blades whose raised central sections are finely decorated with a series of gold spirals. These are clearly objects of luxury. One outstanding example has a lively depiction of a lion-hunt in gold and silver, against a ground of niello – a black sulphide composition. In many cases only the blade remains, but one dagger has survived with most of its handle intact and this is gold-plated with a raised design of lilies. A similar design appears on the central section of the blade, worked in the alloy of gold and silver known as 'electrum'. The handles were attached to the blades by a series of plated rivets – a

Armet, Austrian, c.1510; perhaps by Konrad Seusenhafer. (The Victoria and Albert Museum, London.)

method of attachment which is also found at a later date in northern Europe.

Longer double-edged swords have also been found in Mycenaean shaft graves. Of slightly later date than the daggers mentioned above, the bronze blades have a cast tang to which a bone or ivory handle could be attached, and examples survive in which the handle is covered with sheets of precious metal stamped with scroll designs.

By 700 BC, distinctive types of helmet such as the early 'Corinthian' and the *Kegelhelm* can be seen on Greek bronzes and pottery. The familiar 'Corinthian' helm has the distinctive T-shaped opening at the front with a long nasal bar, whereas the *Kegelhelm* is conical with ear flaps. Circular shields of bronze decorated with friezes showing animals survive from the seventh century BC, and bronze leg-defences are known from as early as 1200 BC, though the classic greave seems to have reached its apogee in the sixth century, when its shape exactly follows the contours and musculature of the leg. Finds from Dendra, which include a bronze corslet dating from the Bronze Age (late 15th century BC), with attached neck and shoulder-guards, demonstrate that metal body armour was an early development. The muscle cuirass, in which the breastplate and back-plate conform roughly to the contours and musculature of the body, was also known by the end of the eighth century BC, as is demonstrated by finds from Argos which included a bell-shaped corslet of bronze which has the characteristic torso shape and was attached to a back-plate over the shoulders and the sides. Some fine early corslets of similar form are known from Crete, and a fine decorated back-plate from Olympia has raised shoulder-blades and an incised design depicting Zeus greeting Apollo, with other figures from Greek mythology. It is from such early examples of defensive arms that the classic Greek armour depicted so accurately on vases and other vessels derives.

Arms and armour taken as spoil in battle were customarily dedicated to temples, and a large quantity of Greek military equipment – sometimes inscribed with details of the dedication by a famous leader such as Militades – has come down to us for this reason. Many of the major shrines such as Olympia have yielded a rich harvest for the arms and armour student. Excavators have also produced many interesting finds, especially from those sites whose history is recorded in contemporary texts. A fine helmet of 'Corinthian' type, for example, was found in the 1950s in Paphos, Cyprus, on

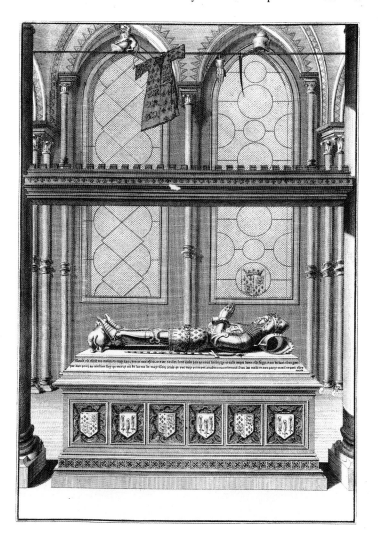

The tomb of Edward the Black Prince (died 1376) at Canterbury Cathedral. Above the tomb are the Prince's helmet, gauntlets, tabard and sword scabbard. (The Royal Armouries, London.)

the site of the Persian seige that took place in 498 BC, described by Herodotus.

The swords carried by the Greek hoplites included a short, inward-curving, sickle-shaped type known as a *kopis* – often depicted on Greek vases – and a broad-bladed, short thrusting weapon with a simple cross hilt.

Greek influence on the Italian mainland at an early date is shown in the arms and armour of the Etruscans. Distinctive helmets survive – curious circular discs of embossed bronze which seem to have been attached to a leather or fabric backing. Many come from the large tombs excavated in the major cities of Etruria such as Praeneste.

The Romans adopted the arms and armour of their adversaries and improved on them. A curious survival of antique fashions in defensive arms is to be found in the weapons and armour worn by gladiators in the arena, which even in the late imperial period had elements of the traditions of Rome's Samnite and Etruscan enemies.

As bronze is a comparatively easy metal to work, arms and armour made from bronze were easily decorated. Armourers used a variety of techniques to decorate their products. Many helmets were embossed with scenes from classical legends. Small cast ornaments were applied to the surface. In some of the magnificent late-Roman parade helmets, cameos and precious stones were set into the surface. Details of ownership by a particular legion or officer were indicated by punched work. The surface could also be engraved. Many Roman helmets show signs of having been given a thin coating of tin, and the more luxurious were often gilded or silvered.

The same luxurious treatment was also applied to weapons. Roman swords in good condition are rare: only a very few of the fine swords shown on architecture and statues have survived – those that have come mostly from Roman military sites. A fine first-century *gladius hispaniensis* found at Rheingönheim, in Germany, has a large hilt plated with silver. Another, from Mainz, survives with most of its scabbard, which is of wood covered with turned bronze, and occasionally swords with grips of turned ivory are encountered. Some fine fourth-century cavalry swords are known from a bog in Denmark, one of which has a distinctive waisted grip of bronze.

Contemporary accounts and a few fragments indicate that Roman helmets and body armour were, in exceptional circumstances, made in silver. Some impression of their appearance can be gained by looking at imperial statues. These often show a considerable use of relief decoration, as does contemporary Roman silver, and it seems likely that some armours were in fact made by Roman silversmiths.

General wear and tear, changes in fashion and especially the reworking of armour and weapons have left us very little from the vast quantity of arms and armour carried by the armies of Byzantium. Byzantine armourers turned to the East for their prototypes for armour design – flexible but complicated constructions of mail, scale and lamellar armour were preferred to the bronze cuirass of imperial Rome. The main sources of information are manuscripts, ivories and depictions of warrior saints. Military commentators such as Emperor Leo VI – 'the Wise' – mention garments of textile, padded and quilted cotton or felt. Shields were of various forms, a large oval shield being used by infantry and the smaller *scutum* being used in conjunction

Drawing of the armour of Sir John Smythe from the Jacobe Album, c.1590. (The Victoria and Albert Museum, London.)

with the spear and sword. The standard sword carried by Byzantine forces was the *spathion* – a straight, double-edged weapon about 36 inches in length, with a cruciform guard. A variety of lances and javelins were carried, ranging from the twelve-foot *contarion* to a short dart weighted with lead known as *martiobarbulus*. Helmets, especially in the later period, were conical and had a distinctive neck defence consisting of a small flap.

Mention should be made of the Varangian Guard of the Emperors of Byzantium. Drawn principally from Scandinavian lands, they had distinctive arms and dress. The very few illustrations in manuscripts show them as bearded and carrying long, broad, single-blade axes, with either round or kite-shaped shields. Their armour usually consisted of mail and a conical helmet, and they must have looked not dissimilar to the armoured figures in the Bayeux Tapestry.

Perhaps the best-known of Byzantine weapons was Greek fire. This was composed of saltpetre with sulphur, tar and other chemicals. It could be fired from a siphon held in the hand, and was also used on ships. It was basically a liquid fire, which was very difficult to extinguish. Its success in naval engagements gave it a fearful reputation, and the recipe for the liquid was kept strictly secret. It was said to have been invented in the seventh century by Kallinikos of Heliopolis.

The arms and armour of the Anglo-Saxon period are no better represented than by the famous ship-burial at Sutton Hoo in East Anglia. Some of the finds were clearly heir-

Gold-mounted swords, c.2500 BC. (Baghdad Museum, Iraq.)

looms from the late Roman period, such as the gold shoulder-clasps set with garnets, but the helmet with face-mask, the shield with its stylized birds and the remains of a once magnificent sword are characteristic of Anglo-Saxon armourers' work at its best. The find also included a mail-shirt and various spears of a typical Anglo-Saxon type.

A type of short knife always associated with the Anglo-Saxons is the 'sceax'. Single-edged with a sharply tapering blade, sceaxs were items of luxury and often carry details of ownership and manufacture inlaid in silver, gold and niello on the back of the blade. Anglo-Saxon craftsmen were particularly skilful at producing finely worked mounts for weapons: hilts often incorporate a pommel with wrythen dragons in silver, or are overlaid in silver and gold in the most delicate ornament. Anglo-Saxon skill in the manufacture of helmets is demonstrated by the recently restored helmet from Coppergate in York.

The characteristic weapons of the Vikings were the sword and the axe. A large number of Viking swords have been discovered, some preserved in outstanding condition. The broad, straight, double-edged blades were designed for cutting rather than thrusting and often carry inscriptions inlaid along the central section. A survey of contemporary sagas show how these weapons were respected, being given names such as 'Fotbitr' – leg-biter – or 'Gramr' – fierce. Individual weapons were often buried with their owners, then subsequently dug up and reused. Thus a blade might well be several hundred years old when in use.

The large, single-edged, long shafted axes favoured by the Vikings and Scandinavian peoples are shown still in use in the Bayeux Tapestry of about 1070, and must have been formidable weapons. The Tapestry is an important source for the arms and armour of a period from which few actual specimens survive. Shirts of mail coming down to the knee, conical helmets with nasal bars, and various forms of sword and spear are all shown. Many of the mounted figures carry large kite-shaped shields. In a few instances the accuracy of the weapons and armour shown on the Tapestry can be confirmed by actual specimens – the famous helmet from Prague Cathedral, which is said to have belonged to St Wenceslaus, who died in 929, is of typical 'Norman' form with a conical shape and a prominent nasal bar.

Armed figures shown in sculpture from the late twelfth and early thirteenth century are often shown wearing a mail coif covering the head. However, the defence for the head was improved at this period with the development of a special flat-topped helmet which, by the 1230s, covered the entire head and was worn over a padded cap. The helmet itself was also lined with some form of padding. Manuscripts such as the Maciejowski Bible of about 1250 present an accurate picture of the arms and equipment of an armed warrior of the period. Knights are shown hurriedly putting on mail over padded undergarments; helmets are shown complete with their rivets and pierced holes to facilitate breathing; and lances, axes and swords are clearly shown.

In addition to mail formed of interlocking rings, scale armour was also used, and towards the end of the thirteenth century a reinforced garment perhaps composed of leather reinforced with iron plates was introduced. These were the origins of the fully developed armoured knight of the following century. Plates were added at vulnerable points on the arms, body and legs, and effigies and monuments indicate that by about 1325 it was customary for the legs, arms and upper parts of the body to be covered with plates. By the end of the century the fully armoured knight had become common, every part of his body was covered in carefully shaped plates. High-quality armourers' work was additionally adorned with gilt copper or latten (copper–zinc alloy) mounts, sometimes engraved with inscriptions.

The fifteenth century really saw the zenith of the armourer's art, in which the entire body was encased in steel, carefully shaped to fit the body. In Italy, Milan especially became a centre of armour production, but excellent work was also produced by the armourers of Augsburg and Nuremberg.

The images of armoured figures are found on sculpture and in manuscripts, but there are also some remarkable survivals of actual armours, especially after the second half of the fifteenth century. Perhaps the most famous family armoury is that of the Trapp family in Schloss Churburg in the southern Tyrol. Armours associated with the Von Matsch family dating from as early as the late fourteenth century have been preserved in outstanding condition. The finest works of the armourers of Milan and of Innsbruck dating from the second half of the fifteenth century can be seen there.

The Gothic style was particularly suited to the craft of the armourer. Fluting, pierced Gothic borders and attenuated shapes can all be found on the best armours of the period. For many specialists, the armour made for Archduke Maximilian I by Lorenz Helmschmied of Augsburg in 1480,

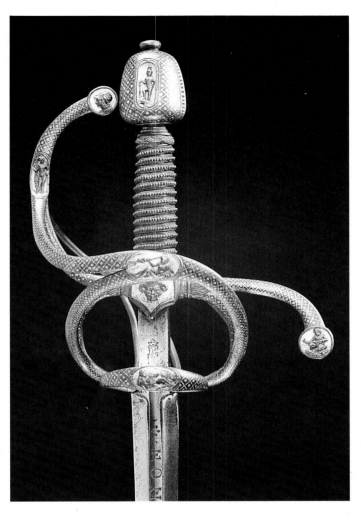

Rapier, the chiselled hilt inlaid with gold; Italian, c.1580. (The Victoria and Albert Museum, London.)

and weapons were invented for these events. Blunt lances, reinforced breastplates and special helmets were all produced – often decorated with the full panoply of heraldry. By the end of the fifteenth century, the rules had become very complicated and formalized. Jousts with sharp lances obviously required heavily reinforced armours. In Vienna is preserved a fine series of these reinforced armours with extra pieces of plate which could be bolted on to the breastplates, large plates covering the vulnerable parts of the body and special supports for the heavy lance.

Gunpowder was probably first brought to Europe from China in the first half of the thirteenth century. Guns first begin to be mentioned in documents in about 1326. An early illustration, from an English manuscript of about the same time, shows a vase-shaped cannon supported on a trestle table and firing an arrow. Handguns start to appear by the middle of the fourteenth century and by the end of the century were reasonably common. Surviving examples have the barrels fitted to primitive wooden stocks and are often fitted with hooks underneath, which could be fastened to a support to absorb recoil. Improvements in the methods of igniting the charge were made throughout the fifteenth century; the matchlock, in which a sprung lever conveys the glowing match into the pan, is first depicted in a manuscript of 1411. By the end of the fifteenth century guns had taken on something of their modern appearance, with stepped stocks and long barrels.

represents the high point of the armourer's art. The surface of the armour is treated with a series of rippling flutes, gilt borders are applied to the edges, and the breastplate tapers sharply in at the waist. The whole effect is one of lightness and strength.

Churches were among the most important havens for arms and armour. From classical times it was customary to dedicate spoils taken in war and personal arms to the appropriate shrine. This custom, in altered form, survived throughout the Middle Ages and is also reflected in our own times with the dedication of military banners in churches. Fine early pieces have been found in many European churches, and in some instances are still preserved there. In English churches, at the funeral of a prominent knight it was customary for the insignia of rank to be carried in the funeral procession and then deposited over the tomb of the deceased. These insignia usually consisted of a helm (complete with crest), a shield, a banner, gauntlets, a sword, a pair of spurs and an heraldic tabard. In Canterbury cathedral are preserved some of the funeral achievements, as they are known, of Edward the Black Prince, who died in 1376. These include a fine fourteenth-century helmet and a pair of gauntlets that almost certainly belonged to the Prince in his lifetime.

Mock battles known as 'tournaments' almost certainly go back to classical times. In the Middle Ages they developed into very formalized encounters going on for many days. To prevent unnecessary loss of life and injury, special armour

Electrotype copies of daggers from Mycenae, 1600 BC. (The Victoria and Albert Museum, London.)

In the sixteenth century, firearms began to play an increasing role on the battlefield. The wheel-lock was invented in the early part of the century – probably by Leonardo Da Vinci. One effect of this mechanical form of ignition was that fire could be 'held' until required, and this produced big changes in tactics.

Improvements in the production and quality of gunpowder meant that firearms became more powerful. Thus armour had to be made thicker and consequently heavier. The elegant shapes of the Gothic period gave way to simpler contours, and unnecessary plates were gradually abandoned.

This was the period when armour became more decorative than functional. Armours were produced imitating the style of ancient Rome. Helmets were embossed with classical figures, breastplates were made to simulate textile and costume, the surfaces of the plates were artificially coloured, and etched designs combined with gilding were used to heighten the effect of the decoration. Because so much armour has been scoured over the centuries, it is often difficult to imagine the rich appearance of a parade harness: vivid peacock-blue contrasted with rich gold, and some armours were entirely silvered or gilt.

Important artists were commissioned to produce designs for the decoration of armour. Very occasionally these designs survive, and it is possible to compare the initial design with the finished product. The well-known Almain Armourer's Album in the Victoria and Albert Museum is a series of sixteenth-century ink and water-colour illustrations of armours made in the Royal workshops at Greenwich under the master-armourer Jacob Halder. Many of the armours survive, and it is possible not only to reconstruct the original decoration of each armour but also to establish for whom it was made. Complete harnesses have often been widely scattered, but the original form of an armour can be reconstructed by comparing the decorative treatments on individual plates. The study of armour decoration is therefore most important – especially where the large armour 'kits' known as 'garnitures' are concerned. Developed fully in the sixteenth century, these consisted of a series of armour all decorated *en suite* which could be used for different types of combat. There might be one armour for use in the field, one for foot combat and types for various forms of joust – all decorated *en suite* and all made for one individual. By adding pieces or removing others, all these different functions could be fulfilled.

The medieval knightly sword underwent several changes in the fifteenth century. Its origins lie in the broad, double-edged blades used by the Vikings, but by the thirteenth century it had become much longer, with a blade gradually tapering to a point. The familiar wheel-shaped pommel seems to have been introduced at some time in the twelfth century and continued to be used in the following centuries.

Changes in fencing techniques – especially in the sixteenth century – had considerable effect on the design of swords. The use of the point became more important than the edge, so swords became longer and narrower. By the middle of the fifteenth century the addition of extra guards to the hilt had become fashionable, and the familiar long rapier is really a development of these hilts. It should be emphasized that the rapier is really a weapon to be worn with civilian dress, *en suite* with a dagger. Great care and ingenuity went into the decoration of these weapons, especially as they were regarded almost as items of costume jewellery. Hilts were chiselled and pierced, damascened in gold, made from precious metal and set with stones, and they were always expensive items. The fifteenth and sixteenth centuries also saw the development of national styles of decoration and form.

Blades were usually imported from one of the main centres of manufacture, such as Solingen in Germany or Toledo in Spain, and mounted up with the required hilt. It is thus very difficult precisely to identify where a hilt was made. As with armour, some of the best artists produced designs for hilts. Those by artists working in the mannerist style must have been extremely difficult to execute in steel, but it is clear from a few surviving hilts that even the most complicated hilt forms were produced by craftsmen. These fragile delicate chiselled hilts would never have been hazarded in the field but would have been reserved for parade or state occasions.

The cross-hilted swords of medieval times did not in fact die out, but the archaic form was reserved for swords of state and for special swords such as those used for execution. However, it now seems clear that many of the so-called executioner's swords are really swords of ceremony to be carried before officers of state and members of important guilds. The rapier in its later, shorter form became in the middle of the seventeenth century the classic civilian sword known as the small-sword, which lasted with little change until the early nineteenth century.

The advantages of curved blades as a cavalry weapon were appreciated very early in the East. Under Turkish influence in the sixteenth and seventeenth centuries the curved sabre was almost universally adopted by European cavalry. A modified version was still being used by some of the participants in the Second World War.

Special weapons and costume for the chase were known in classical times, and hunting was a most important pastime both in medieval times and later. It was very much an occupation of the rich, and large amounts of money were spent on the necessary equipment. Apart from special spears and swords, many of which were very elaborately decorated, firearms used in the chase were also very distinctive. Many hunting-weapons are decorated with scenes of the chase: firearms have lively portrayals of hunting-scenes inlaid into the stock; swords have etched designs showing scenes from the chase on the blades. Because large numbers of retainers were employed in the hunt, huge quantities of hunting-weapons were produced to special order. Many of the long matchlock muskets of the sixteenth and seventeenth century must have been used for hunting, and the few portraits which depict figures in hunting-costume often show these large guns in use.

Another important missile weapon used extensively in hunting was the crossbow, which had the advantage both of range and of silence. Most of the crossbows that survive are in fact hunting-weapons, and variations continue in use up to the present day.

Mention should be made of those curiosities known as 'combination weapons', which were fashionable in princely collections. A knife would be combined with an axe, a sword with a pistol, a multi-shot gun with a walking-staff. An examination of these weapons reveals that many were totally impractical – they seem really to have been made as toys to

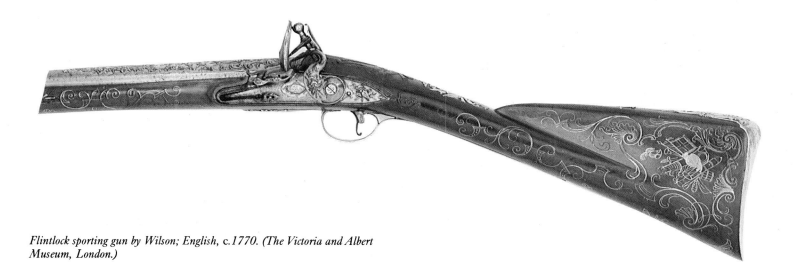

Flintlock sporting gun by Wilson; English, c.1770. (The Victoria and Albert Museum, London.)

demonstrate the supreme technical skill of the gunsmith or swordsmith. Many are beautifully decorated, and they were probably intended more to be admired in a princely collection than for practical use. Some swords even have such unlikely things as watches and miniatures incorporated in their hilts, and the love of mechanical toys, especially in the seventeenth century, led to the invention of special rapiers which extended their blades by about a foot when a lever was pressed.

From the seventeenth century, firearms and arillery had become the dominant weapons on the battlefield. By the middle of the century armour had been reduced to breast-plate and back-plate, and helmet and a single defence for the arm which held the reins. Improvements such as the invention of the flintlock in France in the early years of the century meant that firearms became increasingly more reliable. Certain military commanders such as Gustavus Adolphus of Sweden (1594–1632) realized the devastating effects of volley fire, and this was to become a feature of the battlefield until the nineteenth century. Cavalry armed with swords and lances still had a part to play in warfare, as some of the battles of the English Civil War demonstrate, but the deadly effect of firearms fired from a good defensive position was a lesson that most European armies had learnt by the eighteenth century.

By this period defensive arms had dwindled to a helmet and a small gorget hung around the neck, although there were exceptions among dragoons and cavalry, who continued to wear some body armour.

The Napoleonic wars at the beginning of the nineteenth century still retained some of the elements to be found in the warfare of earlier times – extravagant uniforms, gilded weapons, armour, lances and sword could all be found – but the nineteenth century really witnessed what might be called the end of the parade side of war. However, throughout the century there were some surprising survivals of techniques of war from earlier times. At the beginning of the Napoleonic wars an English gentleman wrote a pamphlet advocating a return to the pike and longbow on the grounds that these had been used with particular success against the French in the fourteenth century, so Napoleon's troops would naturally be afraid of English arrows! (There is in fact at least one verifiable account of a longbow being used in the Second World War.) Cavalry actions fought hand to hand with swords took place in the American Civil War. Armour has on occasion proved useful still more recently – flak jackets were used by aircrew during the Second World War, and the modern infantryman and police use jackets made from a synthetic material, Kevlar, which offers protection against high-velocity bullets fired at close range. Although modern weapons are usually plain and workmanlike, the same can be said of English munition armour and weapons of the seventeenth century.

There is not really such a large difference between the sixteenth-century wheel-lock, with its carved ivory stock and gilt mounts, and the modern top-quality shotgun. Both weapons were made for a discerning customer able and willing to pay large sums for a custom-built luxury product. The prince in his private chamber admiring the crafts-manship and detail on a wheel-lock saw the same qualities of design and function as the wealthy businessman admiring a recently purchased shotgun.

A.R.E. North

INTRODUCTION

The story of arms and armour runs throughout human history. At times it has appeared as the most important thread of this history, as men have attempted to harness the power of destruction in new ways to obtain mastery over their neighbours or security of defence. Yet the history of arms and armour is much more than a catalogue of technical improvements for the field of battle: another aspect is the artist's seeking to make the most pleasing, most fashionable or most impressive piece of armour or sporting weapon. The marks of the knight were his sword, spurs and lance; the sign of the gentleman was his small-sword, and the mace remains a badge of office. Fine arms and armour were thus works of art and the trappings of place in society.

Sometimes the pursuit of excellence and novelty led to absurd lengths and impracticalities. Among these were combination weapons which can rarely if ever have taken their place in war – axes with built-in multi-barrelled pistols, shields with lanterns, and swords combined with pistols. Often decorative effect alone overcame practical purpose: many later armours were intended solely for parade or as a mark of rank. Army officers wore the 'gorget' – a vestige of the knight's neck defence – simply as a badge of rank. Court swords and small-swords were rarely practical fighting weapons but a form of male jewellery and a symbol of status.

The study of arms and armour did not really begin until the late eighteenth century with the publication of a number of works, including Francis Grose's *Treatise on Ancient Armour and Weapons*. During the following hundred years interest increased, stimulated by a number of antiquarians and gentlemen collectors. Perhaps the best-known studies of this period were Samuel Rush Meyrick's *Critical Injury into Antient Armour* of 1824 and John Hewitt's *Ancient Armour and Weapons*, concluded in 1860.

Popular collecting is, however, a predominantly modern phenomenon. Disposable incomes have risen dramatically since the Second World War, and a flood of literature has spread knowledge widely and pushed auction prices high. Tighter laws on firearms make collecting cartridge weapons difficult, and the finest arms and armour of all sorts form a highly specialized international market.

The present work is intended to provide the beginner with an introduction to the subject and to give the more specialized reader food for thought by setting arms in context in a handy one-volume reference. The field is so vast that it has necessarily to be limited in terms of both chronology and the types of weapon covered. We begin,

Leading away prisoners (left); a scene from the Maciejowski bible, c.1250. Apart from the shield, mail was the main defence of the early medieval era. Notice the mail mittens and the caps worn beneath the mail hood or 'coif'. (Pierpont Morgan Library.)

therefore, with the classical period and end on the eve of the First World War. Only items that are man-portable are covered – vehicles and artillery are beyond our scope. Most arms fall into one of three main categories: defensive arms, edged weapons and projectile weapons.

DEFENSIVE ARMS

Under the general heading of defensive arms come body armour and shields. Body armours were not only of metal but used a great variety of materials: linen, leather, silk, lacquer and bone. In the medieval era the term 'arms' was often used to cover armour as well, so an 'armed man' might well mean a man wearing armour, rather than simply carrying a weapon. Plate armour was known to the classical world, but the materials used were too heavy to allow the use of a complete 'cap-à-pie' – head-to-foot – suit.

Padded, scale or mail armours were the most common right through until the fourteenth century. Helmet, breast-plate and leg defences were then joined by articulated – i.e. jointed – arm defences and other plates to make up a complete suit, so that by the mid fifteenth century the popular picture of the fully armoured knight had appeared. Possession of arms was one of the major social distinctions of the era, separating the knightly class from the other divisions of feudal society – the clergy and peasantry. Spurs, lance and sword acquired a symbolic significance and, until bows and other projectile weapons became more important, the nobility fought mounted.

By the sixteenth century, armour was in retreat: suits of overlapping plate were rarer and tended to be made more for the specialist purposes of the tilt and ceremony, where they were a mark of rank. In the seventeenth century it was pointless to try to stop the flight of the musket ball with armour in all but siege situations, where the wearer was not required to move around very much.

After 1700, there was only vestigial use of body armour: breastplates for cuirassiers and household cavalry, full suits for use in portraits of royalty and nobility. Gorgets and helmets helped to distinguish various sorts of troops and officers but had little practical use. By 1914 such armour as remained was an anachronistic encumbrance. Ironically, however, trench warfare – that great four-year siege – was then to make armour a practical proposition again.

THE 'ARMS BLANCHE' EDGED WEAPONS

The earliest edged weapons were 'arms' almost literally, in that they were held in the hand to extend the reach and power of a blow. Some weapons, like the mace or club, were designed to give greater punch in terms of crushing weight; others, like the sword or dagger, achieved greater penetra-

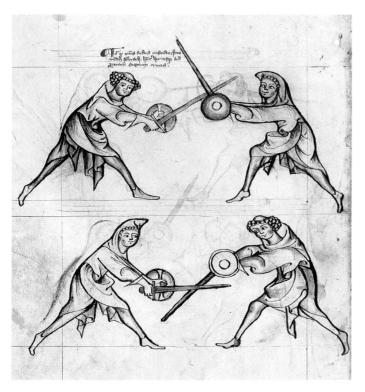

Fencing with sword and buckler from a South German manual, c.1300. The sword was not simply a weapon of war but an arm for the duel, for sport, and finally a status symbol. (The Royal Armouries, London.)

tive ability by sharpness or impact over a smaller area. Long spears, like those of the hoplites, the ancient Greek foot-soldiers, were intended to give advantage by reach. Darts, javelins and other throwing-spears attempted to combine the advantages of a projectile with those of a point or blade.

All these ideas had been developed in the classical era, and refined during the Middle Ages. The sword acquired considerable symbolic power, which was reflected in the offices of state as well as in art and literature. Considerable diversity existed. Knives and 'hangers' were developed for the hunt, and the curved swords of the East began to influence the mainstream of European design. Distinctive patterns of sword came to be identified with different types of troop or the officers of different regiments. Style of sword could distinguish police officer from courtier, or general from customs man.

Spears also developed, from the fire-hardened pointed stick of palaeolithic man, through flint and bronze heads, to iron and the highly organized pike blocks of the Swiss and the seventeenth-century battlefield. The lance came and went from favour with bewildering unpredictability. It was the main shock weapon of the medieval knight but was almost totally neglected in western Europe from the mid seventeenth century to 1800. It made a dramatic comeback in armies of the Napoleonic era in the hands of French, Dutch and Polish cavalry, and was also widely used by Prussian uhlans and Russian Cossacks and lancers.

The bayonet is arguably the most important of post-medieval edged weapons. With this the single-shot musket also became a weapon of close defence and assault. Arranged in squares with bayonets pointing outward, infantry could usually resist charging cavalry. The bayonet charge could also be decisive at the climax of the eighteenth- or nineteenth-century battle, though hand-to-hand action was probably not common – many battalions would break and run before hit with 'cold steel'; other charges would break up or falter under artillery or musket fire.

PROJECTILE WEAPONS

The long-range weapons of antiquity were the sling, dart, javelin and bow. Normally these were associated with light troops, auxiliaries and skirmishers. The earliest bows were not as powerful as the dreaded medieval longbow, and for the sake of convenience the Saxon and Norman bows are sometimes known as 'short-bows'. In eastern Europe and Asia, composite recurved bows were favoured. These were made up in layers of horn, wood, glue and sinew and were not a simple 'bow' shape but curved out again at the tips or 'nocks' when strung. When unstrung, the composite bow curved virtually into a circle until tensioned again with the string. A longbow unstrung assumes the shape of an almost straight stave.

In a Western and especially English context, the bow had a tremendous social significance. It was the only weapon with which the common man could compete with the armoured knight. It is hardly surprising that it should be identified with the legendary Robin Hood – the gentleman in peasant guise striking a blow for the poor. In everyday life the bow loomed large. Practice with the bow was a legal obligation; the bow was the mainstay of hunting and poaching and a healthy, cheap form of recreation.

Firearms existed by about 1300 but made only slow advances. Expensive, slow to load and heavy, they were at first more useful to frighten or to impress than to wound. Firearms did however possess great penetrative power and, as ignition systems and supplies of ammunition improved, they helped to make armour less and less useful.

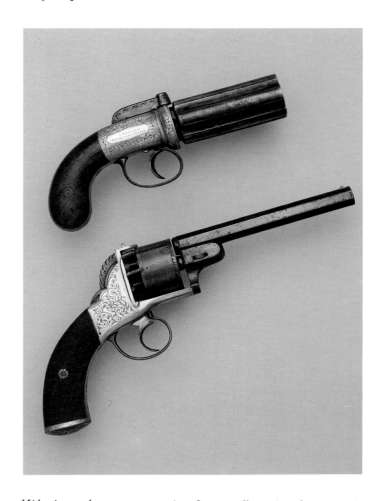

Mid nineteenth century percussion firearms illustrating the two main methods then available to achieve repeating fire. Top, the pepperbox with its multiple barrels. Bottom, the revolver in which a cylinder turned to marry up a series of charges with a single barrel. (Sotherby's, London.)

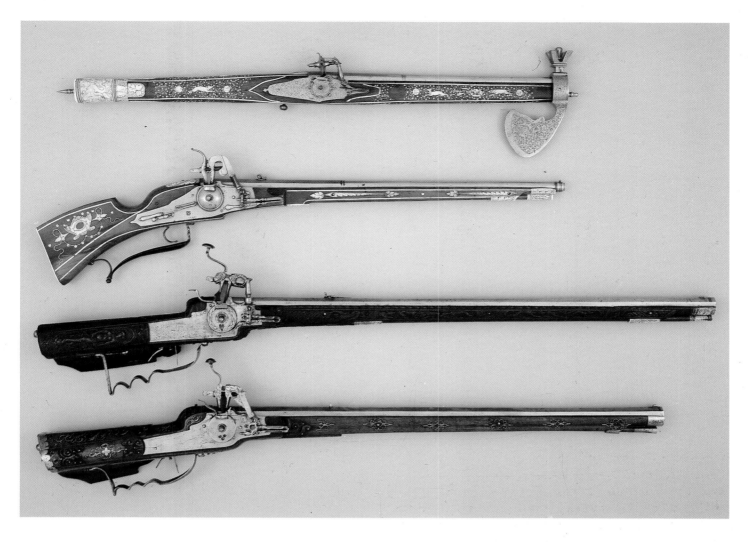

Late sixteenth century wheel lock firearms. Top to bottom, combined axe and wheel lock pistol with ball trigger; wheel lock carbine; and two wheel lock rifles. (Sotherby's, London.)

The 'dag' or pistol became not only a cavalry weapon but a favourite of the assassin and criminal. Handguns such as the harquebus, caliver and musket became the mainstay of the infantry and helped to usher in the 'pike and shot' era from the mid sixteenth century. When matchlock and wheel-lock ignition systems were superseded by the flint-lock, firearms became the universal weapon of war. All states then aspired to standardization, to rapidity of fire and to certainty of supply.

Breech-loaders existed even in the sixteenth century but were not particularly successful, due to the complexity and difficulty of 'obturation' or prevention of gas escape. The new industrial era of the late eighteenth and nineteenth centuries not only put the breech-loader back on the agenda but also made rifling of the bore more common, allowing bullets to be spun in flight for accuracy, and new experimentation took place with ignition systems. Percussion systems took over from flint and steel, and finally solid single-piece cartridges became the norm.

Another big area of development was multi-shot weapons. The earliest efforts concentrated either on multiple barrels or on superimposed loads in the same barrel. One of the first practical alternatives was the revolver, lining up new charges successively behind the barrel. This had been possible as early as the seventeenth century but was not widespread until the age of Elisha Collier, Samuel Colt, William Tranter, and John and Robert Adams, in the mid nineteenth century. Magazine loading became a really practical proposition with the advent of the brass cartridge, at the end of the nineteenth century. There were many different possibilities: tube magazines with springs and levers, pump actions and hoppers. Ultimately, however, a box magazine with a moving bolt was universally adopted by most of the world's armies.

Automatic and semi-automatic fire were the last major hurdles to be crossed before 1900. Again multiple and/or revolving barrels were early favourites. In the Nordenfeldt, a series of barrels was discharged by a forward-and-back motion of a lever. In the Gatling, a series of barrels was revolved in conjunction with a feed mechanism; cranking a handle and supplying ammunition from a hopper, drum or strip enabled continuous fire. Truly automatic fire, in which the recoil of the cartridge reset the mechanism and reloaded the chamber, came only with the Maxim gun in the 1880s. There was nothing to crank and no multiple barrels – the age of the machine-gun had arrived.

These, then, were the main families of arms and armour. In the chapters that follow, we will examine first the mainstream of western European development, with an emphasis on weapons for war and their main methods of deployment. Following these first five chronological chapters are two thematic chapters: oriental/tribal and sporting. Both cover vast areas, and it is intended to do no more than identify important developmental threads and to give an idea of the enormous variety of weaponry that the world has produced.

S.B.

CHAPTER 1

THE GREEKS AND ROMANS

Arms have existed since man first threw stones or struck with a stick. From around 2000 BC the Egyptians, Babylonians and Hittites all had well-developed armies and used armours of scale and textile constructioon – padded, or with plates sewn on to cloth – and wore helmets. Yet it was not until the time of classical Greek civilization that technology was sufficiently advanced to allow large pieces of metal to be fashioned into plates to fit the body.

By about 1500 BC, heavy cylinders of bronze were being fashioned by the Mycenaeans in the eastern Mediterranean. However, the metal 'cuirass' or breastplate seems to have been both unusual and unwieldy until at least the eighth century BC, when the great city-states of Greece – Argos, Athens, Sparta, Corinth and Thebes – were struggling for dominance in the region. At that time, Argos ruled much of the Peloponnese, and continued to do so until challenged in 740 BC by the Spartans under King Theopompus.

It was during this era that the rather 'free-for-all' style of combat of the 'heroic' era, before 800 BC, was superseded by more organized and regimented systems. The most important of these was the archaic *locho*, a compact body of about a hundred acting in concert under the command of a *lochagos* and capable of subdivision into two *pentekostyes* or four *enomotias*.

At about the same time the large round Argive shield was adopted; this not only covered its user from chin to knee but helped to cover the unprotected side of the man to his left. Throwing-spears were also largely superseded by a long thrusting-spear. The heavy bronze cuirass, having been rendered unnecessary by the shield, was now supplanted by a defence of folded linen. Thus it was that the fully developed 'phalanx' or compact block of troops evolved, based on its armoured infantry or 'hoplites'.

The Spartans were the epitome of the Greek military states: harsh discipline from childhood led to liability for military service which lasted from the age of 20 to 60. Recognizable by their red cloaks, the Spartans were organized into divisions or *mora*, each of which contained four *lochos*. These units varied in strength over time, as the army of six divisions dropped in numbers from 9,000 to 4,000. At the beginning of the fifth century BC, helots – subject peoples – were also serving with the Spartan army as light skirmishers; shortly after, small units of cavalry were added to the divisions.

In 494 BC, faced with an external threat from the Persian Empire, the traditional rivalry between Athens and Sparta was buried in the attempt to expel the invaders. Xerxes' Persian army, which may have numbered almost a quarter of a million, was predominantly of light troops – archers and javelin-throwers from the fringes of the empire. The mainstay were the Medes and Persians carrying wicker shields and armed with bows or short spears. The crack troops of the army were the 10,000 men of the 'Immortals' – these were the best equipped soldiers, with both spears and bows, and the most feared.

Greek amphora (left and below), c.530 BC, depicting Achilles killing Penthesilea, Queen of the Amazons, found at Vulci in Tuscany, Italy. Achilles is here armoured in a metal cuirass with swirling decoration over the chest and a full-face 'Corinthian' helmet with a high crest; little else is worn. The spear he is using has a leaf-shaped blade and a long tang.

His opponent is also helmeted, but in an open-faced style with more decoration and an ear cut-out. (It may be that this depiction is influenced by the need to show that the warrior is a woman.) Penthesilea also wears a leopard skin, the legs of which go over her shoulders. Both fighters carry large convex shields. (The British Museum, London.)

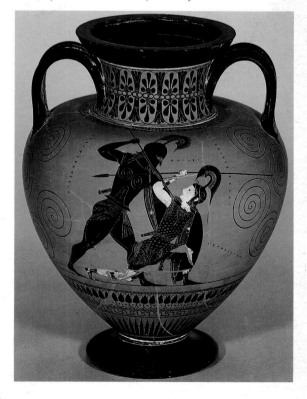

The Dendra panoply (above), from a Mycenean chamber tomb of 1400 BC. The cuirass is a great roughly formed cylinder of bronze of rather limited practicality. The helmet is much lighter, being made of boar's tusk. (The Archaeological Museum, Nauplia.)

In 490 BC the Persians were defeated by the Athenians at Marathon, but ten years later they invaded again. This time they were met by the Spartans, Thespians, Phocaeans and Lorians in pitched battle at Thermopylae. The Greeks were overwhelmed, with the Spartans taking the brunt of the fighting and losing their leader, Leonidas. This was not only a severe blow to Sparta but led ultimately to the fall of Athens.

Only after the great sea battle of Salamis was the tide turned, and the Spartans fully mobilized to assist the Athenians. The Persians and their allies were finally defeated at Plataea in 479 BC. The Greek victory at Plataea was, however, by no means the beginning of a more peaceful age, for the victors soon fell out and were again at war. Between 431 and 416 BC, Athens was brought finally to her knees by Sparta. Next, Sparta was itself challenged by the growing power of Thebes, but already the centre of power was shifting away from the Peloponnese to the north.

The rise of Macedonia heralded a whole new era in both arms and tactics in the ancient world. Philip of Macedonia had spent some time in Thebes and was undoubtedly influenced by Theban methods of making war, but the major sources of information, Diodorus Siculus and Polybius, are frustratingly fragmentary. Nonetheless, enough exists for a convincing reconstruction of the Macedonian army, which was soon to conquer much of the known world.

The Macedonian cavalry had always had a good reputation, but the infantry, lacking in discipline, was reformed into heavy-infantry phalanxes. Strangely, the basic unit of ten men was exchanged for multiples of eight.

Corinthian oinochoe, or wine jug, attributed to 'the Tydeus painter', 560 BC. The subjects here are a horseman and two hoplites in combat. The fighters wear greaves and carry large, round Argive shields. Note how the forearm is slipped through the central ring of the shield while a grip near the rim is grasped. One man wears a cuirass of metal and both have tall-crested Corinthian helmets. (The British Museum, London.)

Eight of these files of eight formed a *tetrach* and four *tetrachies* formed a *syntagima* of 256 individuals. The next level of command was the *taxis* of 1,500 men, which was effectively the biggest sub-unit of the army.

The main weapon of the heavy infantry was a massive *sarissa* or pike. The length of this weapon has been estimated at anything between 16 and 24 feet, but weight, availability of wood and the practical maximum length of later pikes suggest that it was generally closer to the lower of these figures. 'Greaves' – shin armour – and helmets were worn by many troops, and round shields were carried.

Little original source material remains for the age of Philip of Macedonia and his son Alexander the Great – from 360 to 325 BC – but later commentators state that the main body of the infantry was supported by Agrianan javelineers, archers and scouts, and that the Macedonian infantrymen themselves were divided into two types. The bulk of these were the pikemen already described, but there were also *hypaspists* or shield-bearers who protected the flanks of the phalanx.

The cavalry were divided up into *ilai* or squadrons of about two hundred. Their main weapon was a long spear, but their effectiveness must have been limited by lack of stirrups. These Thessalian and Greek horsemen were supported by javelin-armed Thracian and Paeonian scouts. Illustrations and surviving examples show that many horsemen wore the Boeotian-style helmet and that some of the horses had their head protected by a bronze 'chanfron' or plate extending from nose to brow. Another piece of horse armour sometimes used was the *peytral*, covering the breast and sides as far back as the saddle.

'Panathenaic' amphora showing a javelin-thrower, Greek, c.515 BC. This sort of vessel was awarded to successful sporting competitors in the games held in Athens every four years. It demonstrates the very early link between weaponry and competitive sport. The figures depicted are a youth playing a flute, the javelin-thrower himself and another figure holding a javelin, commonly interpreted as his trainer. (The Liverpool Museum.)

Philip of Macedonia defeated the Thebans and Athenians at Chaeronea in 338 BC. Although Philip was murdered in 336 BC, by 334 BC a combined Macedonian and Greek army was ready to invade Persia under the young Alexander. In the next few years Alexander marched through and conquered much of modern Greece, Turkey, Palestine, Egypt, Syria, Iran and Iraq and part of Russia. In 327 BC, he reached the Indus Valley and was opposed by an Indian army equipped with elephants. Although victorious, his army was at the limits of its endurance, and his forces fell back. Alexander died two years later.

Almost inevitably the great Greek Empire now disintegrated through internal power struggles, but several states maintained Alexander's generals as their leaders. This disunity no doubt aided the expansion of a new and even greater empire to the west. Rome was traditionally regarded as having been founded in 753 BC, but it took more than five hundred years for the city-state to establish dominance even over the Italian peninsula.

The arms and tactics of Rome were not sudden new inventions but an assimilation and adaptation of what had gone before; much was owed to the Celts and the Greeks. Rome was a colony of the more northerly Etruscans, but the Romans rebelled against Tarquin the Proud and Lars Porsena to achieve independence as part of the Latin League – a group of allied Italian states. Even then, Rome's very existence was still threatened by the local hill tribes of the Aequi and Volsci, and by a Celtic invasion from the north. Finally, in 343 BC, the Romans became locked in conflict with the Samnites – fellow Italians – a war which was to last for fifty years.

In the earliest days of Rome, the use of armour was limited to a helmet and breastplate, usually in conjunction with a large rounded shield. The helmets were of two main styles – *villanova*, with a distinctive pointed flange or crest, and conical or rounded, often with a central plume-holder.

Swords were of both the long Celtic slashing type and the shorter stabbing variety. Some, with ornate bronze openwork finials at the pommel, have since been christened 'antennae' swords. Daggers, spears and small axes were also in use, mostly with blades or heads of bronze. Round, thin bronze shields from this early period have also been found in some quantity, and these are usually equipped with a central handle and attachments for carrying-straps at the rear. These probably had a mainly ceremonial function, as most of the practical war shields appear to have been of wood and leather.

Relief on a tombstone depicting a warrior attempting to fend off his assailant with a dagger, Greek, late fifth century BC. It is likely that the two figures represent an Athenian and a Spartan during the Peloponnesian War. The prostrate figure wears a 'bell' helmet of a type common throughout Greece and Italy. The standing warrior has a spear, sword and shield. The sword is suspended by means of a strap over the shoulder and the shield is held by means of two loops — one through which the forearm is passed and another which serves as a grip. (The Metropolitan Museum, New York.)

Marble 'herm' or bust of Pericles found at Tivoli, near Rome – a Roman copy of an original (c.430 BC) by Cresilas. This shows a possible alternative way of wearing the 'Corinthian' helmet – pushed well back on the head, clear of the face. In this sculpture the helmet may serve a double purpose, as Pericles suffered from a slightly elongated deformation of the skull which the headgear hides. (The British Museum, London.)

Bronze arrowhead, Olynthian, inscribed with the name of Philip of Macedonia, c.348 BC. There is a common modern saying about 'bullets having people's names on them' but this sort of phrase would also have been familiar to the ancient Greeks. In 354 BC Philip had one eye shot out, and this special arrow was used by archers in the besieged city of Olynthus against the Macedonians with similar results in mind. Bows were an important weapon in early classical warfare but were wielded mainly by skirmishers and light troops. (The British Museum, London.)

Boeotian helmet c.300 BC, found in the River Tigris. This style of helmet appears to have been fairly widespread among the cavalry of Alexander the Great – representations of it appear on the Alexander sarcophagus and on the Alexander mosaic found at Pompeii. The flared skirt and visor provided some protection to the ears and eyes without impairing hearing or vision. (The Ashmolean Museum, Oxford.)

Bell krater (below), for mixing wine and water, showing the departure of two Athenian warriors, Greek, c.460 BC. Both men carry large, round shields emblazoned with animal devices, and one of these shields appears to have a sort of banner attached at three points to its lower part. Both men wear crested helmets, apparently with hinged cheek-guards, for one of them has them tied up clear of the face.

Bronze 'Chalcidian' helmet found at Salonica in north-east Greece, fifth century BC. Evolved from the all-enveloping 'Corinthian' helmet, the 'Chalcidian' is encountered in two distinct types, with either hinged or fixed cheek-pieces. This example has fixed cheek-pieces with a swirling decoration, a deep cut-out for the ear and a shortish nasal bar. This type of helmet continued in use alongside other models in the armies of Philip of Macedonia and his son Alexander The Great. (The British Museum, London.)

The Etrusco-Roman armies also operated a form of the phalanx, with units based on the *lochos*. It seems, however, that the troops were normally divided into classes: at the front were fully armed hoplites; behind them were medium-armed spearmen with sword, helmet, greaves and *scutum* or Italic shield. In a third rank were more lightly armed spearmen, and at the rear were skirmishers with javelins or slings who might move out and on to the flank of the main unit. The typical Etruscan warrior of the period owed much to the contemporary Greek styles and would often be equipped with greaves, Argive shield and helmet. This last could be of a traditional Greek type, like the 'Chalcidian', or of the Italic conical *negau* type. The *kopis* or curved, single-edged sword was also carried; this was popular in Greece and Spain, but its exact origins are obscure, having been attributed both to Etruria and to ancient Egypt.

By the third century BC there is good evidence that not only linen cuirasses covered with lamellae – a series of thin metal plates – were in use but also mail shirts of interlocking metal rings. It is highly likely that mail was a Celtic invention. Similarly, it is likely that the 'Montefortino' style of helmet originated with the Celts and was thereafter adapted by the Etruscans and Romans. The typical Celtic shield was large, long, and either oval or coffin-shaped, and the Celts carried both sword and spear.

By this time the Celts particularly favoured a long slashing-sword – as Polybius described it, good for cuts but not for thrusting. This *spatha* was later widely adopted by the Roman cavalry, for it was an ideal weapon for use from horseback. Many later cavalry broadswords followed a similar pattern. Celtic spears were of two major patterns: a broad-bladed thrusting type and a lighter, throwing variety. Often butts were fitted to the other end of the shaft, to give balance.

The Celts also made use of missile weapons and, though the archaeological evidence is more slender, iron arrowheads of a triangular-tanged form are particularly typical. Slings seem to have been especially popular: digs at Maiden Castle in Dorset discovered a hoard of 22,260 stones for use with slings which had been established in a single deposit by the eastern gateway. Most were beach pebbles of about 1¾ ounces, but some were of specially prepared clay.

The Volsci, Sabines and Samnites used many types of weapon equivalent to those of their Roman adversaries, but some appear to have been unique to the hill tribes. One good example of this is the broad-brimmed 'pot' helmet; another is the round breastplates and backplates which were apparently held in place by leather straps and iron fittings. The Samnites favoured an Athenian or Attic-style helmet, decorated with two or more feather-holders and sometimes a central crest. They also seem to have used squarish cuirasses of metal or a distinctive triple-disc style.

In the middle of the third century BC, the Italian peninsula was under Roman domination. One of the last major efforts to prevent this came from Pyrrhus, King of Epirus in north-west Greece and a kinsman of Alexander, who crossed the Adriatic at the head of a large army in 380 BC. His Macedonian phalanx triumphed over the Romans at Heraclea, but at a cost of losses so vast that any subsequent battle won at great expense has been referred to as a 'Pyrrhic victory'. Pyrrhus was then temporarily forced out of Italy, which gave the Romans time to regroup.

Many tribes now became subject peoples of the Romans. Some were thoroughly integrated, either as citizens or as local administrators, but the Celts were systematically massacred. By 300 BC the Roman army had undergone considerable reorganization and is perhaps best described as 'Roman-Latin' by this time. According to the Roman historian Titus Livius, now known as Livy, the largest unit was now the legion. This was split into three major lines and could no longer be described as a phalanx.

Celtic iron spearhead from the River Thames, c.500 BC. Finds of spearheads in Celtic contexts are fairly frequent, suggesting that spears were one of the Celts' major weapons. Most early Celtic spearheads are broad and leaf-shaped like this one; after contact with Rome, narrower types more like the pilum were widely used. Decoration of the spearhead was not uncommon, and it has been suggested that the most elaborate were used as standards or marks of rank. (The British Museum, London.)

Bronze shield (left), from a bog at Moel Siabod near Capel Curig, Gwynedd, Wales; 500 to 1000 BC. The shape has been created by beating out concentric rings and small pimples or bosses from the rear. It suggests a good degree of sophistication in European tribes before contact with any Greek or Roman civilization. (The British Museum, London.)

The rear line was itself made up of three parts: the veteran *triarii*, behind them the less distinguished *rorarii*, and at the back the reserves or *accensi*. All were equipped with an oval shield, and the *triarii*, at least, were armed with spears. The middle and front segments of the army were of *principes* and *hostati*, heavy infantry covered by *leves* or skirmishers armed with spears and missile weapons.

This organization probably did not last long, for the Roman army now set out on further wars of conquest which brought them into contact with new styles of warfare. Expansion to the south through Sicily led to conflict with the Syracusans and with the empire of Carthage, which covered much of north Africa. The Punic Wars with Carthage were to last 120 years and involve north Africa, Spain and the Mediterranean islands. Meanwhile the Celtic threat still existed to the north, and the failing Macedonian Empire was beginning to offer tempting prospects to the east.

By about 160 BC the Roman legion was established as a primarily infantry force of about 4,000 men. These were divided into classes by wealth and age. The three main divisions were now the *velites*, *hastati* and *principes*, who were respectively the light troops and first- and second-line infantry. A smaller body of *triarii* were the oldest veterans. The smallest independent tactical unit was normally the *maniple* (or handful), composed of two *centuries*.

Most of the legionaries were now armed with the short-sword or *gladius hispaniensis* and two javelins or *pila*. The *pilum* was of several possible designs, and there has been some controversy over their employment. Some appear little different to an ordinary light spear, but other types seem to have been designed to bend or break on impact, leaving enemy shields trailing broken shafts and nothing to throw back. In one variety, the thin iron shaft behind the head is left untempered so that it will bend; in another, the head is held by a wooden peg, likely to break.

Relief from the altar of Domitius Ahenobarbus, showing Roman soldiers and civilians, first century BC. Among the other human figures and sacrificial animals are visible at least six soldiers. Two towards the right of the frieze and two towards the left are obviously legionaries: they carry large oval scuta *or shields and appear to be wearing thigh-length mail shirts over an undergarment. At their waists on simple belts are worn short-swords or* gladi. *Their helmets are of at least two slightly differing types: the 'Montefortino' and a late 'Hellenistic' style which appears to maintain a vestigial visor.*

Near the altar-stone stands a tribune wearing a decorated muscled cuirass, greaves and a helmet. His offensive weapons are the short-sword and a spear. On the far right a horseman appears. He also wears mail and the gladius *and a slightly more elongated pattern of plumed helmet. (The Louvre, Paris.)*

The heavy infantry carried large shields or *scuta* of wood and canvas, often oval in shape. Their armour was usually a small breastplate or *pectorale*, a greave on the left leg and a bronze helmet of 'Montefortino' type. The light troops wore only the helmet and were usually armed with sword and javelins. Their round shield was known as the *parma*.

Each legion had about three hundred cavalry divided into ten small squadrons. These were armed with a spear and round shield and for defence wore a cuirass and helmet. Sometimes mail shirts were used.

The Carthaginian enemies of the legion were as varied as one might expect of a far-flung empire. Many were mercenaries, slingers from the Balearic islands, Celts and Spaniards, but the largest contingent came from north Africa. Best-known of these were the Numidian cavalry, most effectively employed as light skirmishers with their throwing-spears and shields but no armour.

Many of Carthage's best infantry were Spanish or Celtic. The Spaniards were armed with sword, javelin or sling, and those that carried shields had large oval types. Their swords were either the famous short, straight *gladius hispaniensis* or the short, curved *falcata*, which was almost like a large Gurkha kukri in form. Use of armour was limited, but it is believed that the crested caps which some reliefs show being worn by Spaniards were of sinew or leather and therefore had a defensive function.

Another arm of the Carthaginian forces was the famous elephants, employed to great effect not only by Hannibal but in north Africa during the first Punic War, where their impact was occasionally decisive in breaking up the usually well-disciplined Roman formations. Unlike the elephants of Pyrrhus and of Ptolemy of Egypt, which appear to have carried towers containing soldiers armed with bows and spears, the Carthaginian elephants relied on shock effect and horses' natural fear, carrying only a mahout with a prod.

Roman gladiator's helmet, first century AD (far left). This style of helmet, with its wide brim and tall comb, is associated with the mirmillones, *who were also protected by a jointed guard on the right arm and a greave on the left leg.*

Gladiatorial combats were probably first staged by the Etruscans, and it was likely that they took place as part of the funeral rites of the rich and famous. The Romans may have learned the custom from the Samnites, but fights were neither commonplace nor on a large scale in Rome until the second century BC. The greatest gladiatorial sensation came in 73 BC, when Spartacus, a Thracian gladiator, led a revolt against Rome which eventually required ten legions to put it down. (The British Museum, London.)

Roman bronze helmet, first century AD. During the first century AD, two new types of Roman helmet came into use: round, capped bronze helmets with small neck-guards, like this one, sometimes known as the 'coolus', and an iron helmet with a deep neck-guard usually known as the 'Port' type, after the Port bei Nidau site in Switzerland. Both types were often equipped with substantial ear flaps, but those rarely survive complete. Both types also show Gallic influences, and workshops were indeed set up in Gaul and elsewhere for the production of helmets and body armour. (The British Museum, London.)

Tombstone of Sextus Valerius Genialis (below), first century AD. Stones showing Roman horsemen are rare and in this context occur mainly in Britain and the Rhineland. Sextus Valerius was a soldier in the Thracian cavalry regiment and a Friesian by birth. Mounted on a rearing horse, the cavalryman spears his prostrate foe with a long spear or lance. At the rider's side is a long slashing-sword or spatha. *What appears to be a cavalry standard appears behind the figure. (The Corinium Museum, Cirencester.)*

The best-known campaign of the Punic Wars was that of 218–202 BC, when Hannibal crossed Spain, southern France and the Alps to attack the Italian peninsula from the north. He succeeded in beating Roman armies at Trebbia and Lake Trasimenre and most spectacularly at Cannae in 216 BC, where the Roman legions were taken in the flanks by the African pikemen and attacked from the rear by Hannibal's brother Hasdrubal, commanding the cavalry. More than ten years were to pass before Hannibal was finally forced out of Italy and the Roman general Scipio Africanus managed to defeat the Carthaginian forces in north Africa. Carthage itself was finally destroyed in 146 BC by Scipio Aemilianus.

As the Republican era drew to a close, Rome had established supremacy over much of the Mediterranean. The new battlefield for Gaius Julius Caesar was to the north and west: Gaul, Germany and Britain. Rome under the emperors is generally better-documented than the earlier period, and it is possible to get a relatively clear picture of the Imperial Roman Army and its weapons.

Reorganization of the legion largely removed the distinctions between *hastati*, *principes* and *triarii*, and cavalry and light troops were now largely *auxiliares* – non-Roman troops. Baggage trains were pared down to a minimum, and the legionaries – nicknamed 'Marius's mules', after their emperor – carried most of their own supplies. (G.R. Watson of Nottingham University has estimated the weight of the Roman soldier's burden as about 65 lb.) Arms and armour now helped to create the panoply which is the current popular image of the Roman soldier.

It should be remembered, however, that Rome was never centralized or industrialized in the manner of many modern societies, and much local variation must have existed. Thus it is that, though the Imperial legionary helmets all have similarity, they can be of iron or bronze and differ

A modern reconstruction of the Roman Imperial lorica segmentata *or body armour from Corbridge, made by the late M. Russell Robinson at the Royal Armouries, 1964 (top right and far right). A tangle of original plates from two armours was found at Corbridge near Hadrian's Wall. They looked not unlike a pile of rusty lorry springs, but, importantly, parts of the original leather strapping remained which helped make accurate reconstructions possible. The plates were articulated internally with riveted leather straps and were laced and buckled externally. The upper part was fixed to the lower by means of hooks and eyes. Contextual evidence suggests that the armours date from the first half of the first century AD. (The Museum of Antiquities, Newcastle-upon-Tyne.)*

The Roman gladius *(below), first century AD. The* gladius *is believed to have been derived from a Spanish model the* gladius hispaniensis. *The sword shown at top is the so-called 'sword of Tiberius' with an extremely ornate scabbard and is from the first half of the first century AD. It was found at Rheingönheim, Germany. Those shown centre and bottom are slightly later: they are a little shorter in the blade and have short rather than long points. When in use they would have weighed about 2 lb. (Romisch Germanisches Zentral-museum, Mainz.)*

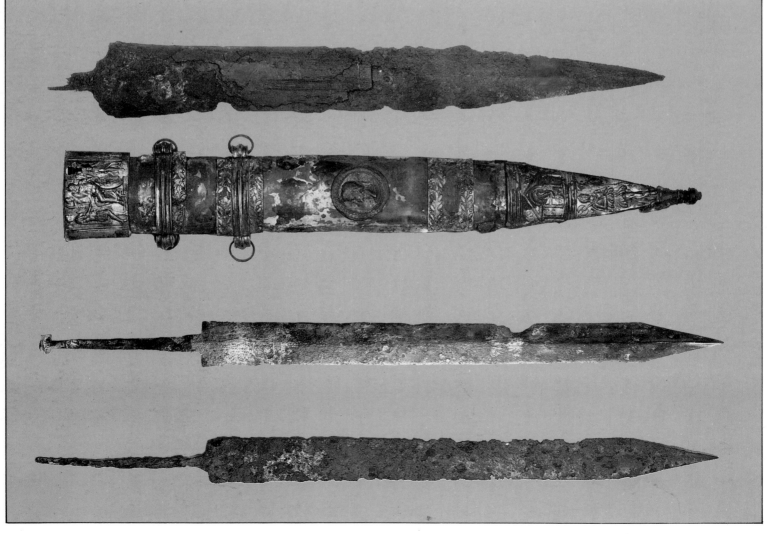

Members of the 'Ermine Street Guard' (below) posing in reproduction Roman arms and armour of the type in use at the end of the first century AD. The figure in the centre is a centurion clad in a scale shirt with greaves to protect the legs. The crest on his helmet is worn transverse across his head as a mark of rank. The musician is a cornicen carrying his long curled horn or cornu around his arm. Over his helmet he wears an animal skin. On the other side of the centurion is the standard-bearer. Roman legions carried three types of standard: the aquila or eagle (one per legion), the signa or company standard (one per 'century') and the imago (an image of the emperor). What is carried here is the signa, faithfully reproduced from that which appears on Trajan's Column in Rome. The other four soldiers are legionaries. They carry rectangular scuta or shields of laminated wood with a hide covering and a square metal boss in the centre. The body armour is lorica segmentata worn with a coolus-type helmet with a stunted peak, wide neck skirt and shaped ear flaps. Similar helmets have been found as far apart as Israel, Germany and Italy. The spears are pila for throwing, designed to bend or break and so prevent the enemy from throwing them back. (The Corinium Museum, Cirencester.)

Tombstone of Marcus Favonias Facilis (below), centurion of the XX Legion, first half of the first century AD. Probably the earliest surviving Roman military tombstone in Britain, this was found at Colchester in 1868. It is thought that the stone was made before AD 49, when the site ceased to be an active garrison and was turned over to retired legionaries, and it may well have been torn down at the time of Boudicca's revolt in AD 60. Facilis carries over his left shoulder a cloak or sagum *and beneath this wears a metal cuirass with long decorative shoulder-pieces; his legs are protected by greaves. His offensive arms are the* gladius, *supported by a belt over the shoulder, and a dagger or* pugio. *In his hand he holds the vine stick or* vitis *as a symbol of rank. Batons have continued in such use for high-ranking officers ever since. (The Colchester Museum.)*

The Ribchester helmet (right, top and bottom), for sports or parade, third century AD. The Ribchester helmet was found in the eighteenth century on the banks of the River Ribble in Lancashire, near the site of a Roman bathhouse, and was subsequently placed in the British Museum. It covers the whole head of the wearer and is moulded in the shape of a realistic human face. Very probably it was intended for use in the hippica gymnasium *or cavalry sports. A number of similar helmets have been found in various parts of the Roman empire, but it seems likely that the cavalry games were of Celtic or Eastern origin.*

In one version of the games, the teams took turns to act as targets while the others threw light javelins at them to score points. In addition to a full-face helmet, a breastplate and greaves were worn and a large round shield was carried. The horses' heads were also armoured. (The British Museum, London.)

Cast of the lower part of Trajan's column (left), showing the early stages of the first Dacian war (AD 101–2). Under the emperor Trajan, Rome made its last substantial conquest in Dacia, now modern Romania. At the conclusion of the successful campaign, a commemorative column was erected in Rome. In the second panel from the bottom we see legionaries cutting and hauling wood, still clad in their lorica segmentata armour. In the third panel Trajan stands amid a group of standard-bearers, being presented with the heads of his enemies. The Emperor himself wears a muscle-cuirass, and a number nearby wear helmets of the 'Imperial Gallic' style. Two of the soldiers immediately behind the Emperor carry oval shields. The Dacians appear as long-haired, bearded and wearing trousers and sleeved jerkins. The whole pillar is shown below. (The Victoria and Albert Museum, London.)

stylistically, from what is often known as the 'jockey-cap' style or *coolus*, to the Gallic type, or to the modified 'Montefortino'.

Body armour was also of several possible types. Best-known of the later Roman armours is the *lorica segmentata*, a Renaissance term describing a series of bands of iron, fastened together on the inside by strips of leather and closed by laces, buckles and straps. However, mail (*lorica hamata*) and scale armour (*lorica squamata*) were also in use, as was a variant in which small scales were attached over mail. Shields were large, curved to the body and usually rectangular. The normal method of construction was of linen and hide over laminated wood. Bosses and often rims were of metal.

The legionary's universal side-arm was the *gladius*, now usually suspended from a leather belt, the multiple ends of which were often adorned with metal plates. These metal plates formed an apron, though the effect was more decorative than protective. *Pila* for throwing were carried, often with a square-sectioned block behind the head, to which the head was attached by means of a flat-sectioned tang.

Armoured cavalry were in use, and these *cataphracti* carried heavy lances. Auxiliary cavalry were often of Greek or Numidian extraction and more lightly equipped. Auxiliary infantry were also usually light troops, often used as skirmishers. Archers of Eastern origin were employed, and these are sometimes depicted as defended with mail shirts.

Though the empires of ancient Greece and Rome eventually fell and disappeared, they left an indelible stamp on methods of warfare and on weapons – as great as that on social organization. The growing use of heavy cavalry was to have far-reaching consequences; the lance, pike, *spatha*, bow and articulated metal body armours were all to reappear in later years in different guises. Greek and Roman military organization were to be rediscovered in the Renaissance and were used as the basis of many drill books and theories.

A panel from the Danish Gundestrup cauldron, c.200 BC. This is one of a relatively few illustrations of the Celtic warriors who were the implacable enemies of Rome. It shows cavalry, infantry and trumpeters.

Polybius, the Greek historian of Rome (c.200–after 118 BC), gives vivid descriptions of Celts who went into battle naked, but it seems that the majority were clothed if not armoured. The infantry here appear to wear breeches and some sort of cap. They carry long shields with round bosses and spears. The cavalrymen have spears and crested helmets.

One dismounted figure between the trumpeters and the spearmen also wears a crested helmet. It may be that he is a leader or a dismounted horseman; he has what appears to be a sword on his shoulder. (The National Museum of Denmark, Copenhagen.)

Celtic bronze shield (above) from the River Thames at Battersea, first half of the first century AD. According to the second-century Greek commentator Pausanias, the Celts had no defensive arms other than their shields. This may not literally have been true, but they were heavily reliant on long shields, usually of wood. This bronze piece is actually a cover for a wooden framework rather than a shield in its own right. It is of high quality and one of the most accomplished pieces of British Celtic art. Most shields were a good deal simpler and for the most part decorated only with a boss or designs applied to the surface. Construction was normally of three planks butted together; a central hole contained the handgrip. One wooden shield found in Littleton Bog, County Tipperary, Ireland, survives in its entirety and is covered all over in leather. (The British Museum, London.)

Celtic horned bronze helmet, first century BC (left), dredged from the Thames near Waterloo Bridge, London, in the nineteenth century. With horns too thin to be in any way defensive, this type of helmet has been variously interpreted as ceremonial or intended specifically for standard bearers. This latter interpretation is supported by the discovery of a relief from Bormio in Northern Italy showing a Celtic standard bearer in similar headgear. (British Museum.)

CHAPTER 2

FROM THE DARK AGES TO THE CRUSADES

After the death of the Emperor Marcus Aurelius in AD 180, pressure on the Roman Empire mounted steadily. The expansion from north-western and north-eastern Europe of the Goths, Franks, Allemans, Vandals and finally the Huns was both military and demographic. In the second century, warfare on the Danubian frontier along the 'limes' – the Roman defensive frontier – was mirrored by internal instability. The last two gains of Rome were Britain, raided in 54 BC and taken in AD 43, and Romania, conquered in AD 101–6, but steadily the empire was falling apart. Foreigners filled not only the ranks of the auxiliaries but of the legions too, and subject peoples now claimed independence.

Rome itself fell in AD 456 but the eastern part of the empire – Byzantium – continued and even developed new forms of warfare. The mainstay of the Byzantine forces was élite heavy cavalry, now using stirrups and clad in mail shirts. These horsemen were backed by swarms of lightly equipped archers and heavier infantry or *scutati*, bearing round shields, helmets, spears and swords.

Each of Rome's enemies had its own distinct cultural identity. The organization of the German tribes, whose most spectacular victory had been that of the Teutoburger Forest in AD 9, was far more individualistic than that of the Romans. Based on family ties, the basic unit was the 'hundred', each one being led by an *ealdorman* or *hunno*. Loyalty was to the prince or *fürst*. Personal bravery was highly valued, but large-scale military organization was lacking.

The Sutton Hoo helmet (far left), Anglo–Saxon, AD c.625. Discovered on a plateau near the river Deben in Suffolk, the Sutton Hoo helmet was one of a number of remarkable treasures unearthed from the ship-burial mound of a Saxon prince. The owner of the helmet, shield, sword, spears and other objects may have been one of a number of men, but the most likely candidate appears to be Raedwald, King of East Anglia. When discovered in 1939, the iron helmet was crushed and corroded and much painstaking work was required for its reconstruction and conservation. The iron plates were covered with tinned-bronze foil sheets which would have given the original a silvery appearance, and the plates of the skullpiece, sides and neck were stamped with four different decorative motifs. Two of these are scenes from Germanic or Scandinavian mythology. One shows a mounted warrior striking down a mail-clad man who stabs at his horse; the other has a pair of warriors with spears and swords.

The face-mask was similarly covered in tinned bronze, with openings for the features and a small moustache modelled on its surface. A low crest runs over the crown of the helmet and is decorated on the brow by animal heads; it then comes down between the eyebrows to end in the nasal bar.

In the opinion of the staff of the British Museum's Department of Medieval and Later Antiquities, 'The Sutton Hoo helmet has its roots in the parade helmets of the late Roman Empire but its immediate ancestry lies in a group of helmets buried in the chieftain's graves of Vendel and Valsgarde in the Uppland region of Sweden.'

It is debatable whether the Sutton Hoo helmet was ever intended for practical use, but it is illustrative of the most ornate helmets of the period. (The British Museum, London.)

One of the pre-Viking helmets from a grave at Vendel in Sweden, AD c.600. Although equipped with an extensive mail face-guard, this shows distinct similarities to the Sutton Hoo helmet. Like the British example, this has a skullpiece marked out into smaller areas, a long comb which joins up with moulded eyebrows, and a pierced face-guard. (Upplandsmuseet, Uppsala.)

The Coppergate helmet, Anglo–Saxon, AD c.775 (far right). Discovered during building operations in York in May 1982, the helmet was an immensely important archaeological find. When uncovered, it lay face down at the bottom of a wood-lined pit, together with some animal bones, pieces of wood and slag.

Careful conservation revealed a practical-looking helmet of four main elements: a skullpiece, two hinged cheek-pieces, and a curtain of mail for the neck. Over the skullpiece ran four brass bands in the shape of a cross. The inscription on these was translated as 'In the name of our Lord Jesus, the Holy Spirit, God the Father and with all we pray. Amen'. The name of either the wearer or the maker – 'Oshere' – also appeared. These inscriptions suggested that the owner and his people were Christian and that the piece dated from after AD 627, when King Edwin of Northumbria had been baptized. Furthermore, the form of the letters and the decoration helped place the helmet towards the end of the eighth century.

The mail neck-guard was one of the most interesting features, having survived surprisingly well due to its having been tucked inside the skull at the time of deposition. It was composed of over 2,000 links of two types: some had their ends butted and welded; others were flattened, overlapped and riveted. (York Castle Museum.)

Though the Batavi and the Tencteri had provided auxiliary cavalry for the legions, most German warriors fought on foot. They were armed predominantly with spears or *framea* for throwing or thrusting. Swords became more common in the third and fourth centuries and were then made in northern Germany and Scandinavia. Many were apparently modelled on the *gladius*, but larger slashing varieties were introduced later. The wooden or wickerwork shield covered in leather with its central metal boss was round or rectangular and could be used to parry and to thrust and throw an opponent off-balance. Armour was rare in this period, but leather and mail protection were not unknown.

In some places the Romans' successors aped their former imperial masters or enemies quite closely, not only in terms of coinage and some facets of culture, but also in arms and armour. The Romano-British princedoms were a good example of this. King Arthur was indeed a real ruler, and a 'knight' in the sense that he and his followers engaged in mounted combat, but he had far more in common with the late-Roman fashion of mounted warfare than with the medieval chivalric tradition which was to embroider his story centuries later.

It may be convincingly argued that the 'Dark Ages' which followed the fall of Rome were seen as dark not because of innate chaos but simply through lack of records and scholarship. From this misty period, a few stunning examples of the armourer's and swordsmith's crafts stand out. From Sweden comes the Vendel helmet – a metal skullpiece with reinforcing bands, a bird ornament forming the 'eyebrows' and a lower face-guard of mail. From Britain come perhaps the best-known examples, in the Sutton Hoo treasures. These include not only an axe, a round shield, a sword and the fused remains of five spears but also a magnificent helmet which, like most others of the period, bears strong Roman influences.

The generic name for the round or conical helmet of the Dark Ages is the *spangenhelm*. Some, like the Sutton Hoo or Mörken helmets, which were of the most expensive type, included cheek-pieces or face-plates. Others were plain and rounded or of two halves with a curved central comb, but later models consisted of a framework of ribs between which were triangular plates.

The Sutton Hoo shield, Anglo-Saxon, c.625. The Sutton Hoo shield was found on the floor of the Woodbridge burial chamber, just west of the helmet, and survived only as a jumbled group of metal fittings and fragments of limewood and leather.

In this reconstruction the leather-covered board has been replaced and the fittings have been applied to it. The central iron boss is decorated with a bronze knop showing animals with eyes of garnet. Either side of the central boss are two mounts in the shape of dragons and also a series of smaller domed gilt-bronze bosses. The rim of the shield was also bound with a gilt-bronze strip.

The general style of the workmanship is very similar to the Scandinavian shields from Vendel and Valsgärde. It has even been suggested that the same armourer might have made all of them. (The British Museum, London.)

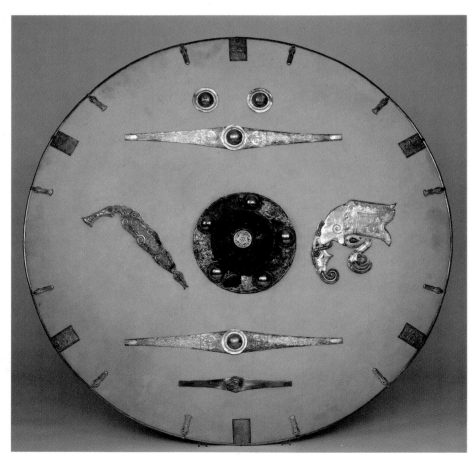

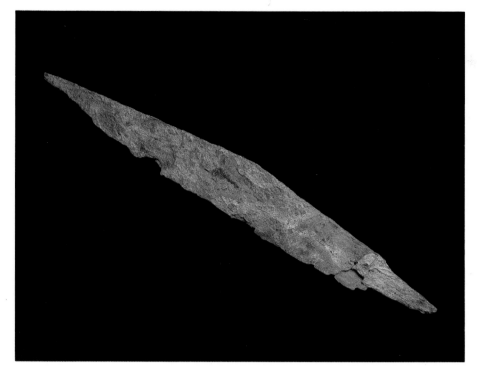

Blade of an Anglo-Saxon scramasax, eleventh century (top left). The scramasax was the most common general-purpose knife and could have been used equally well for a tool as for a weapon. The grips, missing on this example, would originally have been of bone or wood.

The scramasax was not usually over 12 inches in length; longer knives of similar type appear to have been known as the 'langseax' and were favoured as an alternative to the sword by Norse spearmen. (The Museum of London.)

Viking sword hilt (far left) from the Hedeby boat burial, Denmark, tenth century. The decoration on the cross-hilt and pommel is silver inlaid with 'niello'. The black 'niello' is silver sulphide and creates a perfect contrast with the silver.

The next major power to rise in western Europe were the Franks, from Gaul and western Germany. Agathias, the Greek poet, described their early-sixth-century warriors as protected only by linen or leather, with few horsemen but a brave infantry equipped with sword, shield and javelin. Best known of all the Frankish weapons was the *francisca*, a long-bladed axe which could be hurled as well as wielded in close combat. Under the Merovingian Frankish kings the cavalry was developed and the wearing of *brunia* or mail shirts became more common.

Toughest of the Franks' opponents were the Arabs, who, though unsuccessful in their siege of Constantinople from 717 to 718, spread out through north Africa and fought their way across Spain and into southern France. They were eventually stopped at Tours, by Charles Martel.

Only under Martel's grandson, Charlemagne, was the Frankish empire sufficiently unified for the King of the Franks to be crowned Holy Roman Emperor by the Pope.

In 805 an edict of Charlemagne linked the owning of land to the obligation to own a mail shirt, now known as a *birnie*. This was one of the basic planks of feudalism: the warrior classes held land from their king in return for military service, while the other two estates of society – the Church and the peasantry – attended to the needs of the spirit through prayer and to those of the body by growing food. The peasantry could provide infantry, but they were largely limited to club and bow.

The achievement of a universal empire was effectively prevented by the rise of warlike peoples in the north – the Vikings and the Danes. At first, these were only raiders, coming ashore from longships in expeditions of plunder, but increasingly they turned to settlement. These people put great store in arms, giving their swords names and even, like Eric Bloodaxe, being named after their weapons.

The Viking sword was long and straight, and 'pattern-welded' like most others of the period. This means that it was made not of a single piece of iron but of heat-tempered rods or bars, beaten or welded together with untempered pieces. This created a sword with a hard keen edge, but with a flexibility that prevented it breaking easily.

Both Vikings and Saxons used another edged weapon, the 'scramasax'. This term could refer to several types of arm, but generally meant a single-edged, broad-bladed knife with a latched (or stepped) back. Contrary to popular belief, the Viking warrior did not usually wear a horned helmet: a conical design, with or without panels and a nasal bar, was the norm. A few depictions of winged or horned helmets do occur, but these are almost certainly of purely ceremonial helmets for the wealthy.

Norse weapons of the ninth and tenth centuries. Lying on the wooden shield with a central iron boss are a selection of arms of the sort used by the Vikings. Centre foreground are four swords with typical short iron cross-guards and flat or lobate pommels. On the right are spearheads, predominantly long and leaf-shaped, and axeheads. On the left is a helmet with moulded 'eyebrows' similar to those seen on English and Swedish examples. (Universitetets Oldsaksamling, Oslo.)

The coronation sword of the Kings of France, twelfth century (far right). By tradition this is the sword of Charlemagne but, since he died in AD 814, his ownership of it is most unlikely. Nevertheless, it is a triumph of the early medieval armourer's craft. The pommel is large, slightly flattened and intricately decorated; the quillons are straight and end in animal finials; and the scabbard mouth is set with stones. The velvet of the scabbard and fittings is undoubtedly later and bears the fleur-de-lis of France. (The Louvre, Paris.)

Loading arms and armour aboard the invasion fleet (below); from the Bayeux Tapestry, late eleventh century. Strangely the Bayeux 'Tapestry' is not a tapestry at all but an embroidery, for, rather than being woven into the body of the material, its images are built up from stitches embroidered on a backing-cloth. Most likely it was commissioned by Bishop Odo for the new abbey at Bayeux, which was dedicated in 1077. Although quite extensive restoration has since taken place, it remains probably the best single source for information on arms and armour of the period.

Here we see munitions being loaded. The hauberks are conveniently carried by means of poles pushed through the sleeves, helmets are carried by the nasal bars. Swords are slung over the shoulders of the porters in bundles or held by the hilt. The cart to the right carries not only a large 'tun' or 'vat' but spears apparently racked or stacked on top. It is interesting to note that dry vats were later used for the transport of weapons and armour as well as food and wines. (Bayeux Abbey.)

In 911, part of northern France was ceded to the 'northmen' or 'Normans' by the Frankish King Charles the Simple. The Normans later expanded into Italy and played a major part in the first crusade, but their most spectacular success was the conquest of Britain (not just England) from 1066 onwards. The depiction of their arms and armour in the Bayeux Tapestry is the most comprehensive to survive.

The Norman helmet was built up around a framework of bronze or iron and equipped with a nasal bar. The panels which filled the frame were usually of iron, but sometimes of bronze or other tough materials. Occasionally the whole thing was forged from one piece of metal. Under the helmet was often worn a 'coif' or hood of mail. It seems likely that the coif or the helmet, or both, was padded or lined, for otherwise the shock of a blow would have been transferred direct to the skull.

Most of the Norman soldiers shown in the Bayeux Tapestry wear a 'hauberk' or knee-length coat of mail which was put on over the head. Splits at the back and/or front allow the wearer to ride, and a square-shaped reinforcement at the front seems to close the neck opening. The individual links in the suit of mail were riveted closed. Scale armour also appears occasionally during this period. Both mail and scale would have been attached to, or worn over, a long jacket or gown, both to dissipate shock and to prevent chafing.

The legs were normally protected only by cloth or leather bindings, though a few figures in the Bayeux Tapestry do have mail leg defences. The Norman shield was extremely distinctive – long and kite-shaped, of wood with a covering of leather and paint, and with a boss and usually some form of studded decoration. It also appears to have had a rim of metal or wood and a double handgrip and strap arrangement, which allowed the shield to be borne on the forearm or slung on the back.

Norman knights and archers advancing (below); from the Bayeux Tapestry, late eleventh century. Rather than being an homogeneous army, the 'Norman' force was actually made up of several elements. At the battle of Hastings the Norman troops made up the centre, but on the right the French, Flemings and Picards were commanded by Eustace of Boulogne and Robert of Montgomery. The Bretons on the left were headed by Count Alan Fergeant. The whole army numbered no more than 9,000, of which it is likely that no more than a third were mailed cavalry.

The archers were an important element. Those seen on the left have varied styles of dress: one is mailed, but the others have little to distinguish them from civilians, except perhaps for the odd padded cap. The bows themselves are shorter than the later 'longbow' and do not seem to be drawn quite so far in shooting. Spare arrows are carried mainly in quivers, but it was possible to carry a few in the left-hand beside the bowstave. (Bayeux Abbey.)

Bishop Odo riding to battle; from the Bayeux Tapestry, late eleventh century. The prominence of Bishop Odo in the tapestry is another piece of circumstantial evidence suggesting that he was commissioner of this work. He is seen here riding to battle, dressed much as Duke William and wielding a mace. Along the lower border of the tapestry decorative animals have given way to a few examples of the carnage of battle. The strange-looking tree, left, is associated in popular legend with the 'boar apple tree' near which, according to The Anglo-Saxon Chronicle, *King Harold met his fate. (Bayeux Abbey.)*

William of Normandy shows his face to his knights (below); from the Bayeux Tapestry, late eleventh century. During an early assault on the Saxon position at Caldbec hill, a few miles from Hastings a rumour went round that William of Normandy had been slain. Here he tips back his helmet to show that he still lives.

In this illustration William bears a mace or wooden club as a symbol of rank. The man pointing to him has a 'gonfalon' or pennant at his lance head, carried both as a rallying marker and as a symbol of authority. Swords and lances are carried by the other riders. It is noticeable that some of the knights have their lower legs protected by 'chausses' of mail, while others make do with cloth and leather binding. Along the bottom border are more archers. They are not shown with secondary weapons but it is likely that they would have had daggers, hatchets or clubs for close action. (Bayeux Abbey.)

Norman knights attacking the Saxon 'shield wall' (left); from the Bayeux Tapestry, late eleventh century. The Saxons, fighting dismounted and shoulder to shoulder for maximum protection, are armed and equipped in a very similar way to their opponents. Their helmets, mail hauberks and kite-shaped shields appear identical. It is worth noting, however, that a few elsewhere in the tapestry carry round, or even rounded oblong, shields and that axes were a particular speciality of the Saxons. Numerous arrows appear embedded in, or even passing through, the defenders' shields, a testimony to the hail of Norman missiles.

It is worth noting that King Harold's death, portrayed elsewhere in the tapestry, was probably not caused by the famous arrow in the eye. The title over that panel could equally well apply to a figure who is being struck down by a mounted Norman knight. It would in any case be against the social and artistic conventions of the period to show a king being struck down by a man as common as an archer. (Bayeux Abbey.)

Saladin captures the True Cross at the Battle of Hattin, 1187 (top left); from a contemporary manuscript. Saladin was one of the most successful military leaders of the period. Declaring a jihad or holy war against the Christian crusaders, he attacked the Knights Templar and laid siege to Tiberias. This drew out the Christians from their strongholds, and on 3 July 1187 Guy de Lusigan led the crusaders to their greatest defeat, at Hattin on the hills west of the Sea of Galilee.

In the centre of this picture, Saladin wrests the Cross from its guardians. Behind him ride the Saracens in stylized elongated helmets. A number of slightly differing armour styles are apparent: one of the Muslims appears to have scale armour over mail, and there are several types of birnie or mail skirt in evidence. Some of these are short, terminating above the elbow, but Guy de Lusigan (the figure in the surcoat falling backwards) has a shirt with long sleeves ending in mail mittens. Another of the Christians wears a low, rounded Spangenhelm.

On the ground is plenty of evidence of the butchery of medieval combat – severed heads and limbs among splashes of blood. (Corpus Christi College, Cambridge.)

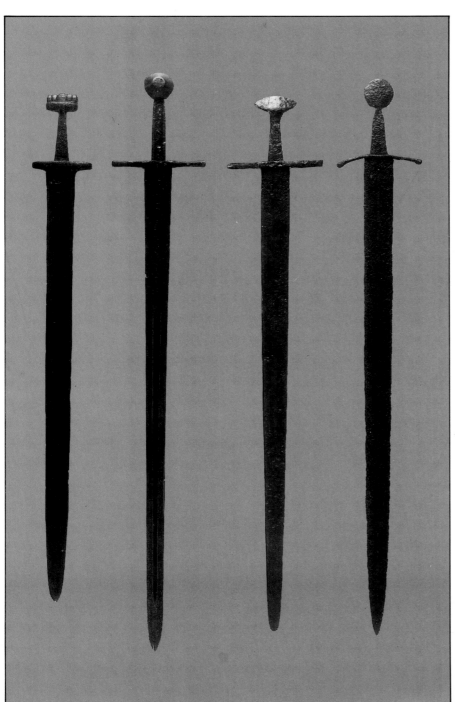

A selection of the sword types in use between 900 and 1300.
Left. Ninth- or tenth-century Scandinavian sword of the type used by the Vikings or Norsemen. The blade is straight and the pommel is divided into five lobes. The quillons are straight and short. The overall length is 30 inches, and it weighs 2 lb 8 oz. One of the quillons is inscribed 'HLI', which may be the first few letters of the maker's name.
Centre left. French knightly sword, c.1300. A straight, slightly tapering blade is here combined with long, straight quillons and a heavy wheel-shaped pommel. It is likely that similar swords were carried during the earlier stages of the Hundred Years War.
Centre right. German sword with a 'Brazil-nut' pommel, c.1000. A number of examples of this type exist from both Switzerland and Germany, suggesting that it was reasonably widespread in central Europe.
Right. Sword with flat 'disc' pommel, probably French or Italian, c.1250. This type of sword with its distinctive pommel appears in many manuscript illustrations of the period and is likely to have had widespread use both in European wars and in the crusades. (The Wallace Collection, London.)

The martyrdom of St Thomas à Becket in Canterbury Cathedral, from a late-twelfth-century Latin psalter (far right). The knights involved in the killing show the main variations in armour and helmets of the period. Foreground left is a figure in a round-topped spangenhelm; beneath his hauberk is visible the hem of a gown, and on his legs are chausses of mail tied at the back of the calf.

Behind and pointing is a man wearing a mail coif with a ventail fastened across the chin. The other armoured figure has a flat-topped cylindrical helmet but no leg protection. (The British Library, London.)

Coloured illustration of the stone effigy of Sir William de Longspree in Salisbury Cathedral, 1226 (below). Sir William is completely clad in mail, but from the flattened appearance of the coif it is reasonable to suppose that the head is also protected by a padded textile or metal cap under the mail.

Sir William was present at the signing of the Magna Carta in 1215 and was one of King John's senior commanders in the Civil War that followed with the recalcitrant barons.

Knightly combat (far right), from The Lives of the Two Offas, *c.1250. The horses of the main participants are covered or 'caparisoned'. There has been a certain amount of discussion over the purpose of the caparison, but there are likely to have been several variations for more than one function. Displaying the arms of the knight was obviously an important use, but it may be that leather or padded versions had a protective function against either arms or the weather.*

Two knights in this illustration wear the 'great helm'. The others have mail coifs. All the riders have high cantles and pommels to their saddles, which hold them firmly in their seats. A number have crowns or coronets around their headgear, indicating rank. The interior of the charging knight's shield is visible, showing that it is held by means of two loops. The forearm is pushed through one loop and the other loop is held. (The British Library, London.)

Like its immediate predecessors, the Norman sword was straight, double-edged and suitable for slashing or thrusting. Cross-guards or 'quillons' were short and either straight or inclined slightly towards the blade. Most of the pommels appear to be disc-shaped or round, but some surviving examples, possibly from elsewhere in Europe, are of flattened or 'Brazil-nut' shape.

In the Bayeux Tapestry, the mail-clad knights carry a number of weapons apart from swords. Lances are carried by many, either couched under the arm or held loosely as a stabbing weapon. Some knights carry pennons or banners: occasionally these were of religious significance and presented by the Pope or bishops; others were probably the personal banners of individual nobles or leaders.

The mace is carried by a number of participants – most notably by William of Normandy himself in one scene, and by his half-brother, Bishop Odo, in another. Tradition has it that the mace was carried by clerics so as not to draw Christian blood, but there is better reason to suppose that it was a symbol of authority and a practical weapon against mail, which had limited resistance against the impact of blunt weapons. Maces of a rough wooden type are shown being used by some of the Saxon infantry, who presumably adopted this sort of weapon for its cheapness and availability.

Axes appear in some number, but seem more popular with the Saxons, who mainly use a long-handled variety, rather like the Viking type. Shorter, smaller axes were better suited to mounted men.

Both crossbows and short-bows were used, but entirely by the lower orders, most of whom had no armour. Evidence exists of crossbows in China as long ago as the third century AD, and they were certainly known to the Roman Empire. Some siege-engines like the *balista* were based on the same principle of mechanically drawing and releasing the string, and the crossbow impinged directly on English history in 1100 when William II (William Rufus) was killed with one in the New Forest. The earliest crossbows were composed of wood, but by about the eleventh century other materials were in use – the particularly springy and resilient 'composite' bow was made of wood, horn and glue. By 1139, the crossbow was thought sufficiently deadly to warrant a specific papal ban on its use against Christians.

The Saxon warrior was not always easy to distinguish from his Norman counterpart, but one particular feature stands out. This is that the Saxons usually fought on foot, whereas the Norman élite charged on horseback. William's army was not homogeneous but was drawn from three different backgrounds: Bretons, Normans and other French. Individual leaders either owed feudal obligations to the Duke of Normandy or were motivated by the prospect of plunder; they brought with them retinues of lesser men. Harold's forces – already exhausted by the defeat of the Norsemen at Stamford Bridge, near York, two weeks earlier, and by the long march from York – were composed of both hand-picked warriors or 'housecarls' and a larger body of 'fyrdmen' who were effectively a peasant levy from the local people.

In the hundred and fifty years which followed the Norman conquest of Britain, there were four crusades whose campaigns together occupied no more than ten years and involved only a relatively small number of knights. Yet the crusades – an embodiment of the Christian knightly ideal – had far-reaching consequences, as the crusaders were brought into contact with Eastern culture and methods of waging war. Most difficult to deal with were the Muslims' highly mobile mounted archers and light cavalry. At first the heavily armed Christian knights were devastating, even against overwhelming numbers, but squabbles between the Christian princes and the growing unwillingness of the enemy to engage in pitched battle ensured that successes were transitory.

The arms and armour of the early crusaders owed much to the weapons

pcunture. ʒ inter sectoꝛu sanguine torrens flu
uius cum loꝛicatu ʒ armoꝛ ponde grauatu
ʒ multipli fatigatum cum multis de suo ex
cercitu simili in comodo speditis: ad ima sub
misit: sine uuluib; miseras animas exala
runt pꝛoditoꝛes: toti posteritati sue pꝛobꝛa
relinquentes. Amnis aut a rigano diuisibus
coꝛuebatur uocabulum: ʒ Riganburne vo
kat uiuat perpetuo memoria: nuncupaꝛ.
Reliqui aut oms de excercitu rigani qui sub
ducatu aymuri regebantur: in abissu des
peraconis demsi ʒ timoꝛe effeminati cum
eoꝛum duce ʒ q̃ magis rigani confidebat:
in noctis crepusculo trucidati: cum uictoria
gloꝛiosa: campu offe strenuissimo ʒ nulla
parte coꝛpoꝛis sui defoꝛmir mutilato. nec q̃
uel letaliter uel periculose uulnerato. licet
ea die multis se letiferis oppoꝛsuisset: periculis:
reliquerunt. Sicq; Offe circa iuuentutis
sue pꝛimicias: a domino data est uictoria
in bello nimis anceipti ac cruentissimo.
ynt alienigenas: uirtutis ʒ induste sue no
men celebꝛe ipsius uentilatum: ʒ odoꝛ longe
lateq; bonitatis ac ciuilitatis: iusto ʒ senuita
es ei circumfusus: nomen ei ad sidera suble
uauit. Poꝛro in crastinu post uictoriam hostiu.
spolia interfectoꝛ ʒ fugitiuoꝛ magnifice comep
nent. ut sibi uolent aliquatenus usurpare ne q̃
modolib; auaricie turpis redargueretur: mi

litibus suis stipendiarus ʒ naturalib; suis ho
minib; peꝛcipue huis quos nouat indigere libe
ralit dereliquit. Solos tn magnates quos ipsemet in
pꝛelio cepat: sibi retinuit incarcandos. redime
dos ut iudicialiter puniendos. Iustosq; ut inter
fectoꝛ duces: ʒ pꝛincipes quoꝛ fama titulos mag
nificauit ʒ peꝛcipue eoꝛ qui in pꝛelio magnifice
ac fidelit se habuerant. licet ei aduersarentur:
seorsum honoꝛifice intumulauit. tciꝛ ei obse
quis cum tamen elaconib;. Excercitus aut popula
ris cadauꝛa: in arduo ʒ eminenti loco ad poster
tatis memoriam: tdi iussit sepulture igno
bilioꝛi. Vnde locus ille hoc noie Anglico estmhul
a strage uidelicet ʒ sepultura interfectoꝛuum
mꝛito meruit intitulari. Multoꝛ eciam et
magnoꝛ lapidum super eos struem excerci
tus offe uoce pꝛeconia iussus congessit emi
nentem. Totaq; circumiacens planies ab ipso
cruentissimo examine: ʒ notabili sepultura
nomen ʒ titulum indelebilem est soꝛtica.
Et blodiweld a sanguine interfectoꝛ denotabaꝛ.
Deletis igitur ʒ confusis hostib; Offa cum
ingenti triumpho ac tripudio ʒ gloꝛia reuertit
ad pꝛopꝛia. Pater uero warinus q̃ sese recep
at in locis tucioꝛibus: rei euentu expectans. ʒ
iam fausto nuncio certificatus. comperiensq;
ʒ securus de carissimi filii sui uictoria: cum
ingenti leticia ei pꝛocedit obuius. Et in am
plexus eius diutissime immoꝛatus: acceptu

Qualmhul
vl Almweld

Gloꝛia triumph.

Samuel · ysai · Bethleem ·

DAVID

· Saul · · Dauid · · golias · dauid

and equipment of the Normans and their contemporaries. Towards the end of the crusades, however, more rounded helmets became common, and there was also a flat-topped variety with sides straight or tapering to the skull. Mail leggings or 'chausses' became more common, and often feet and hands were also covered. Late in the twelfth century the 'surcoat' came into use. This was a long gown, worn over armour. It has been suggested that a light white surcoat was developed during the crusades to reflect the sun's rays, but it was especially useful to show the heraldic arms or devices of the wearer.

It was also during the twelfth century that shields tended to become shorter and flatter across the top, thus developing the modern idea of 'shield-shaped'. Swords became a little more decorative, with elongated quillons and 'Brazil-nut' pommels or inlays, but they retained their long, straight blades.

By the thirteenth century, the crusading movement was more of an ideal than a practical proposition. As the Church and individual states put less into ventures against the infidel, those left behind to carry on the tradition in the East were the new orders of knighthood. The Knights Templars vowed poverty and were descended from those who helped pilgrims to the Holy Land; the Knights of St John began with the founding of a hospital for the travellers in Jerusalem.

The crusades were not the only conflicts of the era. The Capetian kings of France were attempting to consolidate their hold on that country; the Holy Roman Emperors tried unsuccessfully to impose their will on the German states and Italy; and there was constant action in Spain against the Moors. In 1191 on the eastern borders of central Europe was founded the order of Teutonic Knights, who did battle with the Muscovites and Slavs. They were distinguished by a white mantle with a black Latin cross and were led by a *Hochmeister* or Grand Master.

Memorial brass of Sir John D'Aubernoun, Stoke d'Abernon, Surrey, 1277 (below). Apart from being the earliest surviving brass to depict a knight, this effigy is unusual in that the shield was once enamelled in blue.

Except for the knees, which appear to be protected by cops of steel or boiled leather, Sir John is entirely clad in mail. The shield, which is small and short, is suspended over the shoulder by means of a decorated strap or 'guige'. His offensive arms are a sword with a disc pommel and a lance complete with pennon. The sword is suspended by means of a waistbelt worn over the surcoat, and the sword and belt are connected in two places with the aid of a thong, thus ensuring that the sword hangs at a comfortable angle to the body.

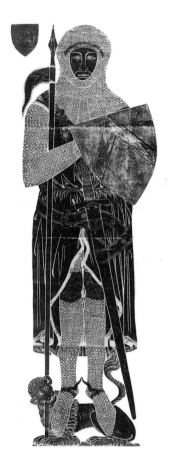

The story of David and Goliath (far left), from the French 'Bréviaire' of Philippe le Bel, thirteenth century. The sling was one of the earliest missile weapons, as the biblical reference suggests. The ancient Egyptians used slings of plaited cord at least a thousand years before Christ, and they were of continuing popularity in the classical era.

As a peasant weapon, cheap and easily constructed, the sling still found some use in early medieval warfare. The most powerful slings were attached to a stave and for ammunition used either rounded stones or lead shot. By 1300 slings were certainly on the wane, perhaps because of the increasing availability of longbows or possibly because of their limited usefulness against armour. (Bibliothèque Nationale.)

Page from a south-German fencing manual, c.1300 (left). These hand-drawn illustrations are two of a much longer series showing various cuts, thrusts and parries with sword and 'buckler'. The distinction between fencing as a sport and fencing only as a preparation for war had not yet been clearly defined by the fourteenth century and it is likely that participants in this type of activity regarded it as both.

The swords portrayed are straight-bladed, double-edged and with typical cruciform hilts. The bucklers vary in detail but are predominantly small, equipped with only one handgrip and easily wielded to parry a blow or throw an opponent off balance with a thrust. That shown bottom left is markedly convex, with a central spike or boss. (The Royal Armouries, London.)

Siege and mounted combat (top); from the Maciejowski Bible, French, c.1250. There is a wealth of detail in this famous illustration. To the right of the picture a castle is under storm; the defenders wearing kettle hats throw down rocks and wield a long-handled axe. Among the attackers one man climbs a scaling ladder, while a miner with a pick covers his back with his convex shield. Behind the miner is a crossbowman squeezing the long trigger of his bow. At his waist is a 'belt claw' to assist in spanning the weapon.

Among the horsemen are visible three wearing 'great helms', a couple wearing conical spangenhelm *(one of which is cleaved by a sword blow)* and others whose skulls are protected only by a mail coif. In the foreground a knight stands in his saddle to deliver a blow from an Eastern-looking falchion or chopper which almost bisects his opponent. *(The Pierpont Morgan Library, New York.)*

Stripping the dead (right); a scene from the Maciejowski Bible, French, c.1250. This is an important reference, for here we see what is worn beneath the armour, and how the mail is joined. The figure at top left who is having his hauberk removed clearly has a cloth smock or gown beneath. Mittens of mail are joined directly to the shirt, but the chausses or mail leg defences are removed separately. Among the men at arms, top right, are a number of different pole arms, an axe, a spear, and a broad 'guisarm' or 'glaive'. *(The Pierpont Morgan Library, New York.)*

Knights leading away prisoners (far right, bottom); from the Maciejowski Bible, French, c.1250. Interesting details on the wearing of mail are apparent here. Three figures at least appear to wear cloth helmets or hoods over which the mail can be pulled up. Several men show a cloth garment projecting from the hem of the mail shirt. A line in the mail, stretching from chin to ear, on a number of the coifs suggests a reinforce or extra defence drawn up to cover the lower face. *(The Pierpont Morgan Library, New York.)*

ualiter Noe uineam plantauit. et inozauo
ebzius a nudatus. ab uno filiozum irrideri
a duobus ne recante contegitur.

ualiter fabilonis erigit. et deus ex alto
pspiciens superbiam humanam confundit lin
quas. ne se inuicem bedisicantes intelligant.
atque ita ceptum opus non possit impleti.

ualiter Abraam iubente deo summa obe
dientia sacrificare filium suum unicum uo
lens. iam eleuato gladio ut feriret. ab angelo
retrahitur. et aries pter spem oblatus sacrifi
cio destinatur.

uomodo excitus regis Elamitarum. tri
um trium regum. uicto rege gomorre cu
alijs quatuor regibus. captiuos ducuit. inter
alios Loth nepotem habzale.

CHAPTER 3

THE HIGH MIDDLE AGES: 1250–1500

At the beginning of the thirteenth century, England lost the Duchy of Normandy to France and now also faced civil war. The Holy Roman Empire was torn with strife between Pope and Emperor, and the Spanish noble houses remained locked in struggle with the Moors. Almost by default, France emerged as a leading power. Three further crusades led briefly to the recapture of Jerusalem from the Muslims, but the crusaders were now on the defensive and the seat of war was in central and western Europe.

During this period the knight passed from being mail-clad to being armed 'cap-à-pie' in plate armour, and the initiative passed from the *arm blanche* to missile weapons. Early in the thirteenth century, the familiar flat-topped helmet was fitted with various face-guards, and ultimately the need for greater protection led to the development of the 'great helm' – an all-enclosing cylindrical helmet. Later this was given a tapering top and reinforcing bands. A crest placed atop the helmet allowed easy identification of the knight, whose face was now totally obscured by his helmet.

Conical or rounded helmets also continued in use, and small skullcaps or plates were sometimes worn beneath the mail coif. Mail enclosed most of the body, and the long-sleeved hauberk now usually ended in mittens. Mail was soon supplemented by the solid plate. The earliest cuirass may have been of leather, but rigid metal plates were soon introduced. Sometimes small plates were sewn to the surcoat, and often discs of metal or 'couters' were attached at the elbow and angular guards or 'poleyns' at the knee. Steel plated gauntlets begin to appear at the end of the century.

Coloured illustration of the memorial brass of Sir Robert de Septvans (or Setvans), 1306, from Chartham in Kent. Save for solid knee 'cops', Sir Robert is clad completely in mail. The coif is pulled back to reveal the head, and the mittens which hang loose at the wrists are obviously slit to allow the hands to emerge. The shield is sharply convex, and the knight's shoulders are fitted with ailettes. The strange device which appears on the ailettes, surcoat and shield is a winnowing fan. This is an allusion to the family motto 'Dissipabo inimicos Regis mei, ut paleam', meaning 'Thus [like chaff before the fan] will I scatter the enemies of my king.'

Mid-fourteenth century stained glass (far left) depicting one of the four Lords of the Manor of Tewkesbury. The period from 1250 onwards saw the rise of plate armour until by about 1450 the knight was fully covered. (Tewkesbury Abbey.)

Memorial brass of Sir William Fitzralph, from Pelmarsh, Essex, c.1323 (left). Sir William's armour shows an interesting transitional stage between mail and plate. Mail appears to be worn all over and on top of it are strapped the solid plates which cover arms, shins and feet. The foot-plates, which are here worn with 'prick' spurs, are sometimes known as 'sollerets'. The shield is deeply convex and bears the Fitzralph arms: 'or three chevrons gules, each charged with as many fleurs-de-lys argent' (a gold shield with three red chevrons, each having three silver fleurs-de-lis). On the right are two effigies from a similar period, those of Sir John de Creke and his wife from Westley, Watterless, Cambridgeshire, c.1325. (The Victoria and Albert Museum, London.)

The Four Lords of the Manor of Tewkesbury, from a mid-fourteenth-century stained glass in the south-west window of the choir of Tewkesbury Abbey. These knights demonstrate several points on the transition from mail to plate which gradually occurred during the fourteenth century. The figure on the left is clad almost entirely in plate, the others wear various mixtures, but all have knee 'cops' and ailettes at the shoulder. All four figures have short lances and swords. The swords are suspended by a variety of means, some at a slight angle to the body by means of a multi-tongued belt. The blades are all straight, and the hilts are cruciform with a round or disc pommel. (Tewkesbury Abbey.)

In the late thirteenth century, additional defences were also added to the shoulder, but the main purpose of the 'ailettes' (or upright shoulder-plates) seen in many contemporary illustrations was identification or decoration. Indeed the ailettes may well have been of wood or leather. They were of varied shapes and were probably held in place by laces.

Horse armour was expensive and cannot but have limited the agility of the mount. Even so, mail 'trappers' covering much of the horse were used by some knights as early as 1250, and often the front of the horse's head was protected by a 'chanfron' or 'chaffron'.

Both crossbows and longbows became of increasing importance. Crossbows were improved with new materials. In the fourteenth century, steel was used for the bow itself, and ratchets were used to maximize the power, providing more pull than was possible by hand alone. In one system a turning-handle was employed, but a simple 'graffle' or hook seems to have been more commonly used. Often the front of the bow was equipped with a stirrup in which the archer placed his foot while the hook, suspended from a belt, was engaged with the bowstring. Pushing down with the foot and/or straightening the body spanned the bow. The 'bolts' or 'quarrels' were short and heavy, often with square chisel-like heads for maximum penetration.

The longbow had the significant advantage of speed over the crossbow. A good archer could have more than one arrow in the air at a time, and ensuring sufficient 'sheaves' (or bundles of 24 arrows) could be a major logistic headache for the medieval army.

Stained glass depicting St Blaise, St George and St Leo, from the north side of the choir clerestory of Wells Cathedral, c.1345. By the mid fourteenth century, St George (centre) was usually portrayed as a paragon of knightly virtue. Here he carries the familiar shield with red cross and a lance, and he is wearing a long surcoat with the same device. The helmet is rather low and rounded, unlike the more pointed basinets which became popular later in the century. (Wells Cathedral.)

Stained glass of the Adderbury knight, English, late fourteenth century. Wearing a mixture of mail and plate, the Adderbury knight presents a fairly typical 'arming' of the period. His basinet is high and pointed, and his neck is protected by mail. The pose shows not only the 'waisted' style of metal gauntlet but also the underside of the vambrace with its dovetailed joint. The knight carries a lance and a rather stylized oblong shield. (The Bodleian Library, Oxford.)

The longbow which was to become legendary on the fields of Crécy, Poitiers and Agincourt was really introduced to Edward I by the Welsh. It was a 'self' bow – i.e. of one wood, rather than a composite of several materials – and it usually reached to eye-level or higher on its user. Illustrations suggest that this was a good deal longer than the so-called 'short-bows' of the Normans and Saxons. Yew was the ideal wood, having a fine, long grain, and was preferably taken from the bole rather than the bough of the tree. It is not by accident that yew comes to grow in so many churchyards: it was actively cultivated for bows. When domestic stocks were low, good wood was imported, and there were even laws stating that so many staves for manufacture had to be brought in with other produce.

Arrow shafts were of several woods, including ash, oak, beech, elder and birch, but the best flights were of goose feather. Logic dictated the best length of the arrow to be that from the archer's nose to the tip of his finger – the 'cloth yard' – allowing maximum 'draw' with aim.

Types of arrowhead were many and various, depending on the purpose. Best penetration was achieved with a heavy 'bodkin' point, small in surface area at the tip and able, at short range, to pierce mail. In modern experiments, arrows from reconstructed medieval war bows have pierced steel helmets under favourable conditions, and a number of contemporary sources suggest that even plate armour could be pierced, given a competent archer and an angle of incidence approximating to 90 degrees. Broad or barbed heads were also used in war and were deemed particularly useful for galling enemy cavalry. Against an unarmoured target they created large wounds and were difficult to extract – some treatises on surgery even suggested that such arrows should be pushed on through the victim and cut

The Warwick chanfron, English, c.1400. Horse armour of all types is rare, and this particular chanfron or head defence is one of the earliest surviving. It is known to have been at Warwick castle in the seventeenth and eighteenth centuries, and was illustrated in Francis Grose's Treatise on Ancient Armour *of 1786. This early type of chanfron has a bulbous and pierced projection for the nose; it would once have had rigid extensions for the ears. Later examples are usually more gutter-shaped. Chanfrons of the bulbous type are illustrated in fourteenth and fifteenth century manuscripts, for example, in the poems of Christine de Pisan and the* Chroniques de France. *(Royal Armouries.)*

off at the far side, rather than be pulled back with the concurrent tearing.

The bow was so useful, and so cheap, when compared with other weapons, that in England it became a way of life. Englishmen were obliged by law to keep a bow, and there was a statutory requirement to practise this sort of archery. Also, fathers were obliged to supply their sons with bows until they came of age.

Despite its great successes in the fourteenth century, however, the longbow was not invincible and required careful tactical handling. If armoured cavalry got among the archers, their only recourse was to the dagger, Welsh knife or 'maul' (hammer), and such conflict tended to be one-sided. It was far better to position the archers behind sharpened stakes on a rise, and to place men-at-arms with pole arms and armour between the 'herses' or wedge-shaped formations of archers.

Better armoured protection was continually sought during this so-called

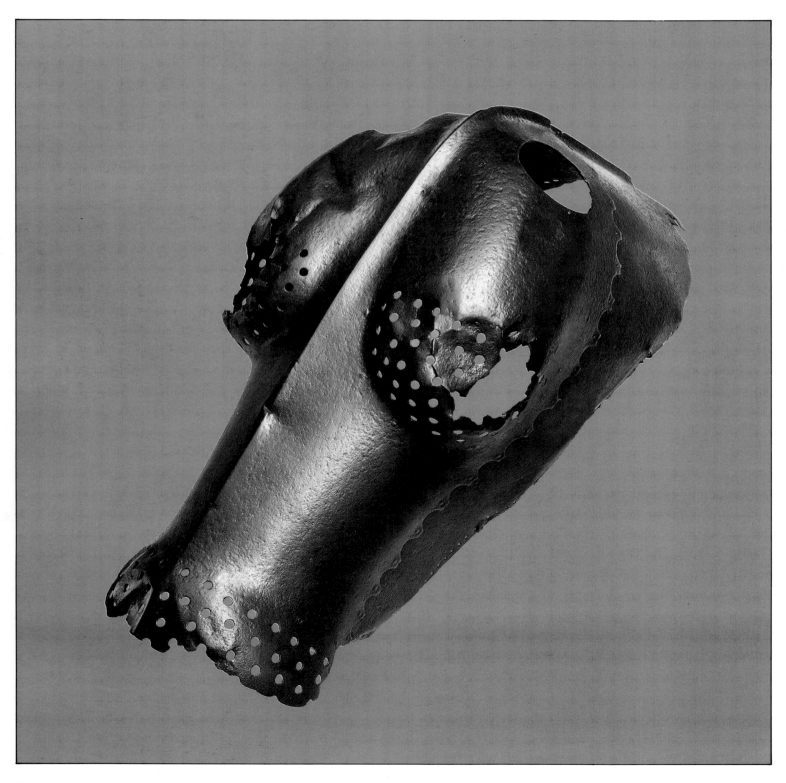

'Great helm' (left), possibly English, c.1375. This helmet is composed of three parts: a crown-plate, a cone-shaped piece and a slightly flattened cylinder which forms the sides. The edges of the 'sight' or vision slot are turned outward to further protect the eyes. The lower right side of the face is pierced by a series of round holes for breathing. Twenty-one other pairs of holes suggest where the lining, mantling and crest were all attached. Similar helmets are portrayed under the heads of a number of English sepulchral effigies, and another is among the funeral achievements of The Black Prince in Canterbury Cathedral. 'Great helms' of this form were probably in use from about 1340 to 1380. (The Royal Armouries, London.)

Coloured illustration of the monumental brass of Sir Hugh Hastyngs, from Elsing, Norfolk, 1347. This particular brass is believed to have been made on the Continent and shipped to England; other parts of the same memorial show figures of Edward III; Henry, Earl of Lancaster; and four other knights. Sir Hugh wears a rounded basinet with a raised visor and a gorget. Much of his body is covered with mail, but there are one or two interesting features. The thighs, for example, appear to be protected by some sort of studded 'pourpoint' or leather defence, and the arms are encased in metal vambraces with roundels at the joints. Over the armour is worn a short surcoat bearing the arms of the knight.

'transitional' period. By the mid fourteenth century, the metal breastplate was becoming more common, as were 'greaves' and 'cuisses' to protect the shin and thigh respectively. 'Vambraces' were now sometimes added to protect the arms. Late in the fourteenth century came the 'brigandine', small plates riveted to a canvas coat – light, flexible and relatively inexpensive. Often the plates were riveted inside or in pockets, leaving a characteristic pattern of rivet heads on the outside of the garment. This covering, and tinning of the plates, helped to prevent rusting. A yet more sophisticated defence was the 'coat armour' or 'jupon'. Shaped like a civilian coat, this was stuffed with wool; used in conjunction with other defences, it was good at absorbing shock or slashing cuts.

The 'basinet' was a typical fourteenth-century head defence, with a conical skullpiece extending to cover the cheeks and neck, often worn with a visor. This visor, which could usually be raised or removed, was of several possible patterns. Best known are the so-called 'pig faces', sharply pointed with 'breaths' or breathing-holes and slot-like 'sights' or vision ports, common towards the end of the century. Various globular types with barred or perforated fronts are also found.

Edged weapons developed further to deal with the increasing use of plate armour. 'Great swords' were made with long blades and grips to allow two-handed or 'hand-and-a-half' use. 'Falchions' or shorter, broad-bladed hacking-swords were also used and must have had an effect not unlike that of a massive meat-cleaver. Daggers were commonly worn on the belt opposite the sword. Some were matched to the sword with straight quillons; the 'ballock' dagger was equipped with a phallus-like grip with round lobes below, and the 'baselard' had a cruciform pommel and a diamond-section blade.

The tomb and funerary achievements of Edward, Prince of Wales – 'The Black Prince' (1330–76) – in Canterbury Cathedral. By tradition, Edward was known as 'The Black Prince' from the colour of his campaign armour. He saw his first major victory against the French at Crécy, where, aged only sixteen, he commanded the right flank of the army, supported by the veteran knights Sir Reynold Cobham, Sir John Chandos and Godefrai d'Harcourt. Poitiers, ten years later, was arguably his greatest action. Here, in command of an exhausted army, he defeated the much larger forces of King John 'The Good' of France and captured him. Destined never to be King of England but leaving behind one of the most formidable military reputations of the age, he died in 1376.

The effigy shows him in a very good-quality armour, almost entirely plate. It is covered with a surcoat and worn with a sword-belt low on the hips. The shield (right) shows the royal arms of the Plantagenets – the lions of England quartered with the fleur-de-lis of France. The 'label' of three 'points' (downward pointing bars) is symbolic of Edward's position as oldest son (other 'labels' could be applied to shields to denote younger sons). The 'great helm' is decked out for funerary use with a massive crest. A less ornate version would have been used in battle, or the crest would have been removed altogether. (Canterbury Cathedral.)

Visored basinet, c.1380. As the 'great helm' lost popularity, it was largely replaced by the addition of visors to the earlier open faced basinet. The pronounced conical and snout-faced helmet shown here was known as the 'hounskull', 'dog-head' or 'pig-faced' basinet. The slots for the eyes are flanged, and there is a group of 'breaths' or breathing-holes on the snout itself. The mail which hangs from the headpiece and covers the wearer's neck and shoulders is known as a 'camail'. This form of headgear probably first evolved in Italy or Germany around the mid fourteenth century, but quickly spread elsewhere. (The Royal Armouries, London.)

Battleaxes and maces were also common at this period. The former were commonly shorter hafted than their early equivalents; the latter were all-metal or metal-headed, often with radiating flanges. For the mace to be effective it was not at all necessary that it pierce the opponent's armour, for it relied principally on 'blunt trauma'. The smashing weight of the head transferred its energy to the enemy's armour, crushing it or simply bruising or concussing the wearer.

Sometimes both weapons and helmets were secured to the breastplate by chains, to prevent their loss in battle. Pikes with long shafts allowed armoured men and cavalry to be engaged at long range.

The fifteenth century saw the apogee of the armourer's craft, with the best-equipped knights now clad from head to foot in plate armour. In many states there were now attempts to break down the war-making potential of the nobility and build up more professional armies loyal to the king. In France and Burgundy, ordinances were issued regulating the composition, pay and discipline of armies. Hired mercenaries formed a sizeable proportion of many forces.

The mid-fifteenth-century knight was commonly clad in back and breast armour, either solid or of a multi-piece construction. Solid types were of several possible designs, one of the most important of which was the *Kastenbrust* – box-shaped around the chest but sharply waisted. The multi-piece constructions often had an upper plate covering the chest and a lower, waisted 'plackart'. The 'fauld' which protected the buttocks and thighs was attached to the bottom of the breastplate and back-plate by means of sliding rivets.

Arms and legs were also commonly fully armoured. The feet were now defended by 'sabatons' of articulated plate and the hands by laminated gauntlets. These could be either of mitten form or with separate fingers – fully articulated. Some were actually designed to lock around weapons.

Two major styles are commonly identified in fifteenth-century armours, which broadly speaking are 'Italian' and 'German'. In northern Italy, clean and simple lines, often of a rounded form, were favoured. The headgear was normally an 'armet' or closed helmet, a close-fitting 'sallet' or a 'barbute'. This last was strongly reminiscent of the ancient 'Corinthian' helmets, with enclosed cheeks but a T-shaped opening at the front. Milan was the major centre of production, and many of the Italianate armours are loosely known as 'Milanese', whatever the exact place of manufacture.

German armour production was mainly in the south, with its great centres at Augsburg, Nuremberg and Passau. Generally, the German armours exhibited elongated 'Gothic' styles and, from mid century, exaggerated fluting, fans and wings. German sabatons were often extremely long and pointed, aping civilian shoe fashion. The helmet worn with Gothic armours was usually a sallet after mid century – large and deep, with a tail to the rear and a half-visor or simple eye-slits. Towards the end of the century some sallets acquired laminated neck-guards. Another type, commonly known as a 'black' sallet, was unpolished and sometimes painted with decorative or heraldic patterns. The sallet was usually accompanied by a 'bevor' or lower face-guard attached to the 'gorget' or neck defence.

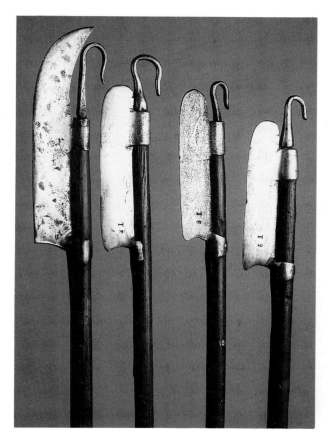

'Lochaber' axes (above), made in Scotland. The lochaber axe was a traditional pole arm of Scottish troops over a long period and examples are encountered from the fifteenth to the eighteenth century. Some appear to have been carried as late as the second Jacobite rebellion of 1746. It has been suggested that the later forms developed from the medieval glaive. (The National Museum of Antiquities, Edinburgh.)

The tomb effigy of Walther von Hohenklingen, killed at the Battle of Sempach, 1386. The sculpture shows the mixture of plate, mail and padded armour in surprising detail. The pointed basinet, breastplate, gauntlets and leg defences are all clearly plate, but underneath the breastplate is worn a padded 'gambeson' or jacket with tight waist and puffed sleeves. The 'aventail' protecting the knight's neck and shoulders is difficult to interpret but may be leather or another padded material, perhaps reinforced with mail. Below the sword and resting on von Hohenklingen's foot is the 'great helm', complete with tall crest. (Schweizerisches Landesmuseum, Zurich.)

Bundle of arrows from the wreck of the Mary Rose. *Making up arrows into 'sheaves' held with a leather spacer with holes was the handiest way to manage large quantities of arrows. That this was not unique to the navy is proved by finds of similar 'spacers' at Bury Castle and elsewhere. (The Mary Rose Trust, Portsmouth.)*

Longbow stave from the wreck of the Mary Rose, *sunk off Southsea Castle near Portsmouth, 1545. The longbow was already gaining ground as a weapon of war at the end of the thirteenth century. Within the next hundred years it became not only the mainstay of English armies but a weapon sought after by most European states. The bow maintained its predominance until the sixteenth century, when it was finally ousted by firearms, but even then there were many who thought it should be retained. Sir John Smythe, writing in 1590, thought that the bow had three really significant advantages: speed of shooting, lack of any mechanism to go wrong and the terrifying effect of massed flights of arrows. The bow being examined here by a member of the diving team is notable not only for its length but for its pronounced taper towards each end. Bows varied not only in length but in 'pull', the most powerful requiring over 100 lb of 'pull' to shoot them. Skeletons found in the wreck suggested to bone-specialists that English archers' bodies were actually slightly physically deformed by continual practice with powerful bows. (The Mary Rose Trust, Portsmouth.)*

The Battle of Agincourt, 1415 (far right); from a later manuscript illustration. Agincourt was the greatest victory of the English King Henry V over the French. This late-fifteenth-century depiction shows the English fighting left to right under the Plantagenet standard. Some of the infantry wear surcoats with the cross of St George. The mounted knights are the main subject, but archers also feature and one arrow is shown piercing the breastplate of a horseman. Almost all the participants are shown with part or full armour and sallets on their heads. The horses wear little armour except for chanfrons on their faces. According to one account, however, most of the English bowmen actually 'had no armour but were wearing doublets, their hose rolled up to their knees, with hatchets and axes or in some cases large swords hanging from their belts; some of them went barefoot and had nothing on their heads, while others wore caps of boiled leather'.

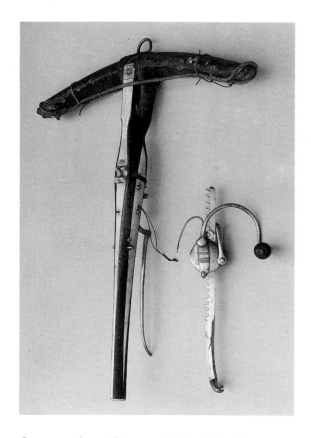

German crossbow with 'cranequin' (above), late fifteenth century. Most military crossbows were too powerful to be spanned by hand and required the use of either a windlass or a 'cranequin'. The cranequin worked on a rack-and-pinion principle. It was attached to the top of the tiller, the claw was hooked over the string, and the handle was turned to span the bow. The cranequin was more expensive than a simple windlass, which was effectively a handle, two ropes and three pairs of small wheels. The cranequin was, however, easier to handle – particularly on horseback. Payne-Gallwey in his book The Crossbow *therefore suggests that mounted troops and huntsmen would have used the cranequin whenever possible, while the windlass remained the common tool of the infantry. (The Metropolitan Museum, New York.)*

High-medieval armour did not rely solely, or even principally, on its thickness or toughness to resist weapons. Design of the plates themselves was critical: the best presented an acute angle to the likely direction of attack, so that missiles and sword cuts were likely to glance off or, if they struck home, were more likely to meet a tough edge than a vulnerable flat. Fluting, carefully used, was also effective, as corrugated materials are usually stronger than flat ones.

The best armours were handcrafted for an individual nobleman, being tailored effectively like a modern bespoke suit, to that one man. The ensemble was usually known as a 'harness'. Cheaper armours were ordered in lots for the less well off, and probably fitted less well as a result. Apart from the great German and Italian centres, armour was also made in the Low Countries, France and England, but stylistically these tended to follow the established designs, occasionally taking Gothic and Italian elements and blending them together.

Contrary to popular belief, stimulated by a Victorian cartoon, the mounted man did not require cranes and cradles to get him into the saddle, nor was he entirely helpless once knocked over. Full harness was heavy, but the weight was well distributed and articulation allowed reasonable freedom of movement. Exhaustion and heat were problems in protracted combat, and so as much as possible of the harness was left off until required, being carried by servants and pack animals. Knights could remove their own armour, but it was customary to have the assistance of a squire or servant.

'Great swords' continued to be popular throughout the fifteenth century, as did the mace, and the war hammer and poleaxe gained in popularity. Both these latter weapons brought more leverage to bear in close combat – to cleave open armour, to pierce it with a spike or to smash it. As armour reached such heights of technical accomplishment, the weapons which were ultimately to bring about its downfall were also under development. Longbows and crossbows were already limiting the effectiveness of the knight, especially when on horseback; but it was to be firearms in their many forms which reduced armour to its last vestiges.

Incendiaries for *pots de feu* (literally 'pots of fire' – thrown or dropped), pumping from tubes, and fire arrows had been known since classical times,

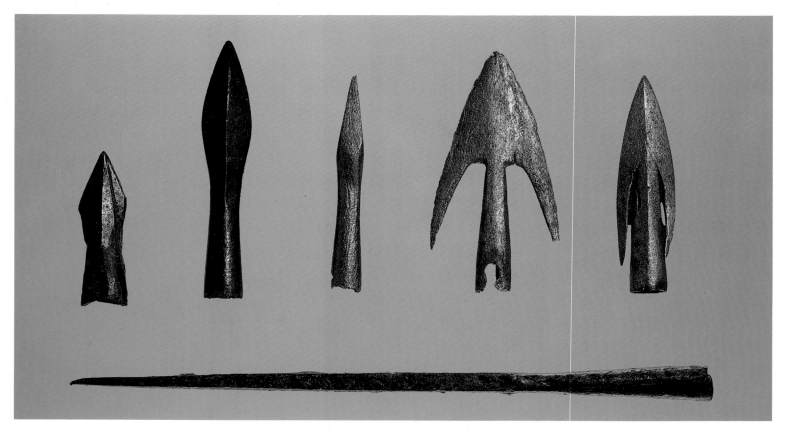

Crossbowman's 'pavise' (left), Bohemian, c.1450. The crossbow was relatively slow to load, and the archer could himself become a target while preparing his next shot. One answer to this problem was the 'pavise', a tall shield which could be propped in front of the bowman when in action. This shield bears the arms of the town of Zwickau in Saxony, and the central monogram may be that of Albrecht of Bohemia. The back of this pavise still has its original T-shaped carrying-handle. (The Royal Armouries, London.)

Crossbowmen sheltering behind pavises; from the Beauchamp Chronicles, *drawn in the late fifteenth century. The shields are slightly concave and held by some sort of prop, and the shooters wear sallets. (The British Museum, London.)*

but isolating and refining the ingredients for a truly explosive material took much longer. Fireworks of various sorts existed in China and the Far East, but there is no reason to suppose that the gun was invented anywhere other than in western Europe, in about 1300.

At no time did the gun suddenly supplant bows and armour, but over a period of three centuries firearms slowly gained their ascendency. The first guns appear to have been vase-shaped, or simple tubes rested straight on the ground or in trestles. Arrows or stones are likely to have been the first projectiles, and indeed cannonballs were known as 'gonne stones' for a considerable period.

The efficiency of these first guns was likely to have been strictly limited, as good powder was difficult to make and extremely expensive. Accuracy was also likely to be low, as was velocity, given the ill-fit of projectile with barrel. These guns were best used in siege situations, where the target was likely to be large and to stay still, or for shock effect against cavalry or inexperienced troops.

Medieval arrowheads (far left) found in London. The two on the left are of a type normally associated with crossbow bolts or quarrels – short, angular and heavy. The two on the right are typical of the longbow shaft, the very broad-headed example being particularly useful against horses. The head in the centre could conceivably be for either longbow or crossbow, but the remarkably long 'bodkin' head at the bottom is unmistakable, being used as an armour-piercing missile. (The Museum of London.)

Coloured copy of the memorial brass of Thomas Beauchamp, Earl of Warwick, at St Mary's Church, Warwick, 1406. Thomas became Earl of Warwick in 1369 and served in France in the 1370s. During the Peasants' Revolt, he helped to crush the rebellion at Bury St Edmunds in 1381. He also took part in an expedition to Scotland, but he was imprisoned for conspiracy against King Richard II in 1397. During the following century, the title of Warwick passed by marriage to the Nevill family, one of whom was 'Warwick the King-maker'. Thomas Beauchamp wears full plate and not only a war sword but also a 'left-hand dagger' at his waist belt. Over the armoured breastplate and possibly attached to it is a short, tight-fitting surcoat or jupon bearing the Beauchamp arms. Around the hem of this projects a skirt of mail protecting the upper thigh and groin.

'Rondel' dagger, western European, c.1400. The 'rondel' dagger – so called because of its disc-like pommel – was probably first carried around 1350 and was very common by 1400. The stiletto-style blade was triangular in cross-section and well suited to a deadly thrust through mail or the gaps between armour plate. Frequently used to finish off an opponent or as a knight's last resort, these and other medieval daggers are sometimes referred to as 'misericordes', from the French for mercy. (The Royal Armouries, London.)

By the time of Crécy in the Hundred Years War – 1346 – guns were a common element, if not a very important one, in English armies and it may be that handguns as well as ground or rested pieces were already in use. In 1400 the commonest form of handgun was a bronze or iron tube between eight and sixteen inches long, held in a straight 'stock' or 'tiller' of wood. It seems that these were not usually held right up to the eye for aim, but were rested on a post or wall, perhaps by means of a hook-like protrustion, for safety and absorption of recoil. Resting also made firing easier, for they were ignited by poking a hot wire or taper in at the 'touch-hole'.

In Germany early in the fifteenth century came the first mechanical means of ignition, which allowed the gunner to keep his eye on the target while shooting. This was the 'matchlock' – a simple pivot with means for attaching a smouldering 'matchcord' to one end. Pressure on a trigger-bar swung the cord to the touch-hole. Later in the century, refinements such as the 'sear-lock' and the 'snap matchlock' were invented; these devices assisted the movement by means of a weak spring, they supported the mechanism with a rudimentary 'lock-plate' and allowed the 'match' to return to its start position.

At the end of the fifteenth century the European military scene was complex indeed. Armies were held together by a mixture of money payments and feudal obligations, and the fighting man varied from the fully armoured lord to the ill-clad peasant, levied to fight for a few days with bow or club. Fighting mercenaries composed a fully established profession, with its best recruiting areas in the poorer parts of Europe like Scotland or Switzerland. High-technology mercenaries with handguns or good cross-bows were also available, predominantly from the Low Countries, northern Italy and the German states. Siege warfare was an important part of most campaigns, and here the siege-engine, larger guns and the crossbow were used to their best advantage.

By 1485 England's position among the leading states in Europe had been largely undermined by defeat in the Hundred Years War and by the intermittent dynastic civil war now known as 'the Wars of the Roses'. Germany and Italy had failed to achieve unity, though individual states possessed wealth and influence. The leading powers in Europe were now undoubtedly France and Spain. The former had acquired a fair degree of unity under Louis XII and Francis I, while the latter finally managed to expel the Moors by 1492 and had united the kingdoms of Castile and Aragon following the marriage of Isabella of Castile with Ferdinand of Aragon in 1469. With Charles I of Spain seeking election as Holy Roman Emperor and Francis I of Valois as King of France, the rivals were on a collision course through their attempts to dominate continental Europe. At the same time, the 'rebirth' of classical ideas, through scholarship, was giving new ideas to soldiers and military thinkers just as surely as it was leading to a 'Renaissance' in art and literature.

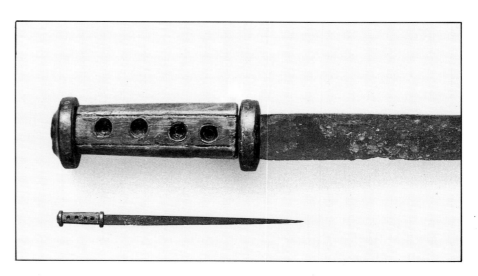

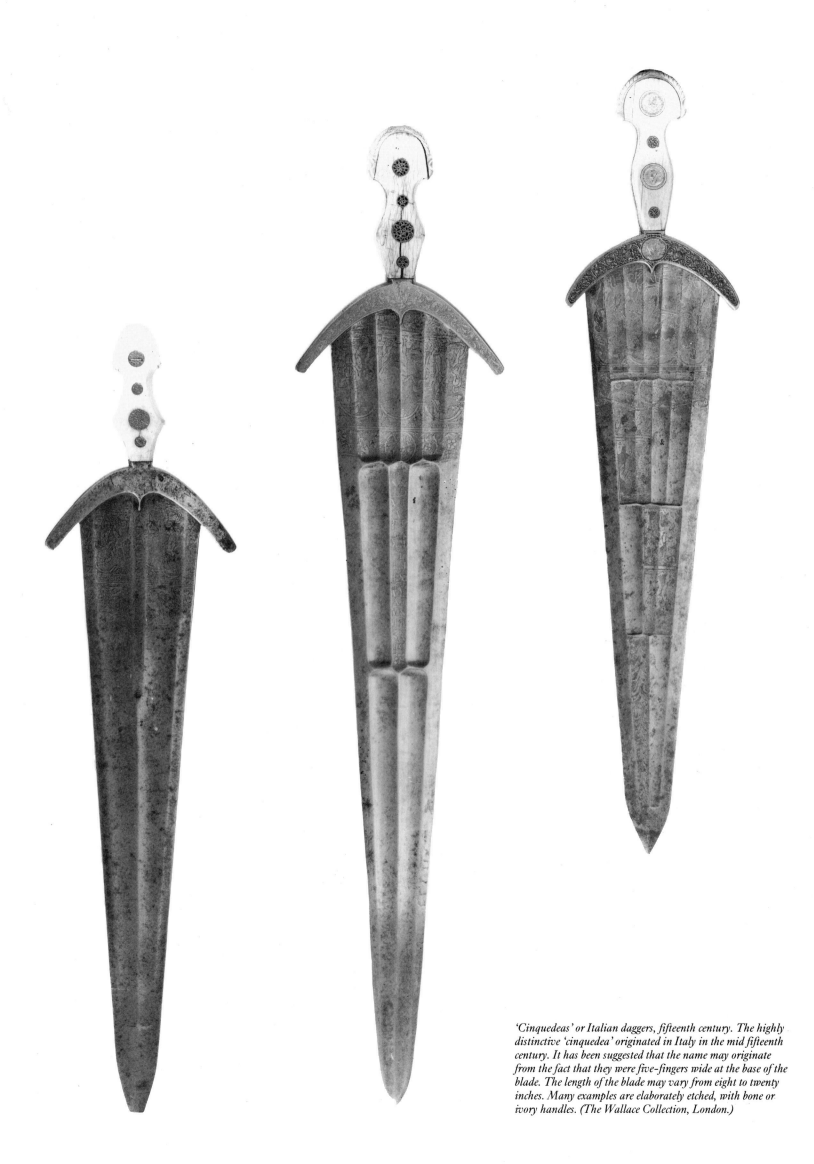

'Cinquedeas' or Italian daggers, fifteenth century. The highly distinctive 'cinquedea' originated in Italy in the mid fifteenth century. It has been suggested that the name may originate from the fact that they were five-fingers wide at the base of the blade. The length of the blade may vary from eight to twenty inches. Many examples are elaborately etched, with bone or ivory handles. (The Wallace Collection, London.)

Scottish 'targe' or 'target' (right). The traditional Scottish shield, in use from the twelfth century to the end of the eighteenth, was made of wood and covered in leather. Decoration was usually of brass bosses or studs, and the shield was held at the rear by two loops. Generally only twenty inches in diameter, it was handy to use in conjunction with a broadsword and to parry an opponent's blade or bayonet. Most surviving examples are later than 1500. (The National Museum of Antiquities, Edinburgh.)

As the medieval era drew to an end and the classical influences of the Renaissance became more widespread, there was an increasing diversity of sword types and more emphasis on style and decoration (opposite page).
Left, fighting-sword with 'fishtail' pommel and copper quillons, Italian, c.1460.
Centre left, venetian sword with down-curved quillons and a diamond-section blade, c.1490. The hilt is probably a replacement.
Centre, Swiss or German 'baselard' short-sword, c.1530.
Centre right, German sword, possibly with a replacement Italian hilt, mid sixteenth century.
Right, Falchion, German or north-Italian, sixteenth century. (The Wallace Collection, London.)

The Rout of San Romano *(below) by Paolo Uccello, c.1450. At San Romano in 1432, the Florentines under Niccolo Maruzi da Tolentino defeated the Sienese. This closely observed work shows a good number of arms and armour details. In the centre of the picture is Niccolo Maruzi himself, easily identified by his commander's baton. His followers are armed 'cap-à-pie' with plate armour, the joints of which are protected by mail. The horses have little armour, but the high saddles and leather furniture are apparent. Along with the lances, which are their primary weapons, some riders carry long, straight-bladed tapering swords or war hammers. Some crests and short cloaks are worn. The most interesting figures occur in the background – a billman with an Italian-style war bill and a series of crossbowmen. The latter include some figures loading – pressing their bows on the ground with or without the use of a stirrup and belt hook. The artist Uccello (1397–1475) is celebrated as an early exponent of the use of perspective. (The National Gallery, London.)*

Spanish brigandine, c.1480 (above). Brigandines were normally constructed of small overlapping plates riveted inside a canvas doublet. Found all over Europe, they came into use towards the end of the fourteenth century and were quite common from the middle of the fifteenth century. It does not seem that they were used much beyond 1600. A significant feature which helps to date this example is the fastening down the centre. Later brigandines often laced down one or both sides. (Musée de l'Armée, Paris.)

Italian armet à rondelle, c.1475 (top right). With a full visor and a closed face, the armet is usually regarded as a direct ancestor of later 'close' helmets. The 'rondelle' on this example is the disc at the back of the neck. This protects the point where the two cheek-pieces join at the back and also provides a support for the strap of the bevor which covers the lower face. (The Metropolitan Museum, New York.)

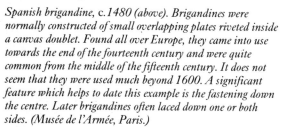

Side view of an Italian barbute, c.1470 (bottom right). The profile of this helmet demonstrates its distinct similarity to early Greek helmets; it also shows clearly the line of rivets by means of which the lining was attached. (The Metropolitan Museum, New York.)

Milanese barbute, mid fifteenth century (far right). Commonly known as a 'barbute', the correct name of this style of helmet in Italian is the celata alla veneziana. Though originating in Italy, this almost classical form of helmet saw fairly widespread use in the mid to late fifteenth century. This example, probably Milanese, dates from c.1460. It has a T-shaped face-opening, is made in one piece and shows evidence that a lining was once fitted by means of rivets around the middle of the skullpiece. (The Wallace Collection, London.)

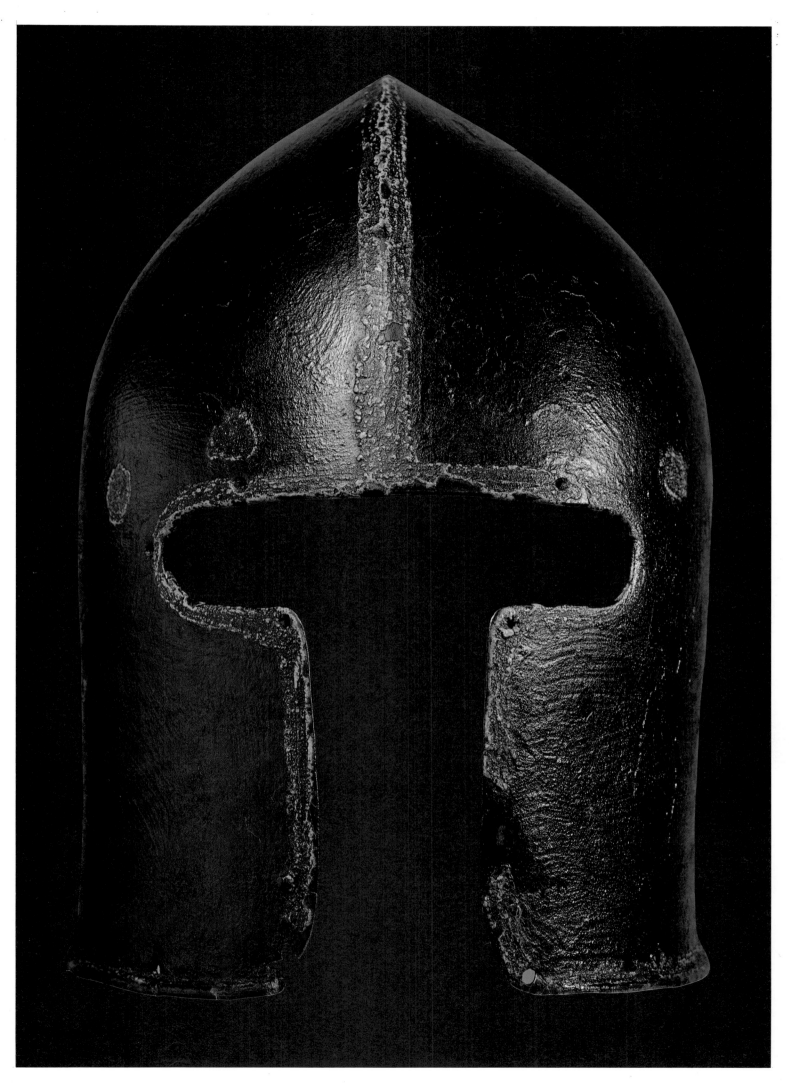

The wearing of a late-fifteenth-century composite German field armour. A good harness was made in the same way as a good-quality suit of modern clothes – it was carefully measured and specific to an individual. Youths who had armour would inevitably require further sets as they grew. Good 'field' armour for use in war had to be light as possible for sustained ease of movement consistent with protection. Field armours are therefore usually lighter than siege or tilt armours. Noticeable here are the fixing details of the armour, which was normally worn over an 'arming doublet' or sleeved jacket. The plates are held together by a mixture of buckled straps and ties or 'points' of waxed twine. Vulnerable points in the harness are covered by extra plates – as for example at the armpit, where there are 'rondelles' or 'besagaws'. The insides of the arms are protected by mail, and the whole of the lower face is covered by a plate known as the 'bevor'. With the helmet in place and the visor down the head would be completely covered. The model for this picture is Graeme Rimer, now keeper of weapons at the Royal Armouries. (The Royal Armouries, London.)

German sallet, late fifteenth century (top). Probably the most common form of headgear in use at the time, the German sallet is recognizable by its pronounced tail, comb and deep skullpiece. When worn with a bevor and the visor in the down position, it gave excellent protection. (The Royal Armouries, London.)

German 'black' sallet, c.1490 with painted decoration (left). The sallet probably evolved in France or Italy early in the fifteenth century. Most German examples have visors and a tail to the rear. The 'black' sallet was left rough from the armourer's hammer and not ground or polished; often, however, other forms of decoration were adopted, like a cloth covering or a painted heraldic design. This particular example has a deep skullpiece with a pronounced ridge running down the tail. The visor is short, locked with a spring stud and equipped with vision slots or 'sights'. (The Royal Armouries, London.)

German equestrian harness in 'Gothic' style, probably
made for Waldemar VI of Anhalt-Zerbst (1450–1508).
The 'barding' or horse armour is a remarkable survival
and includes a chanfron for the horse's head, a 'peytral'
or chest-plate and a 'crupper' for the flanks. The armour
for the man comes from more than one harness but gives a
good impression of a sallet worn with a high bevor or defence
for the throat and lower face and of full armour as worn
by the armoured knights of central and western Europe in
the later part of the fifteenth century. (The Royal Armouries,
London.)

'Puffed and slashed' German armour, c.1525, together with a globular 'close' helmet, c.1530. This armour is attributed to Kolman Helmschmied, and the etching was probably executed by Daniel Hopfer or Hans Burgkmair. The broad horizontal bands, cross-hatchings and gilt work imitate the civilian dress style of the period. The armour comprises a globose breastplate, a fauld of four plates, tassets, a backplate, a 'culet' or rump-guard and arm defences with 'pauldrons' or shoulder defences attached. The gorget and helmet, though in keeping with the whole, were not made to accompany this garniture. The 'close' helmet has a visor with horizontal vision slots and a chin-piece hinged on one side. (The Wallace Collection, London.)

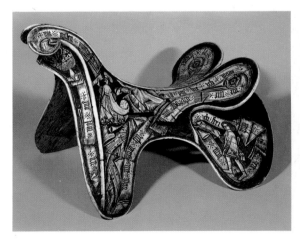

German 'Gothic' saddle, c.1440–80. The late-medieval saddle was typically higher in the cantle or pommel than the modern saddle. This example may have been used by a knight, but is not designed to hold the rider as firmly in place as the typical war saddle with its squared seat and leg bolsters. The decoration on this example is of stag-horn, incised and stained red, green and black. In the pictures, a man and a woman are conversing – they agree to get betrothed but she plaintively asks, 'But what if the war should end?' Doubtless this was one of the less often considered hazards of fifteenth-century warfare. (The Wallace Collection, London.)

Reconstruction of an English billman, c.1480. The bill was originally an agricultural implement intended for pruning and hedging but was pressed into service by levied troops; its long shaft gave it a useful reach, particularly against mounted men. By the fifteenth century, specifically military types of bill with long spikes had developed and were in widespread use in Europe and Turkey.

In the sixteenth century a distinctively English form of bill was in use, shorter in the blade than that seen here. As the Venetian ambassador wrote in 1551, English bills 'have a short thick shaft with an iron like a peasant's hedging bill, but much thicker and heavier than what is used in the Venetian territories, with this they strike so heavily as to unhorse cavalry and it is made short because they like close quarters.'

This billman wears an open-faced barbute, a mail shirt and a leather brigandine or 'jack' on which shows a pattern of rivet heads. The grouping of the rivet heads in threes in this reconstruction was quite typical. The rivets were functional in that they held in place the plates of steel which were the main defence of the brigandine. It is doubtful if many ordinary foot-soldiers or retainers were much better equipped than this. Full plate was largely reserved for the higher orders of society. (The Royal Armouries, London.)

A selection of late-medieval and early-modern hafted weapons.
Left, Swiss halberd, sixteenth or seventeenth century.
Second from left, Italian bill decorated with a rose design, c.1500.
Centre, Boar-spear with leaf-shaped head, German, c.1600.
Third from right, Italian bill with scorpion maker's mark, probably Milanese, c.1500.
Second from right, French or German axe, late fifteenth century.
Right, German halberd, c.1490. (The Wallace Collection, London.)

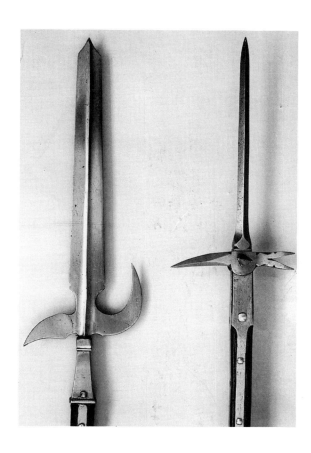

'Lucerne hammer', Swiss, c.1500 (above). Towards the end of the Middle Ages an increasing number of different pole arms were in use. The 'Lucerne hammer' was similar to the poleaxe and the war hammer but was equipped with four prongs on one side rather than a hammerhead or blade. The armoury at Lucerne was well stocked with these arms, and so has given the type its name. (The Metropolitan Museum, New York.)

Gilt Italian war hammer, c.1490 (above). The war hammer was one of the few edged weapons which could tear open or badly dent plate armour. This example has a beaklike blade on one side and a faceted hammer on the other. A spear prong at the tip allows thrusts as well as swings, and down either side are long metal 'langets' or 'cheeks' which prevent it breaking in action. (The Wallace Collection, London.)

Iron handgun 'hackbutt' or 'arquebuse-à-croc', early fifteenth century. Forged in iron with a large 'tiller' or handle to the rear, early handguns were ignited by a separate hot iron or match applied to the touch-hole. This made aiming very difficult, and so resting the gun on a wall, bank or other convenient object became the norm. Many guns were therefore fitted with a hook or stop under the barrel, to be placed over a wall for easy resting and absorption of recoil.

This hook was known in German as a Hak or Haken and in French as a croc, and helped to give the gun its name. In the sixteenth century the term 'harquebus' or 'arquebus' was then applied to other firearms. (The Royal Armouries, London.)

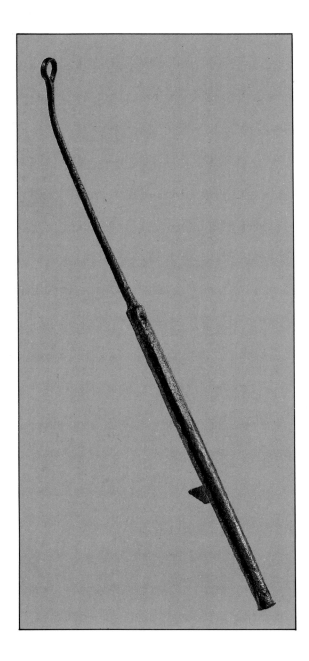

Siege of a town in Africa, from Froissart's Chronicles. Froissart was a fourteenth-century chronicler, but this illustration may be slightly later. Any connection with Africa must be strictly nominal, for the town and the troops portrayed are straight out of a western-European siege c.1400.

In the centre are three 'bombards' or heavy siege-guns laid in trestles; that nearest to the observer is being lit by means of a red-hot wire or primitive linstock. Left foreground are four carefully observed crossbowmen. One of these bends to wind up the windlass or screw on his crossbow while the others take aim. All the bows appear to be equipped with foot stirrups, for easy loading, and long triggers. The bowman far left has hanging from his belt a vicious broad-bladed falchion for close-quarters work. (The British Library, London.)

CHAPTER 4

FROM THE RENAISSANCE TO THE SUN KING: 1500–1750

During the sixteenth century, gunpowder, pikes and paid armies – together with the new learning and the rediscovery of ancient texts – finally transformed knights into 'gentlemen' all over Europe. Horsemen and full armour alike became steadily less useful in war as they were eclipsed by the handgun and cannon. The armourer's craft developed towards an art, as his skills were deployed more for parade and tournament than for war.

The crux of the problem was the penetrative ability of the lead ball, for a common man with a firearm and a pikeman by his side could bring down the noblest in the land. A partial answer was to make armours thicker, and they were indeed increasingly graded 'pistol-proof', 'caliver-proof' or 'musket-proof'. Thicker meant heavier, however, and heavier meant less manœuvrable. Increasingly, therefore, more armour was discarded. Leg defences went first, then parts of the arm covering. Many helmets were made lighter and open-faced as time progressed.

In terms of weapons, specialization was the key, combined with regimentation and a 'discipline' learned from the ancients. Niccolo Machiavelli, the Italian political philosopher, was among the first to scour the classical writings for political and military inspiration, but soon every general and drill-master was doing the same.

The most widespread military hand firearm of the mid sixteenth century was the 'harquebus' or 'arquebus', with a fairly small bore and a matchlock mechanism. Handcrafted and of varying design, harquebuses suffered from difficulty of ammunition supply and lack of standardization. At this date they were likely to be a minority in any regiment or army, being brigaded together with pikes, bows, halberds and also a few 'targetiers' with heavy shields for attacking fortifications.

A little later, the harquebus was joined by the 'caliver', a shoulder arm of slightly larger bore, whose main advantage was that the 'calibre' was more carefully regulated, so that any particular batch was supposed to be able to use the same ball. The term 'caliver' was derived from the expression 'of the calibre of the prince', meaning guns of the prince's bore.

Biggest in this family group was the 'musket'. This was fired from a forked rest, and some authorities suggest that it was originally used by the Spanish with a two-man team. Harquebus, caliver and musket were collectively known as the 'small shot'. Confusingly, the term 'artillery' was often applied to all missile weapons, including bows, siege-engines and small arms as well as cannon.

Louis XIII, King of France, Crowned by Victory, *school of Rubens, c.1630. Throughout the period from the Renaissance to the end of the eighteenth century it was customary for monarchy and nobility to be portrayed with the full panoply of war and leadership. Some of this symbolism – such as the laurel wreath, the commander's baton (seen in Louis's hand) and the wearing of armour in portraiture – dated back to classical times. Other elements in this picture are rather more modern. Under Victory's feet are visible a large 'target' or shield and at least two different sorts of wheel-lock pistol. Under Louis's boots is a cuirassier armour blackened against the effects of weather either by chemical treatment or by painting. Projecting near the helmet is the hilt of a horseman's sword with a pierced shell guard. (The Royal Armouries, London.)*

Italian maces, sixteenth century.
Centre Italian, seven-flanged metal mace with wooden handle,
c.1540. The head is decorated with scrolled foliage.
Left, North-Italian, possibly Milanese, mace with six flanges,
c.1560. Blued steel finish with silver and gold decoration.
Right, Milanese mace of 'morning star' type – that is, with
small spikes radiating from a ball – c.1560. Decorated with
Greek mythological figures and representations of the Muses.
(The Wallace Collection, London.)

'*Henry VIII's walking staff' or 'holy water sprinkle' – a*
combined mace and matchlock gun, English, c.1540. One of
the best-known but least practical of combination weapons, the
multi-spiked mace conceals three gun barrels. (The Royal
Armouries, London.)

Pistols or 'dags' gained importance during the sixteenth century. Their size made them easy to conceal, and contemporary rulers regarded them as particularly murderous weapons and so sometimes banned all firearms under a certain length. In the military sphere they were a weapon of the cavalry and of officers, who purchased their own.

An innovation which made the pistol a viable proposition was the new 'wheel-lock' mechanism. This is perhaps best pictured as similar to the modern cigarette-lighter. A piece of iron pyrites is brought into contact with a rough rotating wheel to strike a spark which ignites the fine 'priming-powder'. The 'priming' creates a flame which passes through the touch-hole, setting off the main charge, the explosion of which propels the ball out of the gun.

The amount of armour worn by the sixteenth-century soldier depended on his function. The 'small shot' wore little or none, except perhaps a helmet. Pikemen and halberdiers were slower to discard their defensive arms, as they were expected to close in hand-to-hand mêlée with the enemy; thus most nationalities wore breastplate, back-plate, 'tassets' to protect thighs and groin, and even arm defences. Cavalry were increasingly divided into 'light' and 'heavy'. 'Cuirassiers' and 'lancers' could well be equipped with three-quarter armour finished off with stout leather boots, and were thus close to the high-medieval knight in the degree of protection. Lighter cavalry like the 'harquebusiers' relied more on firearms and were often limited to a helmet and breastplate, or lighter cloth and metal defences, and would sometimes fight dismounted. Horse archers were largely an eastern European phenomena and, like other mounted skirmishers, used little armour.

Armour manufacture divided ever more sharply into 'munition' and higher-quality products. At Greenwich near London, Henry VIII established a manufactory of the highest-quality armours by importing craftsmen of the best skill for the armour of the royal family and nobility. Similar prestige workshops existed over much of Europe. Meanwhile, a simple standard of protection without embellishment was sought for the humble foot-soldier. These armours became increasingly slab-like and utilitarian.

Popular sixteenth-century military headgear included the 'morion', 'cabasset' and 'burgonet'. The burgonet was supposed to be of Burgundian origin and was an open-faced helmet with a brim projecting over the eyes

The Battle of Pavia, 1525, *by an unknown artist. At Pavia, the Spanish under the Marquis of Pescara defeated Francis I of France in one of the most important engagements of the era. Perhaps most remarkable was the use of the Spanish harquebusiers, who on this occasion did not wait behind cover with their firearms but advanced on the flanks of the enemy cavalry. The King of France was taken prisoner.*

This picture shows the French fighting from left to right under the fleur-de-lis banner. The Spanish and their allies fight from right to left under the double-headed Hapsburg eagle and the arms of Spain. Foreground left is a cavalry action, showing fully armoured knights with closed helmets charging with the lance. Foreground right are visible drummers, halberdiers, pikemen and harquebusiers. In the centre of the picture are siege-guns and pikemen fending off cavalry. (The Royal Armouries, London.)

Silvered and engraved harness of Henry VIII, c.1515 *(previous page). The King's armour shown here was silvered rather than gilt – contrary to prevailing taste – and was made in celebration of his first marriage, to Catherine of Aragon in 1509. It shows a number of interesting features indicative of the period in which it was made. Most obvious is the tonlet, a skirtlike armoured defence of the thighs. This gave great protection and aped the civilian robes of the perioid. The pauldrons or shoulder defences have large upright flanges which help protect the vulnerable regions of the neck and lower face. The sabatons or foot defences are square-toed, in agreement with the prevailing shoe style.*

The horse's armour or 'barding' is Flemish but appears to have been decorated in England and dates from the same period as the armour for the man. Note the high cantle to the saddle, the armour of which protects the groin and thighs of the rider. (The Royal Armouries, London.)

91

and a raised comb to the skull. It was common over much of Europe in varying forms from 1530 through to the early seventeenth century. The cabasset was usually narrow-brimmed and tall, slightly flattened in section and increasingly common from the mid sixteenth century. Some examples have a small stalk-like protrusion on top, and it has been suggested, perhaps erroneously, that the name 'cabasset' is from an Italian word for 'pear', hence the description 'pear-stalk cabasset'. Another derivation says that this helmet is really a form of 'Spanish morion' and that the name is anglicized from a Spanish word for 'helmet'.

The popular term 'morion' is normally applied to the comb morion – open-faced, with the brim forming high peaks front and back and a raised comb. Although many people think of this form as typically Spanish, it was a common pikeman's headgear over much of Europe, including France and Germany from mid-century. It also became popular, in decorated form, for royal and municipal guards. Perhaps best known are those of the Nuremberg and Munich town guards and the Saxon Royal Guard. Similar types appear on the heads of the Lord Mayor's guard during the London Lord Mayor's Show, although later English open-faced helmets were usually known simply as 'pots'.

High-quality breastplates and arm defences followed very much the style of civilian costume. The 'peasecod' breastplate of the later sixteenth century, with its lower part projecting outward and downward, mirrored the shape of the doublet. Others took on a decorative 'puffed and slashed' design and seem to have been popular with the German *Landesknechte*. Sabatons or metal foot defences, which had largely been discarded by about 1540, were generally square-toed or slightly spoon-shaped like contemporary footwear.

Composite horse armour of Otto Heinrich, Count Palatine of the Rhine (1502–59) (opposite page). This armour has been assembled from a number of roughly contemporary garnitures, more than one of which are associated with Otto Heinrich. The burgonet or helmet and the pauldrons, for example, come from an armour now in the Musée de l'Armée, Paris. Nevertheless, the black and gilt effect is stunning and not atypical of a fine armour of the period. Like his contemporary Henry VIII, Otto Heinrich was of considerable stature – much of the armour here dates from the period 1532–6, when he would have been in his middle thirties. (The Wallace Collection, London.)

Memorial brass of Sir Ralph Verney and his wife, from Aldbury, Hertfordshire, 1547. Full plate armour was already rare by the mid sixteenth century yet remained as an artistic convention with the aristocracy. Sir Ralph here wears a harness which was perhaps 30 years out of date by the time it was depicted. Over the armour is worn a short coat of arms displaying several 'quarterings'; earlier heraldic displays, intended for use in war, had been kept simple. Behind his head appears a 'frog-mouthed' helmet suitable for jousting. (The Victoria and Albert Museum, London.)

The Massacre of the Innocents, *by Pieter Bruegel (c.1525–69), Netherlands school, c.1560. Pieter 'the peasant' Bruegel was particularly noted for his observations of ordinary people, their enjoyments and their plights.* The Massacre of the Innocents *is typical in this respect, for, although the ostensible theme is Herod's massacre of children soon after the birth of Christ, the scene is obviously set in the sixteenth-century Netherlands. The parallel with the Spanish behaviour in the Low Countries at the same time is probably too strong to be coincidental. One version of the picture, now at Hampton Court, was thought so shocking that the children in the picture were painted out and replaced with household goods.*

Most of the soldiers in the picture are in full armour and armed with lances; some have a tonlet-style guard or skirt of armour around the buttocks and thighs in typical early-sixteenth-century style. Of equal interest are the lesser figures who wield a variety of edged weapons, including hunting-swords, falchions and at least one boar-spear. (The National Gallery, London.)

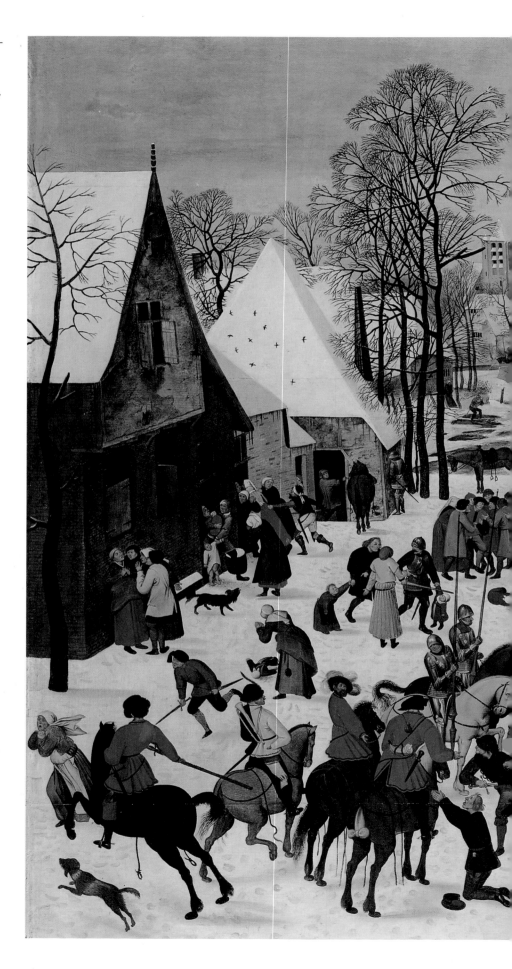

*German 'brayette' or codpiece, mid sixteenth century (top).
Coming into use at the end of the fifteenth century, the codpiece
reached its most extreme forms in the middle sixteenth century.
Some are little less than erections in steel – symbolic rather
than practical defences. Their development mirrors the
development of the codpiece in civilian dress. (The Wallace
Collection, London.)*

Sword development gathered pace, again with a tendency to increased specialization. Two-handed war swords remained popular with the *Landesknechte*, and decorated broad-bladed falchions were common side-arms during the first three-quarters of the century. Additionally, straight swords with more complicated hilts began to be seen more frequently. This was the beginning of what is now known as the 'rapier'. Not all Englishmen adapted easily to this southern European innovation. Sir John Smythe, in his *Certain Discourses Militarie* of 1590, criticized the rapier for its slender, easily broken blade; its great length (which made it difficult to draw) and its 'brawling' hilt.

Where exactly the term 'rapier' came from is unclear: it has been variously ascribed to the German '*rappen*', to tear; the Spanish '*raspar*', to scratch; or even to the Spanish '*espada ropera*' – robe sword. Apart from the narrow thrusting blade, the rapier had a bewildering variety of hilt forms, some of which appear to have little family resemblance. Simple cross hilts continued in use throughout the whole period, but 'swept' hilts with

Half-armour of the Duke of Sessa, together with a parade shield, Italian, c.1560 (right). The half-armour includes a burgonet with visor and high comb, pauldrons, vambraces and articulated tassets and gauntlets, all highly decorated. Shields of the type shown were for display and have since been widely copied for their decorative qualities as well as for their value. The scene on the shield's surface is a classical battle outside a city. (The Metropolitan Museum, New York.)

various knuckle-guards and up- or down-turned quillons appear more typical. 'Cup' hilts and 'shell' guards belong mainly to the seventeenth century. The best modern authority has identified no less than 113 various hilt types for the rapier and the later 'small-sword', with a further 39 types of 'inner guard' which project down from the hilt towards the blade. The same source identifies 93 different pommel types.

By 1618, at the time of the outbreak of the Thirty Years War, European armies had achieved a fair degree of standardization in both arms and armour and fighting methods. Though it still occurred as a novelty, the bow had been largely superseded, and the harquebus was now mainly a cavalry arm. The caliver was also on its way out, and most armies aimed at a force made up of regiments, each of which was half or more musketeers. The smallest administrative unit was the 'company', under the command of a captain, usually assisted by a lieutenant and an ancient or ensign to carry the 'colours'. Signalling was by drum, and a man was usually detailed as clerk or scribe to the company.

Greenwich armour of Thomas Sackville, Earl of Dorset, (1536–1609), made by Jacob Halder, c.1595. This field armour is interesting not only for its quality but in that it is made with additional pieces which can be put on for increased protection. These extra parts shown here are a 'placarte' or reinforcement to the breastplate and a falling 'buffe' or face-guard which can be fitted to close the otherwise open helmet. The decoration is of a zigzag-and-scroll design. Halder was master-worker of the Greenwich armoury from 1576 to 1607. This armour, or one very like it, was the subject of a picture in the contemporary 'Jacobe album' which is now in the Victoria and Albert Museum, London. (The Wallace Collection, London.)

Armet or close helmet, English, c.1600 (right). Closely fitted to the shape of the head, the armet could be shut so as to cover the whole face. It is thought that the modern slang to 'shut your face' has its origin in this type of helmet. This English armet has a moveable chin-piece as well as a visor. The chin is pivoted at the side, and is provided with a locking hook. (The Royal Armouries, London.)

Italian 'pear-stalk' cabasset, early seventeenth century (below). Tall and slightly flattened in section, the 'pear-stalk' cabasset has a narrow brim and a small projection on top which gives it the peculiar modern name. The rivets around the base of the helmet are in the shape of small rosettes and were intended to hold a lining. (The Metropolitan Museum, New York.)

Embossed half-armour attributed to Lucio Piccinino of Milan, c.1590 (opposite page). The use of half-armour at this period was common among both nobility and soldiery but, although the general shape of these plates is usual, their extremely fine quality and the elaborate use of gold and silver damescening put this armour among the best. The breastplate is of peasecod form, with a figure of Mars, the god of war, in the centre and a head of the Greek mythological demon Medusa, with three other figures representing Charity, Fame and Victory. In panels at the sides are Wisdom, Justice, Faith, Truth, Hope and Temperance. (The Wallace Collection, London.)

This system largely grew out of experience gained in the Low Countries during the Dutch revolt against the Spanish, which began in 1560 and continued intermittently until the first decade of the next century. Maurice of Nassau was generally credited with the introduction of the so-called 'Dutch system'.

Infantry gained a primacy on the battlefield, due to their firepower and ability to resist cavalry with the pike. The bigger, stronger pikeman with his armour and usefulness in close combat was seen as the most honourable of the infantry. Cavalry were now predominantly armed with pistols and swords and protected by a breastplate, back-plate and 'pot helmet'. Their main offensive tactic was to ride forward, discharge their pistols and wheel away, attempting to wear the enemy down before closing with the sword.

As the Thirty Years War progressed, more participants came in and military tactics were modified. One of the most important innovators was Gustavus Adolphus, King of Sweden, who fought alongside Dutch and German Protestants against the 'Imperialist' forces of Spain, Austria, Bavaria and other Catholic states. Whether or not Gustavus was personally responsible, the so-called 'Swedish system' began to have a strong influence all over Europe. Musketeers began to fight in shallower lines, three or six deep, and began to be able to discharge all at once as a single 'volley' or 'salvo' rather than having to shoot a single line at a time and fall back. Smaller, handier units were deployed, and cavalry were now encouraged to charge home in a cohesive mass using their pistols after, rather than before, their swords.

Milanese gorget, c.1610 (opposite page). Decorative rather than functional, this neck defence carries a wealth of details of arms and armour in the pictures on its surface. These scenes were copied from the engravings of the Florentine artist Antonio Tempesta (1555–1630) but are reversed. Both front and back plates show an assault on a bridge in which cavalry and infantry are taking part. Also in evidence are blocks of pikemen, boats and siege-guns. The mounted men depicted wear a mixture of open-faced burgonets and 'close' helmets. (The Wallace Collection, London.)

North-west-European cuirassier armour, blackened, c.1600 (above). The final soldiers to lose their full armour were the heavy cavalry, and harness of this type continued to be produced during the Thirty Years War. The last were made not with a 'close' helmet, as seen here, but with a helmet with a peak and wide vertical bars. The colour of the armour shown here is not merely decorative: chemical russeting, blueing or black paint was applied as a defence against rusting. (The Royal Armouries, London.)

Milanese articulated breastplate or 'anime', c.1600 (right). In the sixteenth and early seventeenth centuries there was a fashion for cuirasses which were able to bend. The usual method was to make up the lower part from a series of 'lames' or plates articulated by means of rivets. The articulated and solid parts of this breastplate may have come from separate armours which were later matched. The upper part shows the Virgin and Child, flanked by St Jerome and St Christopher. (The Wallace Collection, London.)

In 1630 the Swedes invaded Germany. After success at Breitenfeld, Gustavus himself was killed in action against Albrecht von Wallenstein's army at Lützen in 1632. The French now bore the brunt of the war against the Imperialists. England, which had largely been kept out of the European theatre of war by Charles I, itself dissolved into civil war in 1642.

Though craft methods were still employed to make weapons, war itself was becoming a very expensive activity. Very large contracts were made for pikes, guns and cannon, and armies were paid – albeit inefficiently – at a national level. The English New Model Army, established in the winter of 1644–5, was a good example of the arming and equipment of the better mid-seventeenth-century armies.

Two-thirds or more of the New Model infantry were equipped with muskets. These were mainly matchlocks, now no longer used with rests but still having a 'bandoleer' of charges. The rest of the infantry long-arms were early flintlocks, variously known as 'snaphances', 'dog-locks' or even 'fierlocks' – a term shared with the wheel-lock. In this type of weapon, a flint was held in the jaws of a 'cock' which snapped down against a 'steel' or 'frizzen', creating a spark which fell into the powder in the 'priming-pan'. This powder ignited, sending a flame through the touch-hole to explode the main charge.

The remainder of the New Model infantry was pike-armed, although the pikemen had now discarded armour altogther. All infantry wore red coats. The New Model cavalry were issued with pot helmets and breastplates and back-plates, though some may have had coats of 'buff' leather – a light and flexible protection against sword-cuts and knocks. The cavalry had swords and pistols and were probably issued with flintlock carbines a little later.

Wheel-lock keys or spanners (right). To fire a wheel-lock required that its spring be tensioned by means of a key. This was certainly a weakness, for wheel-lock weapons could easily be overwound and jammed, or the key could simply be dropped and lost.
Left, Wheel-lock key of octagonal section with tracerywork handle. German, early seventeenth century.
Centre, Italian wheel-lock key, c.1625.
Right, Another German key, mid seventeenth century. The loops midway up each key are for suspension. (The Wallace Collection, London.)

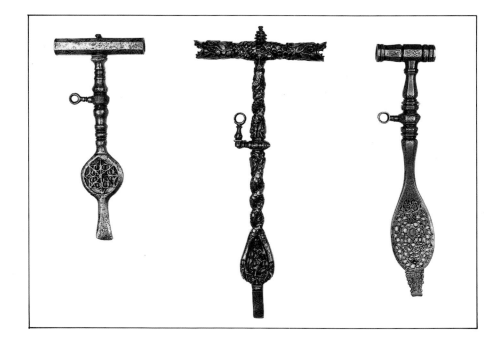

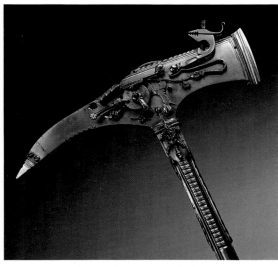

'Axe-pistol', Spanish or German, 1600 (above). During the sixteenth and early seventeenth centuries there was a vogue for weapons combining firearms with edged weapons. This may have come about through uncertainty over the reliability of guns or because there was a desire to boost the effectiveness of a sword or axe by adding a secret weapon. However, most combination weapons are more feats of workmanship than practical battle weapons. This 'axe-pistol', which has no less than five barrels, is no exception, and it may be wondered if the designer simply wanted to use all the available technology in one piece. One barrel is served by a wheel-lock, one by a matchlock and four by a hand-held match. (The Royal Armouries, London.)

German wheel-lock pistols, c.1580 (right). The two at left, though not a pair, demonstrate remarkable similarity in design and decoration. They were probably made at Brunswick or Wolfenbüttel. The decoration is an inlay of engraved stag-horn set into the wooden stocks and shows hares and hounds, as well as an illustration of the Greek myth of Leda being visited by the god Zeus in the form of a swan. All three show the characteristic shape of the period, with the grip at a sharp angle to the butt and an exaggerated pommel. This shape is sometimes known as a 'puffer' pistol. (The Wallace Collection, London.)

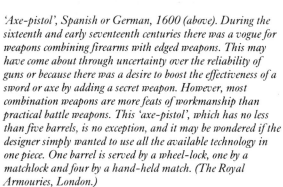

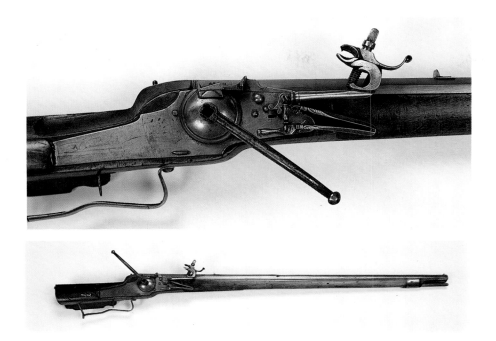

Danish wheel-lock military rifle, dated 1611 (left). The guard of Christian IV of Denmark were probably the first military unit to be armed with rifles. This example is identical to a group, now in the arsenal at Copenhagen, made between 1611 and 1622 by Jørgen Dressler and Reinhardt Pasquier. The calibre is .623 inch and the rifling is six-groove, achieving one complete turn of the projectile in 44 inches. The gun was presented in 1870 by the Danish artillery to Major General Lefroy of the Royal Artillery and was later deposited by him in the Rotunda at Woolwich. (The Museum of Artillery, Woolwich.)

European powder-flasks, sixteenth and seventeenth centuries. The powder-flask in its many forms was a vital part of the musketeer or sportsman's equipment. From larger flasks could be poured out the main charge for a weapon, and often this was done by means of a double spring catch on the nozzle of the flask which let go a measured amount at one operation. Other smaller flasks were designed solely to prime the pan of a weapon, and these are sometimes known as 'primers'. Exceptionally big flasks are seen occasionally and it is likely that these were part of an artilleryman's equipment for the priming of cannon.

The flasks shown here are of the finest quality, using horn, enamel and precious metals for their construction. The collector is more likely to encounter cow-horns, small leather pouches or pear-shaped containers of brass stamped with a simple design. (The Wallace Collection, London.)

Combination matchlock and wheel-lock gun, Italian, c.1620 (below). This unusual weapon adopts a novel solution to ensuring successful ignition of the main charge of powder – initial pressure on the trigger releases the wheel-lock; further pressure moves the match-holder. Far too decorative and expensive for the soldiery of the period, this was once doubtless in a noble armoury, though the story that it was once the property of Louis VIII is probably apocryphal. (The Wallace Collection, London.)

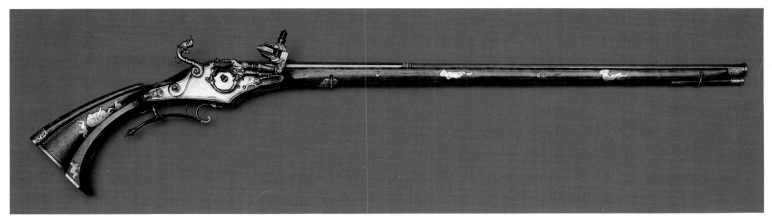

German two-handed swords, c.1580. Commonly associated with mercenary troops and the Swiss **Landesknechte,** *the double-hander was designed to smash through armour and opponents by dint of length and weight. The example on the right with a 'flamboyant' (wavy) blade is by Stantler of Munich; that on the left, which weighs over 14 lb, was probably made at Passau. (The Wallace Collection, London.)*

Gunner's 'stiletto', southern European, c.1600 (below). With its very narrow 'bodkin'-style blade, the 'stiletto' was a particularly popular dagger for thrusting. It was also a gunner's last line of defence after the cannon and any pole arms available to the gun crew had been used. Gunners' stilettos are identifiable by the blade, graduated with engraved numbers. These divisions gave the gunner an easy method of measuring the bore of cannon, to calculate the weight of ball required. Venetian examples are commonly graduated up to the number 120 – hence the Italian name centoventi *for these daggers. (The Royal Armouries, London.)*

A few of the horsemen were designated as 'dragoons' or mounted infantry who rode forward to combat and then dismounted, fighting with short shoulder arms known as 'dragons' or with muskets in the manner of infantry. Few of these features were peculiarly English – 'pike and musket' armed infantry were common over much of Europe, and there was little to distinguish an Austrian or Dutch cavalry trooper from his English counterpart.

One peculiarly English feature was the 'mortuary' sword used by some cavalry and officers. This had a 'basket' hilt and a wide single-edged blade. It was often decorated with portraits of Charles I and/or his wife Henrietta Maria. The term 'mortuary' came from the mistaken belief that these were manufactured after 1649 to commemorate the death of Charles.

After the Treaty of Westphalia had brought a temporary peace to Europe in 1648, the pace of weapons development in the military sphere slowed down. Matchlocks continued alongside dog-locks and the new flintlocks for another fifty years. Pikes also continued to be carried for some time, and some pikemen even maintained their armour. One innovation was the introduction of 'grenadiers' into infantry regiments, armed with hollow iron bombs filled with black powder and fused with a wooden tube of powder.

Another addition to the arsenal was the bayonet. As early as the mid seventeenth century, knives may have been pushed into gun barrels to make an improvised spear, but now these were purpose-made and issued to the infantry. The 'plug' bayonet, as it is now called, was essentially a flat-bladed, round-handled knife which filled the barrel. It was useful but had the disadvantage that the musket could not be fired when it was in place. The soldier's version was normally plain, whereas the officers' items could be decorated with ivory, silver or intricate engraving.

In the civilian field, the second half of the seventeenth century saw significant changes in sword design. The rapier became less popular and was slowly superseded by an essentially decorative type of small-sword. This was a fairly short and narrow-bladed sword, often with a knuckle-bow, a double shell guard and cross quillons. Some early examples have 'colichemarde' blades, wider at the top and tapering suddenly to a pronounced point. Small-swords and short, curved 'hangers' were also popular with officers. Another officer's weapon gaining ground at this time was the 'spontoon' – a form of decorative short pike which was both a mark of rank and a last-ditch hand-to-hand weapon.

Pistols were now made in a wide variety of types and sizes, as Randle Holme described them in the *Academy of Armory* in the 1680s:

Basket-hilted broadsword with blade marked 'Ferara', c.1600 (below). Contrary to popular belief, early basket-hilted swords were not a purely Scottish phenomenon: they are seen in English portraits, occur on English archaeological sites and often have Continental blades. It was only in the late seventeenth and early eighteenth centuries that the basket hilt came to be regarded as the mark of a highlander. This example has a large round pommel and a relatively small number of flattened bars to the hilt, typical of the period. The blade is broad, with three grooves or 'fullers' running down the centre. 'Ferara' was the name of an earlier Italian swordsmith, but by this period the word had become accepted simply as a mark of quality. (The Royal Armouries, London.)

Armour of Sir John Smythe (1534–1607) with wheel-lock pistol (left). Sir John Smythe was one of the best-known soldiers and military theorists of the Elizabethan age. He saw service in France and the Low Countries and in eastern Europe fighting against the Turks. In 1590 he published his treatise Certain Discourses Militarie, *in which he defended the merits of the longbow against firearms. The book was immediately banned – not because the authorities disagreed with his military theories but because of Smythe's comments about the incompetence and corruption of the Earl of Leicester and other English commanders in the Low Countries.*

Smythe was a strong advocate of full armour, and it would be surprising if his armour shown here did not at one time have arm defences also. The salient parts shown are a strongly combed burgonet with a closed face, a breastplate of peasecod form, waisted gauntlets and articulated cuisses or thigh-guards. All are decorated with gilt. The boots are reproductions but are representative of cavalry soldiers' footwear of the period. (The Royal Armouries, London.)

Cup-hilted rapier, Spanish or Italian, c.1630. Rapiers were commonly carried not only by soldiers but also by gentlemen during the late sixteenth and seventeenth centuries. This particular cup-hilted form – with a knuckle-guard, very long quillons and a large, almost hemispherical, cup – was often made and carried in Spain. Gaining popularity in the 1620s and 1630s, such rapiers continued to be made until the first decade of the eighteenth century. The bowls of most cup hilts are either of solid steel or are decoratively chiselled and pierced. The decoration found on the hilts tends to be remarkably uniform and consists mainly of tightly coiled scrolls of foliage with a variety of different flowers and sometimes birds. (The Royal Armouries, London.)

' The pockett pistall, is the least of fire Armes, the Barrell of such pieces being from 4 to 6 inches long.

The Girdle, or belt pistall is a degree larger in the barrell then the former; and is generally hung by the side, by a long piece of iron screwed on the contrary side of the stock to the lock. The barrells of such are from 7 to 9 or 10 inches long.

The troup, or holster pistall, this is longer than the fore said by as much againe, the barrells of these being generall some 16, 18 or 20 inches, all troupers have two of these pistalls put into holsters fixed to their sadles.'

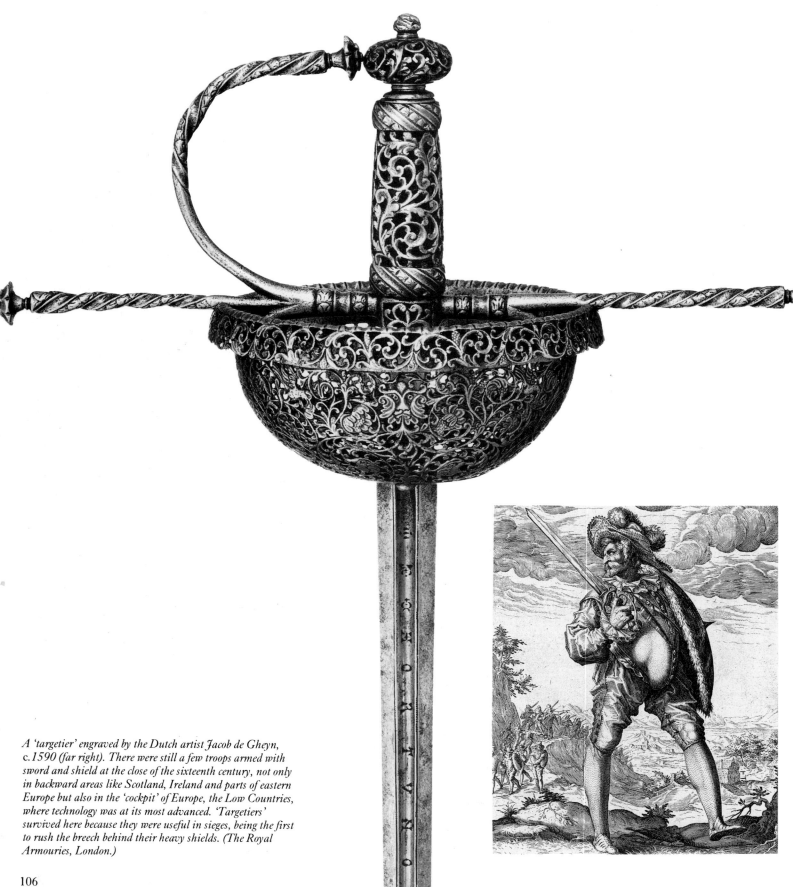

A 'targetier' engraved by the Dutch artist Jacob de Gheyn, c.1590 (far right). There were still a few troops armed with sword and shield at the close of the sixteenth century, not only in backward areas like Scotland, Ireland and parts of eastern Europe but also in the 'cockpit' of Europe, the Low Countries, where technology was at its most advanced. 'Targetiers' survived here because they were useful in sieges, being the first to rush the breech behind their heavy shields. (The Royal Armouries, London.)

Gauntlet of Henry, Prince of Wales, made by Jacob Halder or William Pickering at Greenwich, c.1608. Henry was the oldest son of King James I and would have become King had he not died of typhoid in 1612. The detail shown here is full of Stuart symbolism: together with the Prince's cipher are Scottish thistles, Tudor roses and looped knots. The absence of the badge of the Prince of Wales helps to date the armour to a time before Henry's investiture in June 1610. Other parts of the same armour survive in the royal collection at Windsor. (The Wallace Collection, London.)

The first few decades of the eighteenth century saw a good deal of rationalization in the soldier's arms, as perhaps one might expect in the 'Age of Reason'. In most armies, 'patterns' were established for the flintlock muskets which were their most important arm, and weapons which differed from the established type, even in detail, were rejected. Socket bayonets, which could be used while the gun was fired, were adopted, and the pike finally disappeared. With the pike went all armour except the breastplate and back-plate of some heavy cavalry, a few helmets and the officer's 'gorget'.

The gorget was a relic of the medieval neck defence of the same name; it was now a crescent-shaped piece of brass or other metal hung around the neck with a ribbon. Impractical as a defence, the gorget was the last vestige of the knight's armour and a symbol of rank. It bore upon it the royal arms of the country concerned and/or the name of the regiment.

From the late 1660s to 1715 the European stage had been dominated by France in the person of Louis XIV –the 'Sun King'. Four major conflicts – the War of Devolution (1667–8), the Dutch War (1672–8), the War of the Grand Alliance (1688–97), and the War of the Spanish Succession (1701–13) – had embroiled many European powers in compacts against Louis. Their alliances of many countries and separate interests proved difficult, and, though there were able commanders – such as Prince Eugene, the Savoyard fighting for the Holy Roman Emperor – France was frequently triumphant.

Only towards the end of the period were allied armies successfully coordinated under the Duke of Marlborough. Victories like Blenheim in 1704 were complex cooperative efforts – under Marlborough's overall command on that day were in fact two armies: one made up of Danes, Austrians and Prussians under Prince Eugene and the other comprised of British, Dutch, Hanoverians and Hessians led by Marlborough himself. It seems likely that Sweden and Russia were excluded only because they were engaged in the separate Great Northern War of 1700–21 at the same time.

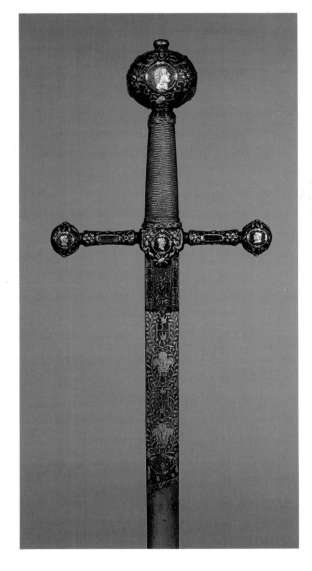

Sword of Henry, Prince of Wales; silver encrusted, with an English hilt and a German blade. The presence of the Prince of Wales' feathers dates this piece precisely to the period 1610–12, between Henry's investiture and his death. The blade is marked with the maker's name – Clemens Horn of Solingen – his unicorn mark and the motto 'Astree Sacrum', dedicating it to the goddess of justice. Horn was maker of sword blades to the royalty and nobility of Europe, and his customers included Philip II of Spain, the Electors of Brandenburg, Charles IV of Sweden and James I of England. The hilt on this example was probably made by Robert South, cutler to both James I and Charles I. (The Wallace Collection, London.)

'Savoyard' or Totenkopf-*style close helmet, north-Italian, c.1635 (below). This type of helmet, offering excellent protection to the face, is usually associated with siege engineers. The derivations of the two names stem from totally different circumstances. 'Savoyard' comes from the fact that a number of these helmets were captured from Savoyard troops at the siege of Geneva in 1601.* Totenkopf *is from the appearance of the helmet, which, due to its eye holes, seems like a 'death's head' or skull. The little spike on the peak is unusual and was probably added simply to make the helmet appear more grotesque. (The Wallace Collection, London.)*

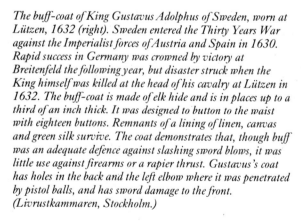

The buff-coat of King Gustavus Adolphus of Sweden, worn at Lützen, 1632 (right). Sweden entered the Thirty Years War against the Imperialist forces of Austria and Spain in 1630. Rapid success in Germany was crowned by victory at Breitenfeld the following year, but disaster struck when the King himself was killed at the head of his cavalry at Lützen in 1632. The buff-coat is made of elk hide and is in places up to a third of an inch thick. It was designed to button to the waist with eighteen buttons. Remnants of a lining of linen, canvas and green silk survive. The coat demonstrates that, though buff was an adequate defence against slashing sword blows, it was little use against firearms or a rapier thrust. Gustavus's coat has holes in the back and the left elbow where it was penetrated by pistol balls, and has sword damage to the front. (Livrustkammaren, Stockholm.)

Pike head, seventeenth century (opposite page, far right). The pike was, after the musket, the second most important weapon of the period, used to protect infantry against cavalry or, at 'push of pike', against enemy infantry. In the middle seventeenth century most English pikes were sixteen feet in length but varied from as little as fifteen to as much as eighteen feet. (The Royal Armouries, London.)

Pike drill (opposite) portrayed in Henry Hexam's 'Principles of the Art Militarie; practised in the warres of the United Netherlands', 1637. When a body of several hundred men wielded their pikes uniform drill was highly necessary. Here, a pikeman in armoured 'corselet' demonstrates the motions to bring the pike into the marching positions, resting positions, and the 'charge' for receiving cavalry. Each line of pikes or muskets was known as the 'rank file' being the number of men standing one behind the other through the depth of the formation. The 'file' was the smallest detachment of men; very often the file leader was also a corporal. When armour was short the men at the front and back of each file were first to receive it, so that the men in the centre had some protection from their colleagues behind and in front. (British Library.)

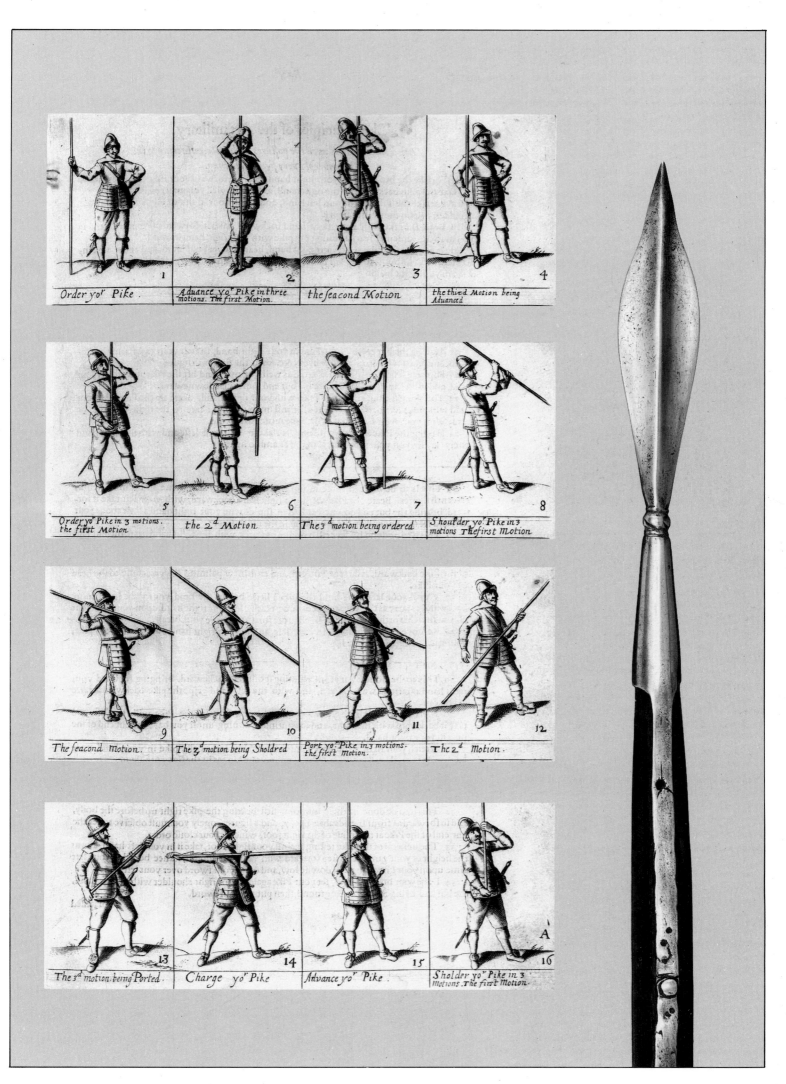

1. Order yo' Pike.
2. Aduance yo' Pike in three motions. The first Motion.
3. the seacond Motion
4. the third Motion being Aduanced
5. Order yo' Pike in 3 motions. the first Motion.
6. the 2d Motion.
7. The 3d motion being ordered
8. Sholder yo' Pike in 3 motions The first Motion.
9. The seacond Motion.
10. The 3d motion being Sholdred
11. Port yo' Pike in 3 motions. the first Motion.
12. The 2d Motion.
13. The 3d motion being Ported
14. Charge yo' Pike
15. Advance yo' Pike.
16. Sholder yo' Pike in 3 Motions. The first Motion.

Memorial brass of Sir Edward Filmer and his wife, Elizabeth, from East Sutton, Kent, c. 1639 (below). Memorial brasses had largely been replaced by three-dimensional effigies or stone-carving in the seventeenth century, and so this is a rare example. Sir Edward is armed with a long, straight-bladed, rapier-style sword suspended from a decorated waistbelt. His armour extends only to mid thigh, below which he wears breeches tied at the knee and riding-boots with spurs. Like the ruff at his neck, the armour is a little out of date; its appearance in the brass is as much symbolic as practical. This is borne out by the fact that of his nine sons only 'Sir' Robert, the son succeeding to the knightly title, also wears armour. (The Victoria and Albert Museum, London.)

Gilt armour of Charles I, King of England (1600–1649) (right). Born in Scotland and Stuart king of both realms, Charles I reigned during one of the most tumultous periods in English history. Lesser wars with Spain and France and a breakdown in relations between Scotland and England were dwarfed by the English Civil War, which engulfed England while mainland Europe remained torn by the Thirty Years War. Charles raised his standard at Nottingham in 1642, and two years of hard but indecisive campaigning followed. In 1644 the Scots joined the side of Charles's parliamentarian opponents, and Charles's nephew Prince Rupert suffered a major defeat at Marston Moor. The Battle of Naseby the following year sealed the royalists' fate. The King surrendered and, despite a second war in 1648, never regained power. He was tried and executed in 1649.

The gilt armour is designed more for parade than for practical use and was made in the Netherlands in about 1612. While many parts of it are similar to other cuirassier armours of the early seventeenth century, it has shin and foot defences which had largely been replaced by boots at this time. The thigh-guards show a characteristic feature of the period, being a series of 'lames' or individual plates. (The Royal Armouries, London.)

European Zischagge, c.1630. Of a distinctively east-European design, this particular helmet from the Wallace Collection has been variously described as Hungarian, Polish or even French. This is perhaps an indicator of how universal a pattern the Zischagge eventually became as a cavalryman's helmet. Other examples were made in the Netherlands and Germany, and some found their way to England. This one is blue and gilt and of outstanding quality – many were of plain steel or blackened or browned against rust. (The Wallace Collection, London.)

The Forge of Vulcan, *by Jan Breughel and Hendrik van Balen, c. 1620. Vulcan was the Roman god of fire, modelled on the Greek Hephaestus, a son of Zeus. He was originally associated with destructive manifestations of fire, such as volcanoes, but by the Middle Ages he was accepted as the patron of blacksmiths and metalworkers such as armourers. In this seventeenth-century Flemish work we see many of the arts of the armourer and gunfounder in a classical setting.*

In the centre are a heap of newly worked arms and armour, with Vulcan himself at the anvil. To the right, workmen use bellows to heat the forge and pound out the metal; on the left are water-wheels which appear to be used to work hammers and grinding-tools. In the middle distance stands an artillery piece. (The Royal Armouries, London.)

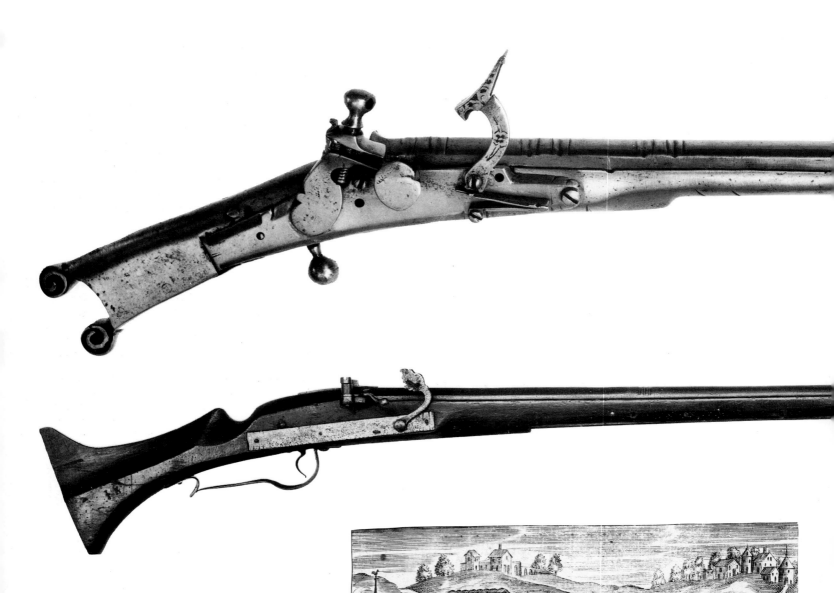

Saltpetre-making, from Thomas Malthus's Practique de la Guerre, *Paris, 1650. By the seventeenth century gunpowder was vital to the military arsenal, not only for hand weapons but also for cannon and engineering. The basic constituents of powder were saltpetre, sulphur and charcoal. Saltpetre formed the largest bulk of any powder: by the seventeenth century, as many as six parts saltpetre were allowed to one each of the others.*

Saltpetre was formed by the action of soil bacteria on proteins exposed to air. It grew best in dung heaps and tombs, which certainly helped the powder-maker to gain a morbid and scatological reputation. In this picture we see the saltpetre together with water in the tubs at 'A'. The resultant liquid is filtered and drained and then boiled down (at B). The man 'C' then mixes the saltpetre with charcoal and sulphur and this is given to his colleague 'D' to work through a sieve with large holes to create grains of powder, this last process being known as 'corning'. Cannon used large grains of powder; hand firearms used small grains. Uncorned or 'serpentine' powder was used for priming. (The British Library, London.)

Scottish 'snaphance' pistol, mid seventeenth century (top). Scottish pistols followed a line of development largely independent of English or European mainstream styles. Characteristic of Scottish weapons was the long-continued use of the 'snaphance' lock, ball or lobate triggers and an extensive use of metal, even in butt and stock. By the eighteenth century many Scottish pistols were entirely metal and equipped with a heart-shaped butt and a belt-hook. Highlanders seldom used holsters, preferring to attach the pistol to a belt or tuck it into clothing. Until 1795 highland regiments carried the native pistols. Not everyone was impressed with them, however, as in 1846 the authors of The Costume of the Clans *described them as 'coarse pop-guns, resembling more the tin toys of the bazaar than the weapons of an army'. (The Royal Armouries, London.)*

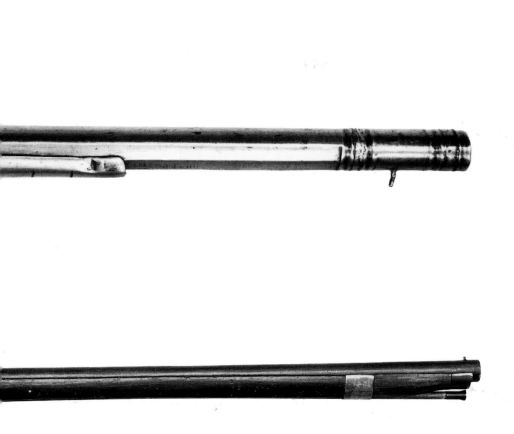

Matchlock musket (left), English, c.1640. Commonest of all infantry arms in the seventeenth century was the matchlock. Similar weapons were in use all over Europe, and some found their way to America in the hands of colonists. This English example has a barrel a little under the regulation 48 inches long and would have cost about ten or eleven shillings (50–55p) when new. The type of butt shown here is known as a 'fishtail', owing to its shape, but within a few years most matchlocks were being made with a more recognizably modern profile – either the 'paddle' or the similar 'French' butt, which was squared off at the end. (The Royal Armouries, London.)

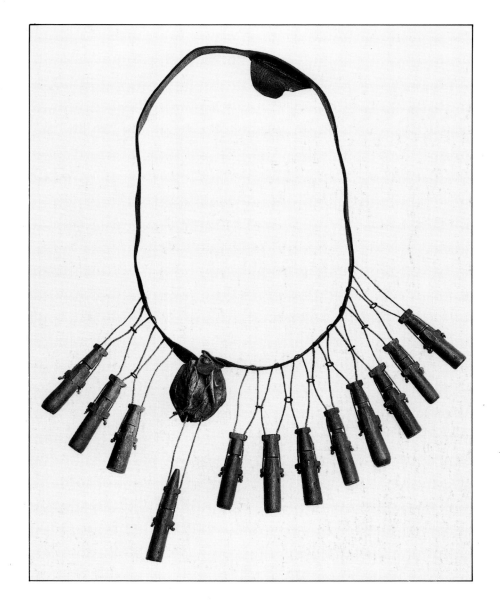

'Bandoleer' or 'collar of charges', English, c.1645. The matchlock musketeers' personal supply of ammunition was usually kept in a bandoleer containing between nine and twelve charges. The large belt slips over an arm and the head, and the flasks hang down at the front, side and rear. Each of the smaller flasks hold a charge of powder, while the longer one has priming-powder. The leather bag was for bullets. It has now become common practice to refer to the bandoleer as 'the twelve Apostles', because there were normally twelve charges. There is no evidence that this term was in contemporary use. (The Royal Armouries, London.)

The Battle of Naseby, 14 June 1645, from Joshua Sprigge's
Anglia Rediviva, 1647. Naseby, where the royalist army of
King Charles I met the New Model Army under Sir Thomas
Fairfax, was one of the climactic battles of the English Civil
War. This plan illustrates well how weapons and tactics
related, both in England and in the Thirty Years War in
Europe. The royalist forces lie to the north and the top of the
plan; those of Parliament lie around Naseby itself.
  Both armies are drawn up in a similar formation: infantry
in the centre, cavalry on the wings. The pikes are in the centre
of each battalion, with musketeers on either flank. Both armies
are deployed in depth, with reserve lines of troops. Artillery is
deployed at intervals along the front line, and two types of
skirmisher are identifiable. Musket-armed dragoons have
deployed dismounted behind Lantford hedges to the top left of
the map and threaten Prince Rupert's flank. In front of the
main parliamentarian forces are the 'forlorn hope', infantry
skirmishers who will deploy in loose order and bring the enemy
under fire. (The British Library, London.)

'Secrete' or 'steel skull' for wear under a hat, seventeenth century, probably English (right). This metal skullcap allowed the wearer invisible protection against edged weapons and was worn both by soldiers and by civilians. The steel skull was of several different types: this solid pattern, one of strips forming a sort of cage, and at least a few which could be folded when not in use. The presence of a large number of a similar type together in the Tower of London suggests that they were at least occasionally an issued military item. (The Royal Armouries, London.)

Cavalryman's buff-leather gauntlet, probably English, c.1630 (below). Although much of the cavalryman's protective equipment had been discarded by the middle of the seventeenth century, the hands were still vulnerable both to edged weapons and to the general rough and tumble of the mêlée. Leather gloves of various sorts remained popular. This example is made flexible but strong by the use of overlapping scales of buff leather. (The Royal Armouries, London.)

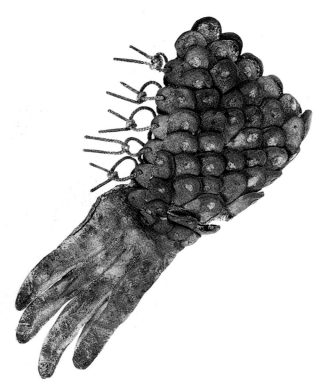

Cavalry trooper's or 'harquebus' armour, English, c.1640. The typical equipment of the English cavalry trooper was 'breast', 'back' and 'pot' helmet. The headgear shown here is usually described as either a 'lobster-tailed' or a 'three-bar' pot. 'Lobster-tailed' was descriptive of the neck-guard, which was divided horizontally into sections by either real or false 'lames'. Originally the helmet would have been lined to cushion the head, and we see here on the inside of the neck-guard three of the many lozenge-shaped rivets which would have been used to hold the binding or lining in place.

The breastplate bears a dent, evidence of the armourer's testing procedure, which was to fire a pistol against it. The waist-strap and shoulder leathers were covered by a single strip of metal subsequently broken into sections rather than a series of widely spaced rectangles as shown here. Most breastplates and back-plates are stamped with the mark of the Armourers Company of London and the initials of the maker. Dating is aided by the fact that up until 1650 the mark was an 'A' surmounted by a crown, but after the execution of Charles I it was changed to an 'A' topped by a helmet. (The Royal Armouries, London.)

English 'mortuary' sword, c.1640 (left). This excellent example shows not only the portraits or heads which often appear on this type of sword, but also other figures, including a pikeman. Much argument still surrounds the identity of the faces on 'mortuary' swords, but the popular explanation is that they represent Charles I and his wife Henrietta Maria. Equally, they might be taken to represent Frederick of the Palatinate and his wife Elizabeth, who were driven from Bohemia in the opening stages of the Thirty Years War. Elizabeth elicited particular sympathy in England because she was a daughter of King James I. The pikeman shown here is also interesting. He wears an armoured corselet and long boots and grasps the shaft of his pike. Only a fraction of the pike is visible – most pikes of this period were sixteen to eighteen feet in length. (The Royal Armouries, London.)

English infantryman's sword, c.1640 (above). During the seventeenth century, most foot-soldiers were issued with a sword in addition to their pike or musket. Plain and cheap English examples often followed the general shape of the 'mortuary' sword, and for that reason are occasionally called 'proto-mortuary' swords. This specimen is engraved with the legend 'For the Tower' and a running wolf. 'For the Tower' may well mean that it was made for a government contract for delivery to the Tower of London. The wolf symbol was first used by the German makers of Solingen and Passau, but by the seventeenth century it was also appearing on arms made in England. One of the reasons for this use of the wolf mark in England appears to have been the emigration of German cutlers to Hounslow, near London. (The Royal Armouries, London.)

119

*Equestrian portrait of Colonel Alexander Popham, from
Littlecote House, Wiltshire. Popham served as a
parliamentarian officer in the English Civil War (1642–9),
and Littlecote House retains its armoury of weapons relating
to the Civil War and the following century.*

*Here Popham wears full armour, and among his
accoutrements are a pistol, a 'hanger' and a commander's
baton. 'Three-quarter' rather than full armour was more
usual at this period, so it may be that the leg defences shown
are an artist's convention. Popham's left, or bridle, hand –
vulnerable to sword blows – is clad in a metal gauntlet; his
right hand, requiring greater flexibility, is protected only by
a leather glove. The pistol butt appearing from the saddle
holster may belong to either a wheel-lock or a dog-lock pistol.
The holster, with its decorative fabric 'caps', is definitely of
'officer' quality but, like most holsters of the period, is attached
to the horse harness rather than to the rider. Conspicuous on
Popham's thigh is the hilt of a curved 'hanger', complete with a
'grotesque' pommel and a double suspender running to a
waist-belt. Behind the subject are visible parts of a cavalry
action near a fortress. (The Royal Armouries, London.)*

Polish 'winged' hussar helmet, mid seventeenth century. Some of the most colourful troops of the period were the hussars of eastern Europe, whose flamboyant dress and curved swords were later adopted in the west. Except for the perforated 'wings', however, this helmet is very similar to the German Zischagge *and the English lobster-tailed 'pot'. (The Metropolitan Museum, New York.)*

The Deliverance of St Peter, *by David Teniers the Younger (1610–90). Perhaps the best idea of the dress and equipment of mid-seventeenth-century soldiery is given by Dutch paintings of the period. The religious subject-matter is just visible through the archway, while the dominant position is given to a realistic portrayal of soldiers. The passage of the Bible which the scene illustrates is Acts 12. Peter has been captured by Herod and is guarded in jail by four squads of four soldiers. However, an angel appears to him and a light shines in his cell, and the angel leads Peter through the guards and the iron gate of the city to his escape. Herod then orders that the guards be executed for carelessness.*

In this depiction one of the squads play dice. One of the seated figures wears a cabasset ornamented with a feather. On the ground lie a gorget and a gauntlet. These and the richly decorated coat may belong to the seated figure with his back to us — the quality of his clothing suggests that he may be an officer. The standing soldier wears a rapier at this waist. (The Wallace Collection, London.)

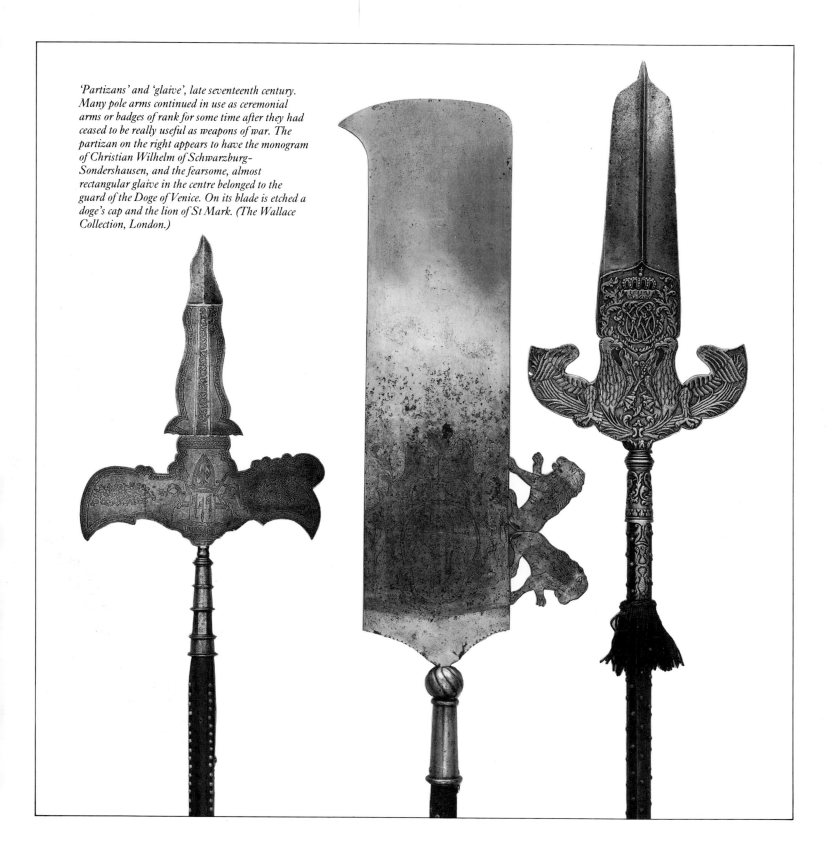

'Partizans' and 'glaive', late seventeenth century. Many pole arms continued in use as ceremonial arms or badges of rank for some time after they had ceased to be really useful as weapons of war. The partizan on the right appears to have the monogram of Christian Wilhelm of Schwarzburg-Sondershausen, and the fearsome, almost rectangular glaive in the centre belonged to the guard of the Doge of Venice. On its blade is etched a doge's cap and the lion of St Mark. (The Wallace Collection, London.)

Flintlock 'grenade gun' by James Ermendinger, c.1690 (right). German by birth, Ermendinger spent part of his working life in London, where he was gunmaker to the Prince Regent and to the Hudson's Bay Company. This weapon was one of eight made for Prince George of Denmark. The exact function of these extraordinary guns has been much debated, but it seems fairly certain that they were not for firing military anti-personnel grenades – these would have been too heavy for the relatively weakly constructed barrel. It seems much more likely that grenade guns were for shooting fireworks or flares. Fireworks were very popular in the seventeenth century and were let off to celebrate royal birthdays and military victories as well as other festivals. (The Royal Armouries, London.)

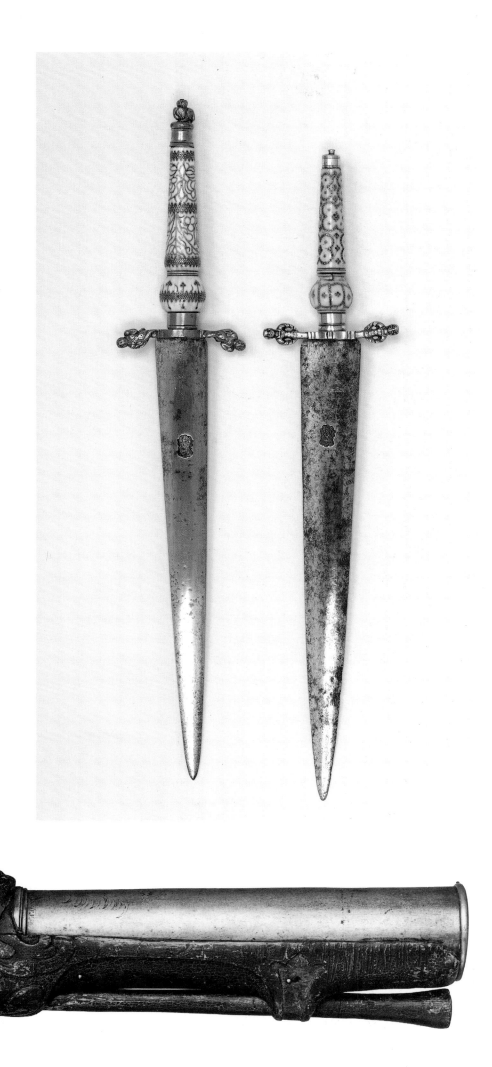

Officers' or sporting 'plug' bayonets, English, c.1690 (left). Essentially similar to the soldiers' weapons, these are of better quality with ornamented ivory grips and decorative quillons. The finials of the quillons are cast into the shape of human figures. A number of portraits from the late seventeenth and early eighteenth centuries show officers with similar bayonets worn on a frog at the waistbelt, and they appear to have been used as an extra mark of rank. (The Victoria and Albert Museum, London.)

Infantryman's 'plug' bayonet (below) by Timothy Tindall of London, c. 1680. The 'plug' bayonet is so called because it 'plugs' the barrel of the musket, which cannot be fired when it is fitted. Converting the muskets to short pikes in this way did, however, mean that the firepower of units could be increased, as few if any pikemen were now required. The bayonet may have been invented as early as 1647, but was not a general issue until the 1660s. Many of the earliest bayonets were purchased by the colonels of their regiments, rather than on issue by the Crown. This example is typical, having a wooden handle and brass quillons and pommel. The hole through the handle is not original and is probably the result of being part of a wall decoration. (The Royal Armouries, London.)

Officer's 'plug' bayonet inscribed 'God save King James the Second', English, c.1685 (above). Although fairly plain and not ivory-handled, examples such as this are usually thought of as officer's bayonets. The King James referred to was the last of the Stuart monarchs, deposed in 1688 by William of Orange and his wife Mary. Inscriptions found on other bayonets mention William of Orange or officers' names, often with a date. (The Royal Armouries, London.)

Trooper's armour or 'harquebus' armour, English, c.1650.
Shown here are a breastplate, back-plate, pot helmet and
buff-coat – the typical idea of a Cromwellian soldier's
equipment. Recent research into documents of the period
suggests, however, that a buff-coat and breastplate were not
often worn together by the rank and file. The cuirass cost about
13s (65p) and a buff-coat could be £5, so it was easier and
cheaper to issue only the breastplate.

The helmet shown here is a typical 'three-bar' or 'lobster-
tailed' pot with a pronounced central comb and hinged ear
flaps. The breastplates and back-plates are linked by a
waist-strap and by articulated armoured shoulder-straps
which are closed by hook-and-pillar catches at the front. The
shoulder-straps were usually made by placing a strip of metal
over a strip of leather and breaking the metal into rectangular
plates which then protected the flexible strap.

Around the neck of the breastplate is a raised ridge which
helped protect the wearer – especially if no gorget or neck-plate
was worn. The dent in the breastplate is a test mark to
demonstrate that the plate had resisted a firearm. Few could
withstand a musket, and breastplates were usually claimed
only to be 'caliver-proof' or 'pistol-proof'. (The Royal
Armouries, London.)

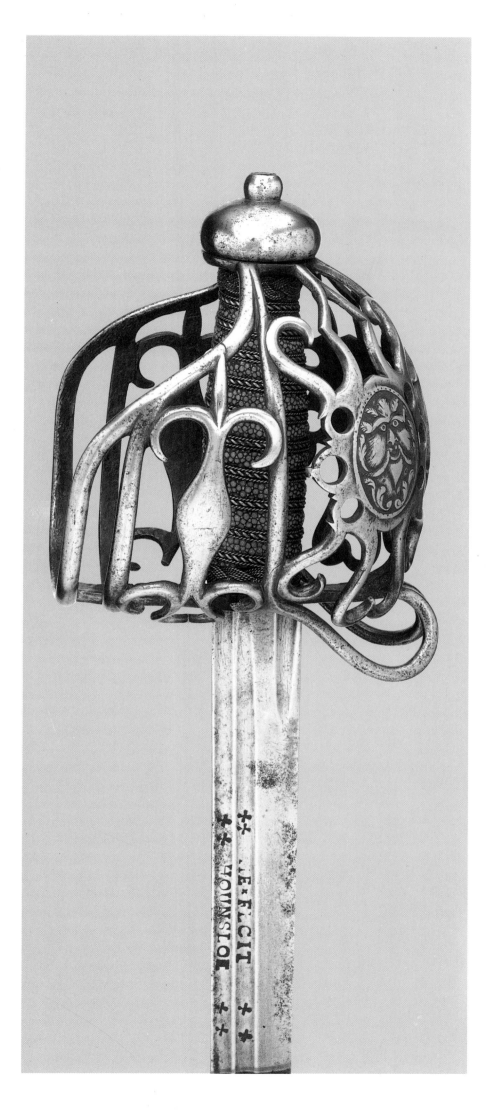

English basket-hilted broadsword, early eighteenth century (left). Although now popularly associated with the highlander, basket-hilted broadswords were also made in England from the sixteenth to the eighteenth century. This example, with its flattened pommel and cartouches decorated with faces, is clearly stamped 'me fecit Hounsloe' – made at Hounslow. (The Victoria and Albert Museum, London.)

French silver-hilted small-sword, made in Paris, 1726 (above). The style of decoration with panels of stylized flowers seen here is sometimes described as 'Berainesque', after the designer to the French court Jean Bérain the Elder (1637–1711). Similar patterns were applied later in England, Germany and the Netherlands. Swords were commonly worn by gentlemen in civilian dress until the third quarter of the eighteenth century, and for some time afterwards on formal or court occasions. (The Victoria and Albert Museum, London.)

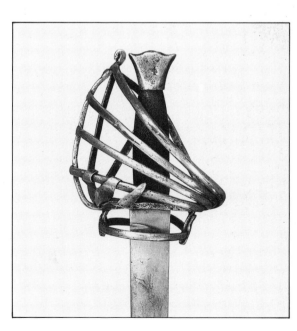

'Schivonia', north-European or Italian, late seventeenth century (above). Particularly popular with the Venetians, the distinctive 'Schivonia' style of sword was notable for its complex barred guard which extended forward of the crosspiece or quillons. The use of the Schivonia was quite short-lived and was limited essentially to the late seventeenth and early eighteenth centuries. (The Royal Armouries, London.)

CHAPTER 5

FROM 'BROWN BESS' TO MAXIM: 1750–1900

B y the mid eighteenth century, military arms were highly specialized, to match the type of troops for which they were intended.
The cavalry, for example, were now divided into 'cuirassiers',
'horse', 'dragoons' and 'hussars' – the first two being essentially
'heavy' types, the others 'light'. Different national armies favoured different mixes of the types. Hussars – fast and armed with curved swords –
were particularly popular in eastern Europe.

'Dragoons' had originally been intended as mounted infantry – paid less
and riding smaller, cheaper horses than the cavalry proper. England
steadily converted all horsed troops to dragoons, but this was little more
than a change of nomenclature, for the mounted troops were intended to
perform both the light-cavalry duties of scouting and pursuit and also the
massed actions of heavy cavalry. Between 1760 and 1815, British cavalry
were again redesignated – this time as 'light dragoons', 'dragoons',
'dragoon guards' and 'hussars'.

*Photo-portrait (opposite) of a Union infantryman armed with
a .58 inch rifled musket and revolver, by Matthew Brady,
c.1864. The American Civil War (1861–5) was an intensely
bloody struggle, due at least in part to the universality of rifled
and revolving arms. Artillery and heavy mortars were also in
use, leading to a decline in the offensive use of cavalry and a
more widespread use of troops in skirmish order. The regular,
blue-clad, U.S. army was tiny at the outbreak of war and
required massive expansion to bring the conflict to a successful
conclusion. The Confederate forces adopted the grey of the
volunteers and reservists and, having little control over
industrial areas, were forced to use a wider and less uniform
selection of arms – both native and imported.*

A report produced in 1860 entitled Manufacturers of the
US *noted 239 establishments producing firearms in America.
In total, these employed 2,056 people who between them made
two and a half million dollars worth of arms per annum. Only
41 of these factories were in the South, with a total output
value of 72,652 dollars.*

*The long-arm shown here is probably either an 1861 or an
1863 model of US-issue percussion rifled musket. One and a
half million such guns were made by the North, half of them by
the Springfield armoury. The photograph gives a good view of
the fixing of the socket bayonet, which is slipped over the
muzzle and held by a locking ring. The exact type of pistol is
unclear, but the most likely manufacturers would be Colt or
Remington, who produced a number of .44 inch army and .36
inch navy models. (Library of Congress, Washington DC.)*

*English 'pepperbox' percussion revolver, c.1850. Seen here in
its case is a typical mid-nineteenth-century pepperbox, complete
with its equipment. At the top of the case are a bullet mould
and a nipple wrench, and above and behind the butt are
containers which may hold grease, wadding or percussion caps.
Below the gun are the lead balls and a powder-flask. (The
Victoria and Albert Museum, London.)*

British 'long land' pattern musket, mid eighteenth century (bottom). Affectionately known as the 'Brown Bess', the musket in use by the British army and many of Britain's allies between 1730 and 1830 was actually of several different types. All were smooth-bore flintlocks capable of taking socket bayonets, but they varied in details of lock, furniture and barrel length. The 'long land' was so called because it was designed for land service and had a 46 inch barrel. Government-issue models are identifiable by the presence of the 'Tower' mark and the 'broad arrow' on the lock. Private-purchase, export and volunteer arms commonly have only a maker's name or nothing at all on the lock. Sometimes the top of the butt-plate or an escutcheon are found engraved with regimental marks. The 'short land' was a very similar weapon, distinguished only by a barrel four inches shorter. Early 'land' patterns are notable for their wooden ramrods and lack of a fore-end cap. Post-1750 and refurbished examples have a steel ramrod and a brass fore-end cap finishing off the woodwork under the barrel. (The Royal Armouries, London.)

Heavy-cavalry swords all over Europe were essentially long and straight-bladed. Many had different forms of basket hilt to protect the hand. Light-cavalry swords were often curved and equipped with a simpler hilt, many having only a plain knuckle-bow. Carbines – commonly shorter than the infantry musket and often of smaller bore – were carried by most cavalry and allowed for some degree of dismounted operation.

The infantry also became more specialized in their weaponry as time progressed. Most noticeable was the formation of 'light' infantry units. The model for many of these was the German *Jäger*, commonly armed with a comparatively small-bored, long-barrelled 'rifled' arm. Rifles were slow to load but accurate over greater ranges than the smooth-barrelled musket and therefore ideal for skirmishing. 'Rifling' was simply a spiral groove inside the barrel which made the close-fitting ball spin in flight. The shot was therefore stabilized, in the manner of a modern gyroscope, and less liable to deviate from the mark. The technique had been known for two hundred years, but expense and difficulty of manufacture had to be overcome before it could be used for a practical military arm.

During the eighteenth century, many German settlers took their rifles to America with them, where further evolution produced a distinctively American style. This was usually known to contemporaries simply as the 'long rifle' or 'American rifle' and was prevalent in Pennsylvania, Virginia and North Carolina as well as Kentucky. Later, such rifles were all known by the general, if inaccurate, title of 'Kentucky rifles'.

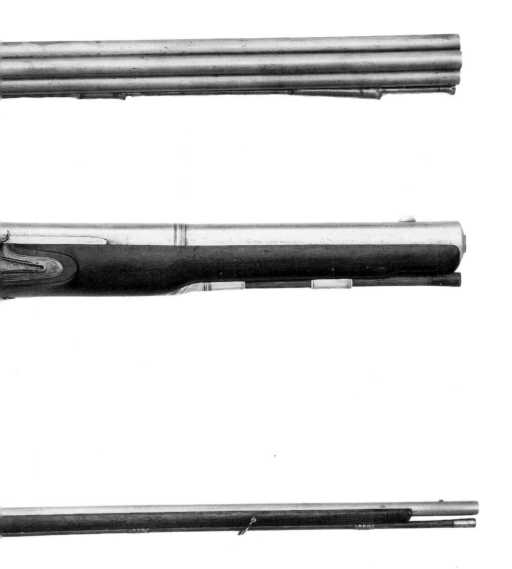

Wars in the mountainous and wooded areas of Europe, and also the American War of Independence (1775–83), were the province of the rifleman, who found good targets in the lines of troops which had been the hallmark of the armies of Frederick the Great and his contemporaries earlier in the century. Small units of riflemen had existed as long ago as 1611 in the guard of Christian IV of Denmark, but widespread use had to wait until the late eighteenth century. Even then, the main users were the Americans and Germans – the French and Russians were not common users until the mid nineteenth century.

One of the best-known British experiments in rifle design was Patrick Ferguson's screw-plug breech-loader, patented in 1776. Ironically, this was broadly based on a design by Isaac de la Chaumette, a French émigré. Turning the trigger-guard of this weapon allowed a plug to fall, opening the breech which was then loaded with ball and powder. Ignition was via the normal flintlock with priming-pan. Despite its fame, the Ferguson was only one of several rifle designs thought too expensive and complex to be generally adopted. Another, perhaps even more remarkable, was Durs Egg's breech-loading rifled Volunteer carbine. In this model there was a 'tip-up' breech, based on a design by Giuseppe Crespi of Milan, and a long spear-type bayonet. Finally, the British adopted the Baker rifle in 1800; essentially, this was a British version of the old muzzle-loading German 'Jäger' rifle, but it did help to add home-grown riflemen to the mercenaries and allies on which the army depended.

Militia 'hangers' (right), Denbighshire Militia, third quarter of the eighteenth century. The side-arm of the British militia from the middle of the eighteenth century was a brass-hilted 'hanger' – short, and with a slightly curved blade. The number of side-bars on the hilt and the type of grip and pommel differed from unit to unit and with time. This collection of 24 from the same unit decorates the ceiling of the servants' hall at Erdigg, near Wrexham. This method of display – the decorative 'trophy of arms' – was common in stately homes of the seventeenth and eighteenth centuries. Continued by the Victorians, it helped to preserve many specimens which might otherwise have been lost. (The National Trust.)

'Spadroon-style' sword, British, c.1780 (below right). Before the introduction of a standard 'pattern' infantry officer's sword in 1796, a 'spadroon' was carried by many officers, both army and navy. Gaining popularity in the 1770s, spadroons were made both plain and with regimental distinctions. Occasionally the cartouche on the grip is marked with a regimental number; sometimes the name of a regiment will appear on the knuckle-bow. The signal features of the 'spadroon' are the straight, slender blade, the 'stirrup-style' knuckle-bow and the faceted grip, usually of ivory or ebony. (The National Army Museum, London.)

British 1796 pattern light-cavalry sabre (below). Designed for slashing and cutting, the 1796 pattern was one of the most successful swords of its time. Common to all swords of this type are the knuckle-bow, forward-swept quillon and the curved, broad blade, but there are many variations in details. Officers' examples, privately purchased, are often decorated with regimental badges, names, coats of arms and classical figures, sometimes in blue and gilt.

Troopers' weapons, like that shown here, may carry a regimental mark and a maker's name. Many blades were made in Birmingham, and names commonly encountered from that city include Gill, Dawes, Osborn and Woolley. Officer's blades were often imported from Germany and many carried the name of the importer Runckle of Solingen. They may also have the name of an outfitter or tailor like Andrews or Brunn of London. Technically superseded in 1821 by a new type of sword, the 1796 pattern continued in widespread use, particularly in Yeomanry and colonial units. Variations on the theme may well have been fabricated as late as 1840. (The Royal Armouries, London.)

Although there had been undoubted advances in rifle technology, the military rifleman was still a breed apart. Most of the infantry still relied on the muzzle-loading smooth-bore musket, which varied little over much of Europe and America. The French had the 'Charleville', of which there were several slightly varying models, though they were all identifiable by their broad brass barrel-band at the fore end. There were several different Prussian models, of which the best-known was probably the model of 1782; during the revolutionary and Napoleonic wars of the early nineteenth century, this was succeeded by the 'Northardt' and the 'New Prussian'.

The British relied on their short and long 'land' patterns – i.e. muskets for 'land service' – which were supplemented at the end of the eighteenth century by the 'India' pattern. There was no single type known as a 'Brown Bess' – this is simply a popular but inaccurate designation for all British

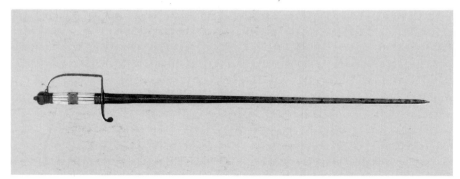

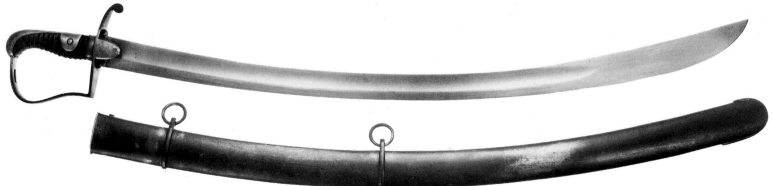

flintlock long-arms of the period. The 'Brown Bess' muskets were still being used by the British Infantry throughout the Napoleonic Wars.

Extensive tests with the various military flintlocks were carried out by the Prussian general Sharnhorst in 1813, with interesting results. The target was an inch-thick wooden board the height of a man and a hundred yards long. Against this, most muskets scored between 40 and 75 per cent hits at 100 yards range. The Swedish musket proved least effective, while the 'New Prussian' pattern and the French 'Charleville' did best. At 200 yards, hits varied between 25 and 37 per cent; this time the British muskets scored best, alongside the Swedish, which was obviously happier at this range. Some hits were still obtained at 400 yards, with the British, French and Prussian arms in the lead. Only the Prussian 1782 model scored any hits at all at 500 to 600 yards, and these were few indeed.

It can fairly be suggested that these tests showed that the individual muskets of the nations did have some different characteristics which varied with range, but the effectiveness of all dropped off sharply at 200 yards. Penetration of the ball through the target was virtually certain at this range. Actual numbers of hits in battle would have been considerably lessened by misfires, smoke, wet and the soldier's natural fatigue and stress in battle. Most muskets were finished off by a socket bayonet of iron and steel between one and two feet long and usually triangular in section. When the troops were in 'square' formation, this could be used most effectively to discourage cavalry.

Officers continued to carry swords, supplemented both by pistols and by some pole arms such as the spontoon. Increasingly, however, junior officers also took to carrying shoulder-arms, which were essentially lighter, better-quality versions of the other ranks' muskets. These little weapons were known as 'fusils'. Most weapons carried by the officer classes were

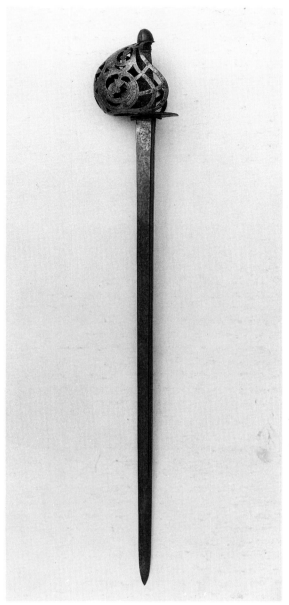

Basket-hilted broadsword (above), 116th Highland Regiment, c.1794. By the late eighteenth century, most nations had evolved individual types of sword, either for particular classes of troops or for the officers of individual regiments. In the case of the Scots, most officers retained a traditional broadsword, but there were dozens of individual regimental patterns. The 116th existed for only a year before being disbanded as a result of mutiny. The officer's sword has a bulbous steel hilt, made in two parts and decorated with thistles. A central cartouche carries the regimental number. (The National Army Museum, London.)

Basket-hilted broadsword (left), 'Bredalbane Fencibles' regiment; Scottish, late eighteenth century. As regular Scottish regiments all had their own distinct sword types, so too did the volunteers and militia. 'Fencibles' differed from the militia in that they were raised in time of war and put on a permanent basis like the regulars, but were intended for local defence. Even so, many served in Ireland in 1798 and others volunteered for service overseas. This basket-hilted sword has a deep bowl completely enclosing the hand. The bowl is constructed of two parts jointed in the centre and has cut-out designs of Scottish thistles. The regimental initials 'BF' appear in the central cartouche. (The National Museums of Scotland, Edinburgh.)

The Grande Armee on the retreat from Moscow, 1812. Napoleon's attempt to hold the Russian capital and force his enemy into surrender failed in the face of scorched earth, refusal to give battle and bitter weather. It cost him the bulk of his men, allies as well as French. Apart from the Charleville muskets, notice also the varying sword types. The seated figure, right, has at his belt the short, curved, brass-handled sabre briquet of the elite infantry. In the centre foreground lies a straight-bladed half-basket of the sort used by heavy cavalry. (Musee de l'Armee, Paris.)

not issued but were privately purchased from gunsmiths or outfitters. The result was a good deal of variation both in quality and in type.

Cavalry arms were now carbine and/or pistol and sword. During the nineteenth century, the lance – a traditional weapon of the Cossack and eastern Europe – began to regain popularity further west, where it had virtually passed out of use. During the Napoleonic era it was re-adopted in Prussia, Poland, France and a host of minor states. Britain followed suit only after the Napoleonic wars.

There was now a bewildering variety of swords in use. Each class of troops had its own, although they were largely dropped by the line infantry around 1800 to 1820. Until the late eighteenth century, brass-handled short 'hangers' had been popular, grenadiers keeping theirs somewhat longer than the rest. For the heavy cavalry, the 'pallasch' (or 'palache') style was usual. This was long, stiff and straight-bladed, and often had a 'half-basket' to protect the hand. The Prussian cuirassier's arm was most typical of the type, but the French, Russians, Spanish and Scandinavians all had similar swords. British heavy cavalry were reliant on the 1796 pattern – disc-hilted and clumsy-looking, subsequently much vilified, but capable of delivering a shattering blow from horseback.

Before the Napoleonic wars ended in 1815, there were already experiments under way to produce a new ignition system for military small arms. 'Fulminates' of various metals like silver, gold and mercury were known to be highly explosive but were sensitive, unstable and difficult to control. It was not until Alexander Forsyth's experiments with them as a means of ignition rather than as a means of propulsion that their potential was unlocked. Some of his earliest efforts resulted in a scent-bottle-shaped reservoir which rotated to release a few grains of 'percussion powder' which was struck by the hammer to cause a flame to ignite a black-powder charge. Later military designs were much simpler and safer. Most were based on a metal pillar with a hole through the centre. On top of this pillar was put the 'percussion cap' – a tiny copper top-hat-shaped cap in which was a little fulminate of mercury. A squeeze on the trigger of the gun released the spring-loaded hammer which hit the cap, causing a flame which passed through the metal pillar or 'nipple' to ignite the main charge.

Other variations on this theme were the 'pellet lock' and the 'strip primer' or 'tape primer'. In the first, a pellet of fulminate was released from a magazine to be struck by a hammer; in the second, small measures were set on a moving tape in the manner of a modern child's cap pistol.

The copper-cap and pillar model was undoubtedly the most practical and robust for the military market and was widely adopted from the 1830s. At first, many of the arms to which the system was fitted were simply old flintlocks, many of them smooth bores. Later, however, the percussion system was fitted to new rifled weapons to form a new purpose-built military arm.

One of the best-known of these was the 'Brunswick' rifle. Though the original model was German, it was adopted in slightly varying forms in many countries, including Britain and Russia. Other highly influential designs were the French *minié* and the British 1853 pattern Enfield rifle. The French *minié* in particular proved its worth in the Crimean War. A special feature was its bullet – elongated in shape, with an iron cup to the rear. On firing, the cup was driven into the lead, forcing it to expand and fit exactly the bore of the gun. The result was greater accuracy.

The 1853 pattern Enfield, or 'three-band' Enfield as it is now popularly known, was imported into America during the Civil War and was also a model for the Springfield and other US arms. Despite the distaste of indigenous troops in India for the animal grease used on its bullets, it was a serviceable arm and highly accurate. Even the present author has succeeded in making tolerably good practice with an example 130 years old.

The percussion system was applied equally well to the civilian market and was adopted across the range of weaponry. Pepperbox pistols with their multiple barrels were fitted with percussion locks, as were shotguns, sporting rifles and duelling pistols of all qualities.

In many ways, the American Civil War of 1861–5 and the Franco-Prussian War of 1870–1 mark a significant watershed in small arms development, signalling the end of muzzle-loading percussion arms and the rise of the self-contained breech-loading cartridge. Many US-issue model flintlock muskets had been converted to percussion systems from 1840, and these had been joined by the 1841 model percussion rifle. By 1862 these were substantially superseded by new rifled percussion types such as the 1855 and 1861 models, large numbers of which were made by the Springfield and Harper's Ferry arsenals.

From then on there were a large number of experiments with various breech-loading systems, most of which were known after their inventors. In the Miller, Mont Storm and Needham conversions, a .58 rim-fire cartridge was used with various 'tip-up' or swinging-breech mechanisms. More successful were those using centre-fire cartridges which succeeded them, such as the 'trap-door' Springfield which came in a large number of lengths and calibres.

Equally important in developmental terms were the magazine lever-action types – the Henry rifle and the legendary Winchester, both of which originally used a .44 rim-fire cartridge. The Henry did see some service in the Civil War but was made only in small numbers. The better-known

Lieutenant of the 8th Regiment de Cuirassiers, France, c.1810. By the Napoleonic period the cuirass and helmet of the heavy cavalry were useless against musket and cannon but still of some worth against edged weapons. Note the classically inspired helmet and the long, slightly curved half-basket sword. The cuirass shown here was worn by Lieutenant Leclerc of Thigué when wounded at Friedland in 1807. French troops continued to wear such equipment in action until 1914, and similar styles were adopted in Austria, Russia, Prussia and the lesser states of western Europe. British Household Cavalry took up the cuirass after the defeat of Napoleon. (Musée d'Armée, Paris.)

British naval presentation swords (below) of the Lloyd's Patriotic Fund. In July 1803 the Patriotic Fund of the marine insurers Lloyd's of London decided to award swords to officers who had distinguished themselves. Originally there were intended to be three designs: a £30 sword for mates and midshipmen, a £50 sword for lieutenants and a £100 example for captains and flag-officers. This basic plan was complicated by a variant of the most expensive sword given to the captains who were present at Trafalgar and by the fact that a small number of swords were given to army officers.

All types have similar hilts, the main differences being in the scabbards, blades and inscriptions. The swords were given in wooden boxes under the lids of which was a notice explaining the symbolism involved: 'National union producing Herculean efforts, which aided by Wisdom lead to Victory'. The Roman fasces of the hilt stood for national union, the club of Hercules stood for the powerful giant, Wisdom was represented by a serpent, and the skin of a lion was for Victory. (The National Maritime Museum, London.)

City of London gold presentation sword of Vice-Admiral Lord Collingwood (right), by Ray & Montague of London, 1807. The Corporation of the City of London voted to give Collingwood a highly decorated sword 'for the brilliant and decisive victory' at Trafalgar, where command of the fleet devolved to him on the death of Nelson. This extremely fine sword has a gold hilt decorated with enamel and studded with diamonds. Around the outside of the knuckle-guard written in diamonds, is Nelson's signal 'England Expects Every Man to do his Duty', and on the inside is 'Trafalgar'. (The Royal Armouries, London.)

Winchester was very similar but was produced in greater quantities and was essentially a civilian arm.

European developments of the period show distinct parallels. In England the 1853 pattern Enfield was converted to breech-loading by means of the Snider method, using a hinged breech and a one-piece centre-fire 'Boxer' cartridge. The Prussians made early advances in the breech-loading field with the adoption of Johann Nikolaus van Dreyse's *Zundnadelgewehr* or needle-gun, but the French had probably the greatest success with their 'Chassepot' rifle. This used the simple expedient of a rubber seal on the face of the bolt to help prevent gas from escaping rearwards.

In the 1870s, breech mechanisms and magazine loading continued to be the main preoccupations of military gunmakers. 'Falling blocks' were the solution in the American Peabody and the better-known British Martini–Henry rifle. The latter used a .45 bullet and, although only a single-shot weapon without a magazine, achieved considerable range and accuracy without a significant loss in stopping-power. It was this arm that the British took to fight the Zulu and inflicted such a terrible toll at Rorke's Drift and Ulundi. The disaster at Isandhlwana in 1879 was not so much due to any defect in the Martini–Henry but to disorganization in the main British square and poor ammunition supply. It is often said that ammunition dried up in this action due to an inability to open the boxes, but, according to the official manual, these could be kicked open if the necessary tools were lacking!

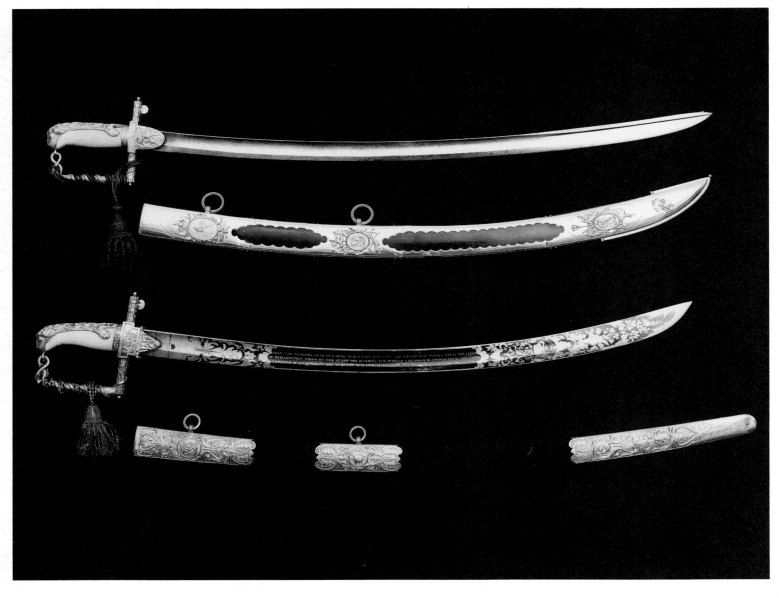

French Cavalry Attacking British Squares at Waterloo *by Denis Deighton (1792–1827). The Battle of Waterloo, fought near Brussels on 18 June 1815, was the end of Napoleon's long struggle for hegemony in Europe. Held all day by Wellington's allied army of British, Hanoverian, Dutch and Belgian troops, his attacks were already faltering when Blücher's Prussian army appeared and turned the defeat into a complete rout. The three main elements of the Napoleonic army all appear in this picture: cavalry, infantry and artillery. The musket-armed British infantry (right) have formed a square with the front rank kneeling and are succeeding in fending off the French armoured cavalry or cuirassiers with the bayonet. The field gun (left) is shown abandoned, but it was common practice for artillerymen to leave their guns in the face of a cavalry charge and seek safety within infantry squares.(The National Army Museum, London.)*

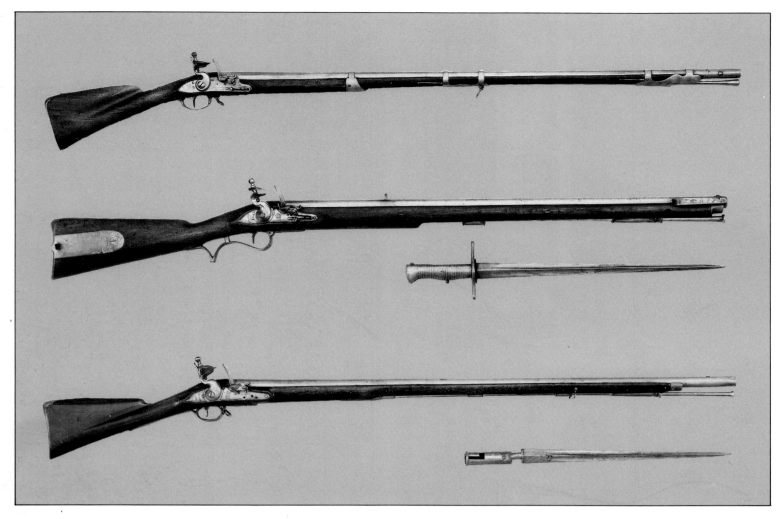

French 'Charleville' musket, c.1800 (top). The French were among the first to adopt 'pattern' arms, settling on a muzzle-loading flintlock of universal type as early as 1717. The popular name 'Charleville' came from one of the French government arsenals. At the height of Napoleon's power there were ten such official manufactories, the other nine being Culemborg, Liège, Maubeuge, Mutzig, Roanne, St Étienne, Tulle, Turin and Versailles. A notable feature of the 'Charleville' patterns was their broad brass barrel bands holding together the barrel and the fore-end; English muskets were secured only by metal pins through the wooden furniture. The United States musket adopted in 1795 was basically a copy of the 'Charleville' design. (The Royal Armouries, London.)

Government-issue Baker rifle, British, c.1800 (centre). Designed by Ezekiel Baker and chosen for service as a result of a test at Woolwich in February 1800, the Baker rifle was produced in both musket and carbine bore. The former type was soon dispensed with as too clumsy, but the lighter weapon was used to equip not only the rifle regiments like the famous 95th and 60th but also a number of militia and volunteer units, and a few cavalry. The Baker was used throughout the Napoleonic era by both British and German troops, and during the course of its life it underwent a number of minor changes. Most obvious of these was the bayonet. The original 'sword', as the riflemen called it, was long with a flat blade and a knuckle-bow. Later on, socket bayonets and a rather dagger-like bayonet, shown here, were also used. (The Royal Armouries, London.)

British 'India' pattern musket, c.1800 (bottom). Originally designed for use by the Honourable East India Company, the 'India' pattern was one of several muskets brought into British army use as a result of war with revolutionary France. Ordnance workshops were unable to keep pace with demand for 'land' patterns and so East India Company muskets were bought in. Discovering that this simply-made 39 inch barrel musket was easier to produce, large orders were then placed by the Ordnance Office. (The Royal Armouries, London.)

By this time, most small handguns in both the military and the civilian sphere were revolvers. In America, the Colt in all its guises – 'Army', 'Navy', 'Dragoon' and 'pocket' models – had begun to corner the market, but there were many other manufacturers at work. Among these were Smith & Wesson, Remington and Marlin. In Britain, the native 'Tranter' and 'Adams' types retained pre-eminence, although Samuel Colt did set up a factory in London and managed to obtain a modest defence contract which resulted in a few Colts accompanying the British army in the Crimean War.

All these revolvers had a basic similarity in that a number of rounds were held in a revolving cylinder that presented a new cartridge to the hammer with every working of the action, but there were a mass of details which distinguished each individual type. For example 'single-action' revolvers required the hammer to be cocked manually before firing; 'double-action' models were both cocked and fired by pulling the trigger. Some guns were loaded via a 'gate' which opened to the side; others were 'tip-up', the frame 'breaking' about its centre point to allow the barrel to drop forward (or alternatively be pulled forward) so that the cylinder could be loaded from the rear. They were also in every conceivable calibre, from as little as .22 to .65, though most military types were between .32 and .455.

Perhaps the most extraordinary revolver of the 1860s was the French Le Mat. This gun had two barrels, the upper one being equipped with a fairly conventional .44 revolving cylinder with a nine-round capacity. In the centre of this cylinder was the second barrel with a mighty 'man-stopping' .65 charge.

One group of pistols totally outside the revolver tradition consisted of the so-called 'howdah' pistols, many of which were made by Charles Lancaster of London and his successor Henry Thorn in the 1870s and 1880s. In these weapons, a multi-shot capability was achieved by the simple age-old expedient of multiple barrels, but they were equipped with a revolving striker. Thus it was that one squeeze of the trigger produced a single discharge twice or four times, depending on the number of barrels.

Particularly popular with officers and big-game hunters in India, 'howdah' pistols were particularly valued for their great stopping-power. Most had a calibre of .476 and were perfectly capable of dispatching a charging tribesman or a wounded tiger.

A name of increasing importance in the British revolver market was Webley of Birmingham. The family and its associates had been in the gun trade since the early nineteenth century, but in 1877 Philip Webley took over the well-known firm of Tipping & Lawden and soon after was examining many of the methods of mass production pioneered by Colt. Ten years later the firm received a major British government contract which began a tradition which lasted well into the twentieth century.

The Webley Mark I, which replaced the service Enfield revolver in the British army, was a remarkably robust weapon. Its great strengths were a very strong breech fastening, the ability to eject the spent cartridges as the gun was broken open and a hefty .455 round. Soon not only the army but the navy and the Royal Irish Constabulary were also equipped with the impressive Webley models.

Improvement in small arms and artillery naturally meant changes in military tactics. Columns and dense lines of troops gradually came to make less sense in the face of increased firepower. European armies were at first reluctant to accept the evidence of the American Civil War and British colonial wars as conclusive – after all, these were 'irregular' conflicts fought over vast non-European terrains. The Franco-Prussian War brought the message rather closer to home, and here the effects of the Chassepot and *Zundnadelgewehr* were reinforced by Krupp artillery and the *mitrailleuse*.

Gunner's 'linstock', French, eighteenth century (below). Until the invention of 'cannon locks' and percussion ignition, cannon had to be lit with a slow match to set them off. The 'linstock' gave the gunner somewhere to place a smouldering slow match out of the way of powder and a means of protection in case of attack. This example has a small leaf-shaped head engraved with the sun in splendour and has two pairs of jaws on either side to hold the match. The holders are in the form of monsters, and their mouths are a serrated slit to grip the matchcord. Similar items existed for many years over the whole of Europe – the head of a similar match-holder in wood has been found in a Spanish Armada wreck, and there are widespread illustrations from the early sixteenth century onwards. (The Wallace Collection, London.)

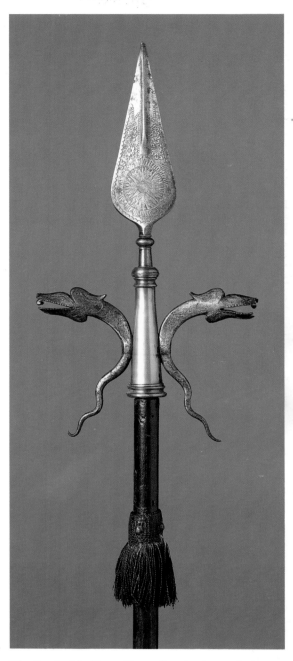

The Sentinel by Horace Vernet, French, nineteenth century (opposite page). A wealth of detail is provided by many paintings of this period. Here, a grenadier of the Imperial Guard carries a flintlock musket with a socket bayonet and a short sabre. The exact model of musket is not clear, but the way in which the bayonet fixes over the foresight without obscuring the bore is apparent, as is the small, worsted tufted plug inserted into the barrel. These plugs were used with many firearms of the nineteenth century, to prevent the barrel rusting or the ingress of debris. (The Wallace Collection, London.)

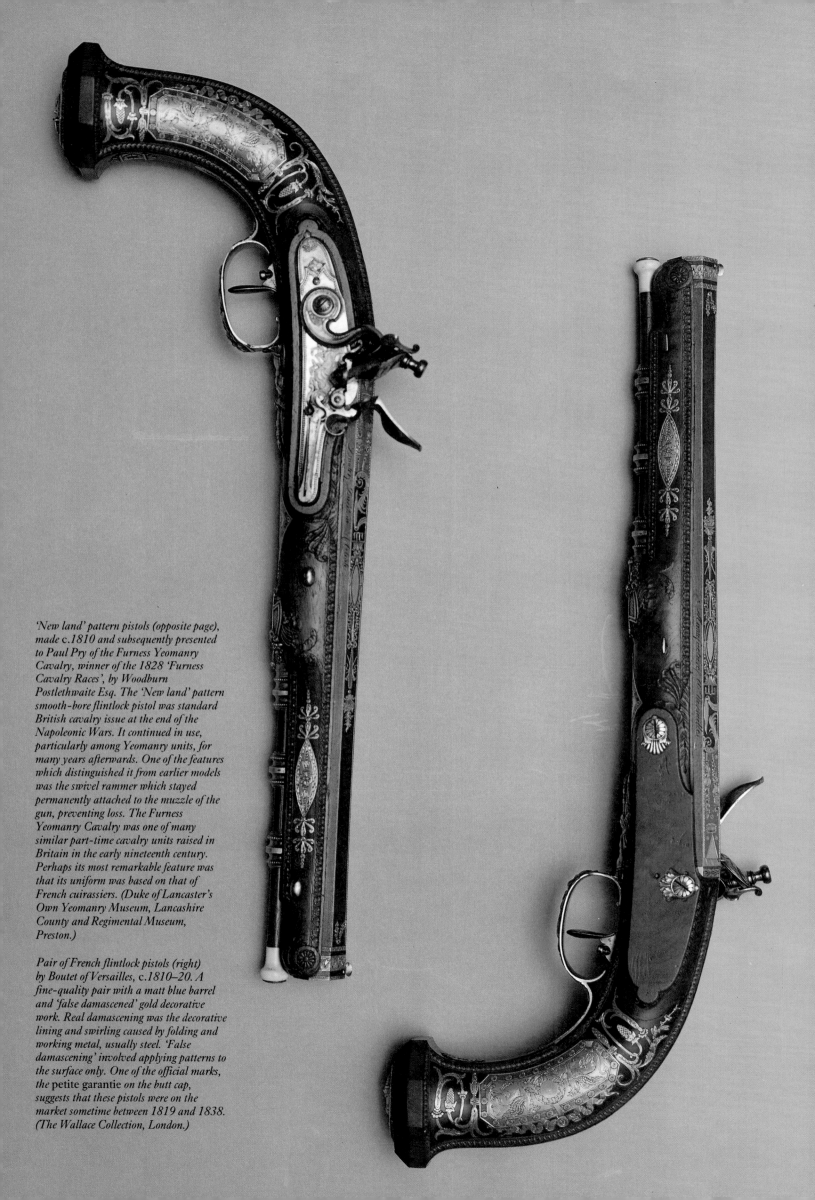

'New land' pattern pistols (opposite page),
made c.1810 and subsequently presented
to Paul Pry of the Furness Yeomanry
Cavalry, winner of the 1828 'Furness
Cavalry Races', by Woodburn
Postlethwaite Esq. The 'New land' pattern
smooth-bore flintlock pistol was standard
British cavalry issue at the end of the
Napoleonic Wars. It continued in use,
particularly among Yeomanry units, for
many years afterwards. One of the features
which distinguished it from earlier models
was the swivel rammer which stayed
permanently attached to the muzzle of the
gun, preventing loss. The Furness
Yeomanry Cavalry was one of many
similar part-time cavalry units raised in
Britain in the early nineteenth century.
Perhaps its most remarkable feature was
that its uniform was based on that of
French cuirassiers. (Duke of Lancaster's
Own Yeomanry Museum, Lancashire
County and Regimental Museum,
Preston.)

Pair of French flintlock pistols (right)
by Boutet of Versailles, c.1810–20. A
fine-quality pair with a matt blue barrel
and 'false damascened' gold decorative
work. Real damascening was the decorative
lining and swirling caused by folding and
working metal, usually steel. 'False
damascening' involved applying patterns to
the surface only. One of the official marks,
the petite garantie on the butt cap,
suggests that these pistols were on the
market sometime between 1819 and 1838.
(The Wallace Collection, London.)

Dress uniform of a lieutenant of the Lancashire Hussars (right), c.1856, with 1821 pattern sword. The Lancashire Hussars were a Yeomanry unit raised in 1848 and converted to artillery after the First World War. The uniform shown here is that of Arthur Farrel, who served with the regiment from 1851 to 1853 and again from 1855 to 1859. The 1821 pattern sword is also sometimes known as the 'three bar', after the number of bars in the hilt. Similar swords were carried by troopers and by artillery officers and continued to be made in the twentieth century. (The Lancashire County and Regimental Museum, Preston.)

British sergeant's spontoon, 1800 pattern (below). A regulation issue for sergeants in line and many volunteer regiments, the so-called '1800 pattern' was nine feet in length with a broad blade and a transverse bar under the head. Little academic work has been published on pole arms, but collectors are aided by the fact that the regiment's name or initials were often inscribed down the metal 'cheeks' or 'langets' which protected the top of the shaft. Though of limited offensive value, the spontoon was useful defence in a mêlée, was a mark of rank and could be used to herd private soldiers back into line. (The Royal Armouries, London.)

Interestingly, neither the Gatling nor the *mitrailleuse* was a true 'machine-gun'. Richard Jordan Gatling's gun, which first saw action in the American Civil War, required constant hand-cranking; the Montigny *mitrailleuse* was more like a volley gun, with a 37-round plate fitted to the rear. Much the same was true of the Nordenfeldt gun, invented by a Swede but built in England: with this, a horizontal sweep of a lever produced one discharge from each barrel. True 'machine' weapons, which used the power of the cartridge to cock and operate the mechanism while a trigger was depressed, had to wait for the work of the American inventor Hiram Stevens Maxim.

By 1890, most European countries were experimenting with, or had already adopted, the magazine bolt-action rifle. The basis of the action was a bolt, like a door bolt, which moved back and forth in the breech. Pulling back the bolt allowed a cartridge to rise from the magazine into the chamber; pushing the bolt forward again and closing it locked the mechanism, and then the trigger was squeezed. A striker hit the cap of the cartridge and discharged the round. Another working of the bolt ejected the spent cartridge and let another up from the magazine.

Such were the basics, but – predictably enough – every state seemed to have its own make or model, in many slightly varying calibres. The Mauser-type bolt action was undoubtedly most widespread – before 1900, Belgium, Germany, Luxemburg, Montenegro, Serbia, Spain, Sweden and Turkey had all adopted it. Outside Europe, not only China and Japan but also virtually every South American state used their own variations on the Mauser theme.

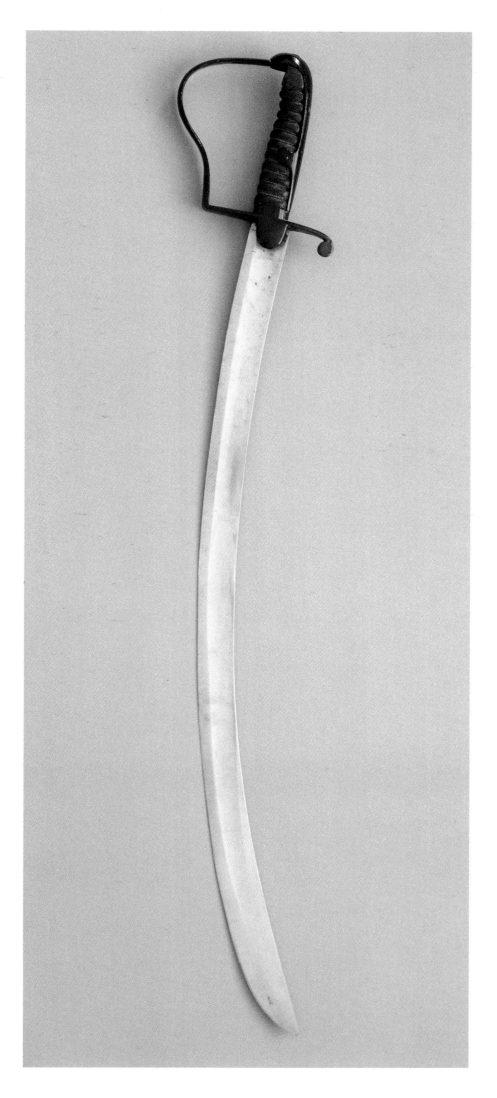

Sword based on the 1796 light-cavalry pattern, presented to Major Hugh Birley as a result of 'Peterloo', 1819. The 'Peterloo' massacre occurred when a crowd gathered in St Peter's fields near Manchester to hear the radical reform speaker Henry Hunt. The crowd was fairly peaceful, but the authorities wanted Hunt arrested and so sent the Manchester and Salford Yeomanry into the crowd. Fearing that these 100 men would be overwhelmed, the 15th Hussars were then sent in to support them. Eleven people died and hundreds were injured. Birley, commander of the Yeomanry, was put on trial for his part in the disaster, but was acquitted. His men presented him with this sword in commemoration in 1822. Based closely on the 1796 pattern weapons, it has a highly curved wide blade and an exceptionally large knuckle-guard. (The Lancashire County and Regimental Museum, Preston.)

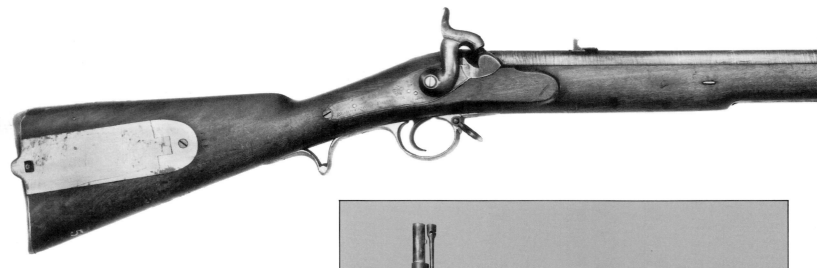

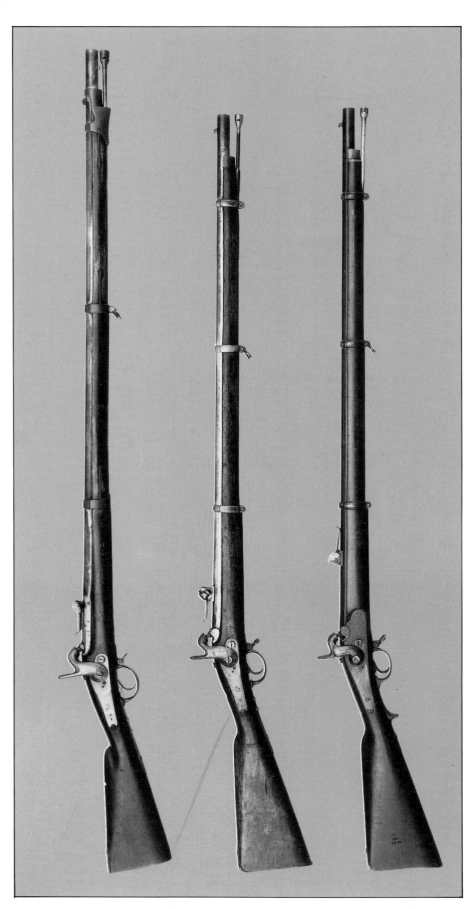

Russian military-issue percussion muskets (right), Tula arsenal, c.1840. The cannon factory at Tula had been converted to the production of small arms by Peter the Great in 1705; thereafter it produced both sporting and military arms. Despite the fairly poor reputation of Russian military arms in the Napoleonic wars and the Crimea, the use of machine-made parts was pioneered at Tula and many foreign craftsmen were employed in the production of fine-quality arms. The arms seen here are typical of the patterns used by the Russian army in the Crimea. (The Royal Armouries, London.)

William Tranter's 'double-trigger' revolver in case, c.1855 (below, opposite page). William Tranter (1816–90) was a Birmingham gunmaker who made a notable contribution to the evolution of 'double-action' revolvers. The 'double-trigger' model patented in 1853 could be cocked and have the cylinder turned by pulling the lower trigger which projected through the trigger-guard. Squeezing the upper trigger fired the shot. The 'Tranter' was popular with army officers but was also used by civilians and was available in many calibres, including .50, .45, .44, .38, .36 and .32 inch. In this cased set are included a box of Tranter's own patent 'lubricating bullets', percussion caps, nipple wrenches, a bullet mould and a powder-flask. The lever visible on the gun barrel was a loading aid, the bullet being rammed down from the front of the cylinder by raising the lever. (The Victoria and Albert Museum, London.)

1853 pattern, .577 inch muzzle-loading Enfield rifled musket (above, opposite page). The standard firearm of the British army, the 'P53' was essentially a development of the French minié rifle. The remarkable feature of both weapons was the use of a bullet designed by the French captain Delvigne which expanded to fit the bore of the rifle when fired. The P53 was a strong, reliable and accurate gun with surprising qualities of endurance. One weapon, kept at the Tower of London, was fired twenty times a day from August 1863 to May 1866 without serious malfunction! Cavalry and artillery were issued with carbine versions of the P53, and it was not until the early 1860s that the authorities considered muzzle loading a sufficient handicap to require a new arm to be adopted. After extensive experiment, and bearing in mind the huge number of P53 rifles in existence, it was decided to convert the old rifle to breech loading. The method used was to cut out a section of the existing breech and insert a new hinged block designed by the American designer Jacob Snider. This was used in conjunction with a metallic cartridge designed by Colonel Boxer of the Royal Laboratory at Woolwich. By 1867, 150,000 old rifles had been converted to the new system. The P53 then soldiered on in its new guise until eventually replaced by the Martini–Henry. (The Royal Ordnance Pattern Room, Nottingham.)

Brunswick rifle, British, c.1840 (left). Like its predecessor – the Baker – the Brunswick rifle had strong German connections and seems to have been adopted as a result of the experiments of George Lovell with a number of different designs, including a Hanoverian percussion rifle. Two really significant features separate the Baker and the Brunswick. Most obviously the Brunswick is a percussion arm, using copper caps rather than flint, steel and priming-powder. Secondly and less apparent is the fact that the Brunswick has two-groove rifling and uses a 'belted' ball. The ridges on the ball fit into the deep grooves of the barrel, leading to better accuracy. The Brunswick continued in production until 1850. (The Royal Armouries, London.)

Decorated version of the Colt model 1861 percussion navy
revolver, .36 inch (right). With white grips and etched frame
and barrel, this pistol exhibits the main techniques applied to
presentation and first-quality civilian weapons. A similar
model was used by James Butler (Wild Bill) Hickok. Samuel
Colt (1813–62) of Hartford, Connecticut, did not invent the
revolver but he probably did more than anyone else to make the
revolver principle practical and widely available. His first
factory was set up at Paterson, New Jersey, in 1836 but the
initial venture failed – at least partly due to lack of demand.
Not daunted, Colt tried again – this time with a plant in his
home town. Mexican, civil and Indian wars provided the
necessary demand, and Colt kept pace with new models and
high production. Although a limited number of weapons were
made at Paterson and in London, England (1852–7), the vast
majority of Colt pistols were made at Hartford. (The
Smithsonian Institution, Washington DC.)

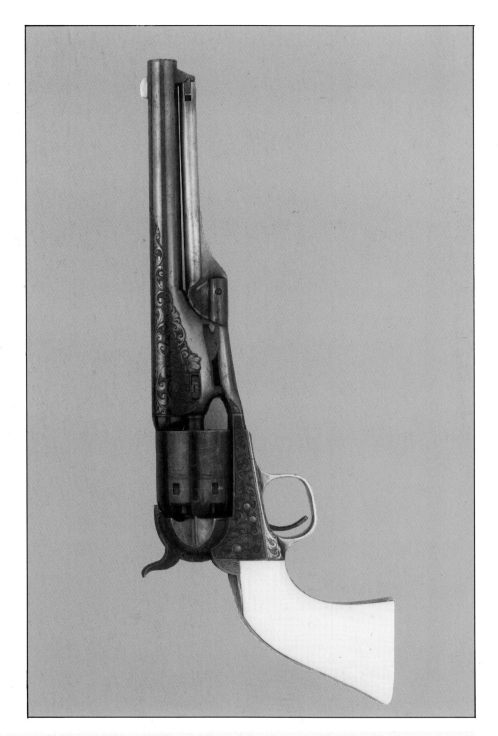

Collier patent flintlock revolver, Anglo-American, c.1820
(below). The principle of using several charges in a cylinder and
realigning them in turn behind a barrel to achieve more rapid
fire was an old one, going back until at least the late sixteenth
century. Early 'revolvers' were scarce and had many problems,
not least of which was the fact that a poor fit between cylinder
and barrel would result in a good deal of the explosive powder
issuing as flame and smoke at the break. Another significant
difficulty was that priming for each discharge required a little
priming-powder in a pan outside the chamber to ignite the
main charge. Elisha Haydon Collier was an American citizen
living in London. His patent of 1818 produced an effective
revolver which overcame a good number of the drawbacks
associated with earlier models. Most importantly a single
priming-pan and steel served all five chambers and the
priming was supplied by a small magazine which supplied
powder to the pan when it was shut. Another big advantage of
the Collier system was that it achieved a good gas-seal at the
rear, because the cylinder head was countersunk and keyed into
the barrel. Collier also designed a cylinder to be mechanically
rotated, but none now survive complete. Collier himself
observed during a test at Woolwich in 1819 that he 'considered
the gun better without it.' (The Victoria and Albert Museum,
London.)

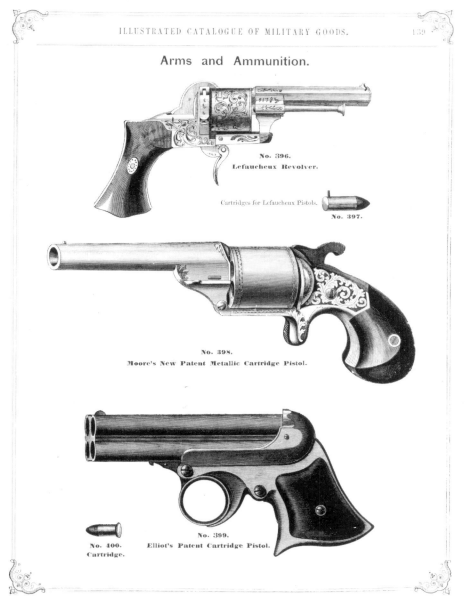

ILLUSTRATED CATALOGUE OF MILITARY GOODS. 139

Arms and Ammunition.

No. 396.
Lefaucheux Revolver.

Cartridges for Lefaucheux Pistols.

No. 397.

No. 398.
Moore's New Patent Metallic Cartridge Pistol.

No. 399.
Elliot's Patent Cartridge Pistol.

No. 400.
Cartridge.

Daw patent percussion revolver, British, c.1860 (above). G. H. Daw was a London gunmaker whose main claim to fame was the use of a particularly effective 'double-action' lock first devised by Charles Pryse and Paul Cashmore of Birmingham in 1855. In a 'double-action' lock, trigger pressure not only releases the hammer but also cocks it and rotates the mechanism. In the Daw pistol it was possible to operate the mechanism either with the trigger or manually via the hammer. Moreover, a slow deliberate pressure on the trigger would bring the gun to full cock, allowing deliberate aim and a pause to steady the hand before a further slight pressure fired the gun. (The Royal Ordnance Pattern Room, Nottingham.)

A page from Schuyler, Hartley and Graham's Illustrated Catalog of Military Goods, USA, 1864. This valuable catalogue gives a good idea of the sort of arms and equipment available for private purchase by Union officers and volunteers during the Civil War. Top is the French Lefaucheux 'pin-fire' revolver. Casimir Lefaucheux (1802–52) designed this pistol around the 'pin-fire' cartridge which he had developed in the 1830s. In this cartridge, a pin was so positioned that when struck by the hammer of the gun it set off the primer which immediately ignited the main charge. 'Pin-fires' were never popular in Britain or the USA but did gain a substantial market in continental Europe. The Lefaucheux was adopted by the French navy in 1856, and millions of pin-fire guns were also produced by the Belgian arms industry.

Centre is Moore's patent pistol, popularly known as the 'teat fire' gun. Daniel Moore of Brooklyn, New York, whose Patent Firearms Company was active between 1864 and 1882, designed this gun in an effort to circumvent Rollin White's patents on rear-loading cylinder revolvers. The barrel and cylinder tipped sideways, clear of the frame, and then special cartridges were inserted from the front. It was the cartridges, designed by Moore and David Williamson, that had the 'teat-shaped' ends. Bottom is Elliot's patent pistol. William Elliott, once an employee of Remington, designed this neat pistol during the Civil War. It achieved repeated fire by having four separate barrels and a striker which activated each in turn. The model shown here was produced in .32 inch calibre and a rather small and unmilitary .22 inch. (The Library of Congress, Washington DC.)

The Charge of the Light Brigade, Balaclava, October 1854, *by Richard Caton Woodville (1856–1927). There has been much argument as to whether the Crimean War was the last of the Napoleonic-style campaigns or the first 'modern' war. In truth it had elements of both – war correspondents, rifled muskets and trenches existed alongside cavalry charges, set-piece actions and elderly generals. Balaclava was one of many actions fought by the allied armies against the Russians for the control of the sea port of Sevastopol. After the British Heavy Brigade had charged successfully under the command of Colonel James Scarlett, impetuosity and garbled orders led the Light Brigade to charge massed Russian artillery in one of the most celebrated incidents of the war. Five British regiments were involved: two light dragoon, two hussar and one lancer. Visible here at the Russian gun line are members of two units: the 11th Hussars or 'Cherry pickers' (so called after their red overalls) and the 17th Lancers, who here earned their motto 'Death or Glory'. In 1853, all types of British cavalry began to receive a standard-pattern sword, but it is likely that many carried the old 1821 pattern light-cavalry weapon at Balaclava. On the left of the painting is just visible a Russian infantryman in a spiked leather helmet – one of the few vestiges of armour which survived the nineteenth century. (The National Army Museum, London.)*

Scottish 'skean-dhu' (top) (also 'skene-dhu' or 'sgain-dubh'), 92nd (Gordon Highlanders) Regiment of foot, third quarter of the nineteenth century. The 'skean-dhu' or 'black knife' is a traditional small knife carried in the top of the stocking by highlanders. It is normally short with a flat, dark grip and is often set with a 'cairngorm' or smoky quartz stone in place of a pommel. From the mid nineteenth century, various patterns were adopted for use by British highland regiments. The 92nd were formed at the end of the eighteenth century, serving against the French in Egypt, Spain and the Low Countries. During the reign of Queen Victoria, they fought in Afghanistan, Egypt and South Africa. (The National Museums of Scotland, Edinburgh.)

Constabulary 'hanger' (centre), English, mid nineteenth century. Modern police forces use both the truncheon and firearms as the need arises, but edged weapons were commonly issued in the nineteenth century. The 'hanger' shown here was typical, having a short, broad, and slightly curved blade; a simple knuckle-guard; and a grip covered in fishskin. The scabbard is leather with a brass chape, or scabbard end, and mouthpiece. Coastguards and customs officials often had similar swords, and the manufacturers were normally those who also supplied the army and navy. (The Royal Armouries, London.)

A page (right) from Schuyler Hartley and Graeme's Illustrated Catalog of Military Goods, USA, 1864, showing a selection of decorative sword blades available to US forces. This picture helps to show that even in the mid nineteenth century 'Solingen' German steel was still appreciated, and that many of the highly decorated blades still thriving are not unique but produced to a pattern. The 'Damascus' blades would have a 'watered' appearance, created either by the original twist in the metal as it was forged or reproduced afterwards by means of etching. (The Library of Congress, Washington DC.)

'Albert' pattern helmet (opposite page), Lancashire Mounted Rifle Volunteers, c.1860. By the middle of the nineteenth century, helmets and body armour were mainly decorative in function. The 'Albert' pattern helmet was worn not only by Mounted Rifle Volunteers but also by heavy cavalry and some Yeomanry Cavalry units. Along with the cuirass, a similar helmet remains in use with the full dress uniform of the Household Cavalry. (The Lancashire County and Regimental Museum, Preston.)

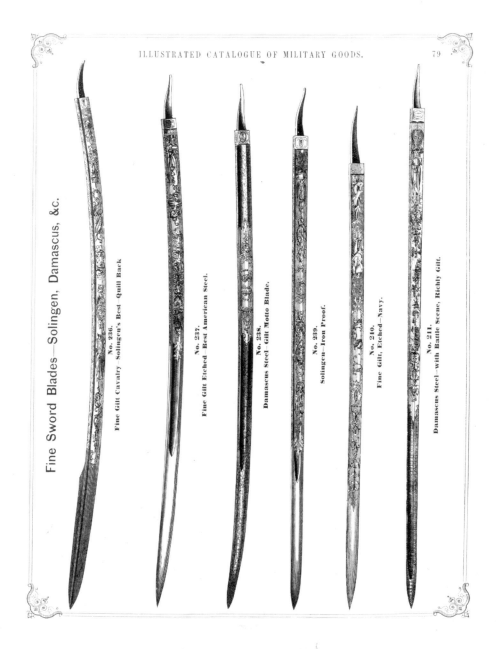

ILLUSTRATED CATALOGUE OF MILITARY GOODS.   79

Fine Sword Blades—Solingen, Damascus, &c.

No. 236.
Fine Gilt Cavalry—Solingen's Best Quill Back.

No. 237.
Fine Gilt Etched—Best American Steel.

No. 238.
Damascus Steel—Gilt Motto Blade.

No. 239.
Solingen—Iron Proof.

No. 240.
Fine Gilt, Etched—Navy.

No. 241.
Damascus Steel—with Battle Scene, Richly Gilt.

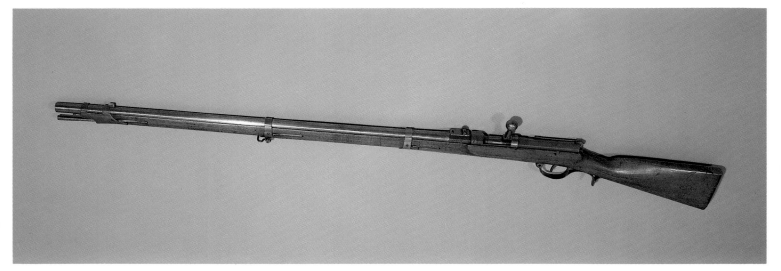

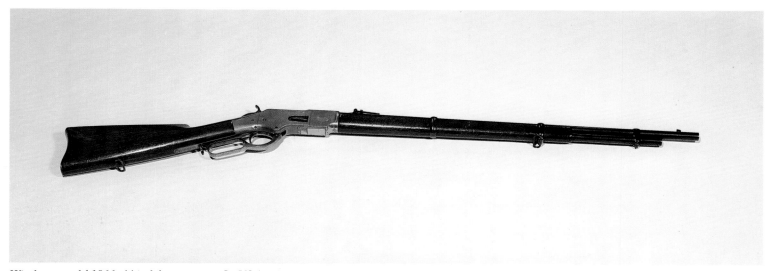

Winchester model 1866 .44 inch lever-action rifle, USA (above). Oliver F. Winchester (1810–80) reorganized the New Haven Arms Company in 1866 and put his own name to the company, creating the Winchester Repeating Arms Company. The model 1866 rifle was the first new product, but in reality it owed much to its predecessor the Henry rifle. The most important improvement was the addition of a loading-gate which allowed the under-barrel tube magazine to be loaded from the rear. The cartridge used was a .44 inch rim-fire. Production of the 1866 model continued alongside other types until 1898; most of the early production have octagonal barrels, but late examples, like that shown here, have round barrels. The Winchester achieved its popular fame from the American West, where it became known to the Indians as 'Yellow boy'. Strangely, however, the Winchester repeater really proved its worth as a military arm in the hands of the Turks, who used it to inflict heavy casualties on the Russians at the Battle of Plevna in 1877. (The Royal Armouries, London.)

The *Zundadelgewehr* and the Chassepot had both been bolt types, but were only single-shot weapons. Parent to all the Mauser bolt-action repeating magazine types was the 1884 model, which was a modification of the existing single-shot 1871 pattern. The '*Gewehr 71/84*', as it was technically known, had an eight-round tubular magazine under the barrel and fired an 11 mm round. For reasons of secrecy, the designation 'repeater' was at first forbidden.

Actually, Mauser had not been the first to introduce repeaters to the military, as they were already possessed by the Swiss and the Turks, but the quality of the Mauser action and the enormous market share it soon achieved convinced many that this was the weapon of the future. The US army, which had initially adopted the Danish-designed Krag-Jorgensen, changed to a Mauser-type action in its 1903 model Springfield rifle.

One of the major alternatives to the Mauser was the Lee action, taken into service by the British army in the Lee–Metford rifle in 1888. The Germans claimed greater long-range accuracy, but the Lee had an edge in speed and sustained firepower due to a slightly shorter bolt pull and an eight-round (subsequently ten-round) magazine. Other bolt-action types of the period were the French Lebel, the Austrian Mannlicher and the Russian Mosin–Nagant. The strange name of the Russian rifle stemmed from the fact that the bolt had been designed by a Russian colonel, Mosin, while the magazine had been the work of a Belgian, Monsieur Nagant.

Fully automatic firepower finally became available in 1884, when Hiram S. Maxim declared the results of his research to a disbelieving world. In the words of his autobiography, 'over six hundred rounds a minute, everyone thought it was too good to be true – a bit of a Yankee brag'. Though an American, Maxim was working at the time at Crayford in Kent. Both a showman and a skilled promoter, he was able to get many dignitaries to visit him and he solicited many opportunities to put on displays of his 'little gun' abroad. Among those to whom the gun was shown in the middle 1880s were Edward, Prince of Wales; the German Kaiser; a Chinese ambassador; and Turkish and Russian officials. This systematic lobbying paid handsomely, for different versions of this 'devil's paintbrush' were adopted all over the world within the next ten years. Indeed, so universal did the Maxim design become that machine-guns working on this principle were often referred to simply as 'Maxims' whether made at Vickers in Kent, Spandau in Germany, or the Tula arsenal in Russia.

Prussian Zundnadelgewehr or needle-gun, c.1850 (opposite, top). Invented by Johann Nikolaus von Dreyse of Sömmerda in 1841, the needle-gun was one of the first attempts to use an opening bolt mechanism for the breech of a rifle. In the Dreyse system, the cartridge was a self-contained unit wrapped in paper with primer at the base of the bullet. With the cartridge loaded and the bolt closed, the trigger was then squeezed. A long spring-loaded firing-pin penetrated the cartridge and hit the primer, firing the gun. The needle-gun was highly successful in the War of the Danish Duchies fought between Prussia and Denmark in 1864 and in the Austro-Prussian War of 1866. By 1870 it was beginning to be rather dated when faced by the Chassepot rifle of the French. (The Royal Ordnance Pattern Room, Nottingham.)

Chassepot breech-loading rifle, French, c.1866 (opposite, centre). This rifle, invented by Antoine Alphonse Chassepot in 1863, was very similar to the Prussian needle-gun but included two significant refinements. Firstly, the primer of the cartridge was its base rather than immediately under the bullet, which allowed the use of a shorter, more robust firing-pin. Secondly, a rubber disc in the breech helped to create an efficient gas-seal. Both the firing-pin and the rubber seal required periodic replacement, but the weapon performed very well. The Chassepot was adopted by the French army in 1866 and remained standard until 1874, when it was replaced by the Gras rifle which used modern metallic centre-fire cartridges. (The Royal Ordnance Pattern Room, Nottingham.)

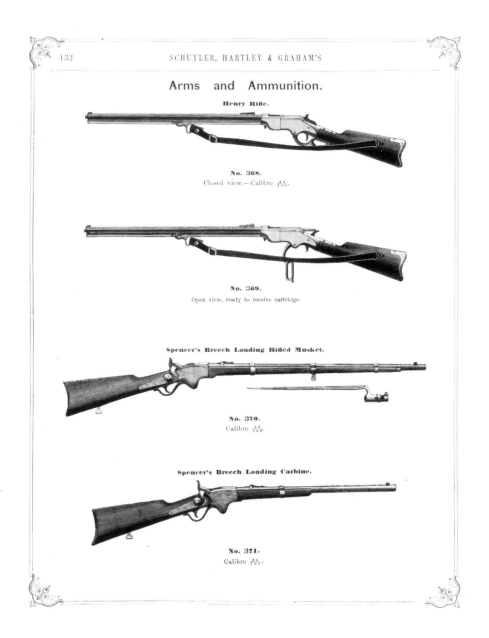

A page (left) from Schuyler, Hartley and Graeme's Illustrated Catalog of Military Goods, *USA, 1864. The Henry and Spencer rifles shown here were excellent performers both against game and on the battlefields of the Civil War. Top is the Henry rifle, first produced by B. Tyler Henry in 1860, which was manufactured by the New Haven Arms Company of Connecticut. An improvement of the 'Volcanic' carbine produced by the company in the 1850s, the Henry was a really practical lever-action repeater using .44 inch metallic rim-fire cartridges. Total production before the company reorganization in 1866 was about 13,000 perhaps 2,000 of which were immediately purchased by the US government.*

Bottom are the Spencer rifle and carbine, first devised by Christopher M. Spencer (1833–1922) and made by the Spencer Repeating Rifle Company of Boston, Massachusetts. Similar weapons with different rifling were made by the Burnside Company at Providence, Rhode Island. The Spencer was a repeater, seven cartridges being carried in a tube magazine in the butt. Quick and reliable, this weapon was given the personal endorsement of President Lincoln; over 100,000 were bought by the US government and after the Civil War it saw long and hard use in the Indian wars. (The Library of Congress, Washington DC.)

Martini–Henry Mk II rifle, .45 inch, c.1879 (above).
Approved for service by the army in 1877, the Mk II was one
of several Martini–Henry types used by British troops. There
were also carbine versions for artillery and cavalry, and from
1890 a number were manufactured in the new .303 inch
calibre. All Martinis had a basically similar action. Pulling
down the lever opened the breech and ejected any used cartridge
there. A round was then slid in from the top and the hinged
breech-block was closed, again by means of the lever. The rifle
was then ready to fire its single shot. The cartridge was
powerful and could be used at targets up to 1,000 yards distant
but was something of a weak link in the system as it was made
of rolled brass and easily deformed. The Martini–Henry Mk II
weighed 8 lb 10½ oz and was 49 inches long. For close action
it could be fitted with either a sword or a socket bayonet. (The
Royal Ordnance Pattern Room, Nottingham.)

Krag–Jorgensen 8 mm rifle, US army, c.1893 (top). The Krag–Jorgensen was developed in the late 1880s by Captain Ole Krag of the Royal Norwegian Artillery and Erik Jorgensen of the Norwegian state arsenal. Similar weapons were adopted by the Danish, Norwegian and American forces. The rifle is bolt-action but has a highly unusual magazine. This is loaded laterally through a hinged trapdoor, visible here under the bolt. The magazine contained five rounds and the weapon was sighted to 2,200 yards. (The Royal Ordnance Pattern Room, Nottingham.)

Lee Enfield magazine rifle, c.1900 (centre and below). Great Britain adopted the Lee Metford bolt-action magazine rifle in 1888. This and its .303 inch bullet were to have a profound impact on British military weapons for almost a century. Minor modification produced first the Lee Enfield, which had slightly different rifling, and then the short-magazine Lee Enfield, a standardized arm for infantry and cavalry which was to serve in both World Wars. Earliest versions used a compressed black-powder cartridge, but smokeless nitrocellulose propellants increased the muzzle velocity and made shooting easier. Reduction in smoke both helped to keep the target clear and made it difficult for the firer to be seen by the enemy. Bolt-action rifles could achieve very impressive ranges, and the sights were often graduated up to and beyond a mile, though battle range was usually closer. (The Lancashire and County Regimental Museum.)

Pair of percussion pocket pistols, c.1850. Small and handy for concealment, the pocket pistol was popular with travellers. Those shown here even have folding triggers to minimize the inconvenience and danger to the user when in a pocket. Large numbers of this type of pistol were made, particularly in England and Belgium, and many survive. These are still in their original case, together with their equipment which includes a powder-flask and a bullet mould. (The Victoria and Albert Museum.)

Colt single-action army revolver, Hartford, Connecticut, United States, c.1880. One of the best-known weapons of all time, the Colt single-action army revolver was produced in large numbers and given many nicknames, including 'the Peacemaker'. Production started in 1872 and continued into the twentieth century. This gun is seen in many different barrel lengths, grip configurations and calibres. The most extraordinary and sought after is the flat-topped 'Buntline Special' with a folding rear leaf sight and a barrel anything up to 16 inches long. Standard models, like that shown, were made with barrels of 4³/₄ inches, 5¹/₂ inches, and 7¹/₂ inches, and the commonest calibres are .45, .44, .38 and .32 inch. (The Smithsonian Institution, Washington DC.)

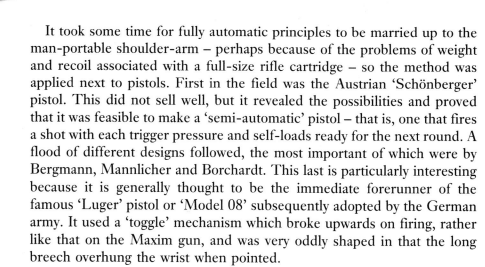

It took some time for fully automatic principles to be married up to the man-portable shoulder-arm – perhaps because of the problems of weight and recoil associated with a full-size rifle cartridge – so the method was applied next to pistols. First in the field was the Austrian 'Schönberger' pistol. This did not sell well, but it revealed the possibilities and proved that it was feasible to make a 'semi-automatic' pistol – that is, one that fires a shot with each trigger pressure and self-loads ready for the next round. A flood of different designs followed, the most important of which were by Bergmann, Mannlicher and Borchardt. This last is particularly interesting because it is generally thought to be the immediate forerunner of the famous 'Luger' pistol or 'Model 08' subsequently adopted by the German army. It used a 'toggle' mechanism which broke upwards on firing, rather like that on the Maxim gun, and was very oddly shaped in that the long breech overhung the wrist when pointed.

Perhaps the best-known semi-automatic pistol to be manufactured before 1900 was the Mauser model C96, commonly known as the 'broomhandle' after its distinctive wooden grip. This had a number of interesting and innovative design features, including an exposed hammer, a magazine mounted forward of the trigger and an unusual wooden holster which, when clipped on to the back of the pistol, formed a detachable shoulder stock.

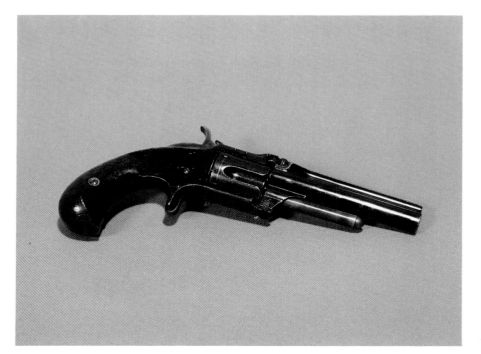

Smith & Wesson 'tip-up' pocket revolver, c.1870. Horace Smith and David Baird Wesson went into partnership in the mid 1850s in anticipation of the expiry of Colt's patent on all revolvers with mechanically rotated cylinders. Smith & Wesson's first really innovative venture was to combine the revolver principle with a metallic cartridge of their own design (which fired when struck on the rim) and a bored-through cylinder which could be loaded from behind. Loading a 'tip-up' revolver of this type requires that a catch be released and the whole front of the weapon turned upwards through 90 degrees. The cylinder can then be removed and filled. Most 'pocket' models are of small calibre – often .22 inch and usually not more than .32 inch. (The Royal Ordnance Pattern Room, Nottingham.)

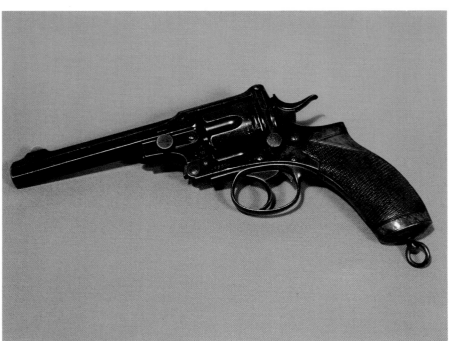

'Webley-Pryse' revolver, British, c.1880. In 1876, Charles Pryse of Birmingham patented a new type of revolver designed to overcome an old problem. Loading a revolver often meant either that the frame had to be broken open to get at the cylinder or that the cylinder had to move out to the side. Both systems were a source of weakness. In the Pryse system, which may have been inspired by contemporary Belgian weapons, a spring-loaded latch on each side of the gun acted to lock the breech firmly in place. When these latches were squeezed, the frame could open and tip forward. A number of different models were produced by Webley using the Pryse catches, and similar weapons were also produced by Thomas Horsley and Christopher Bonehill. A number of Continental manufacturers, including the Belgians at Liège, also made guns of this type. (The Royal Ordnance Pattern Room, Nottingham.)

Gasser revolver, 11 mm, Austrian, c.1870. Using a reduced-charge version of a carbine cartridge and weighing a massive 3 lb 2 oz, the Gasser was one of the biggest revolvers of the period. The firm of Gasser was founded in 1862 by Leopold Gasser, who made revolvers for both the civilian and the military markets of the Balkans and south-eastern Europe. The model seen here, patented in 1870, and others similar, continued to sell in considerable numbers almost to the end of the century. Like the early Colts it is an 'open-frame' model, with no top 'strap'. A loading-gate at the back of the cylinder hinges out to allow the insertion of six cartridges from the rear. (The Royal Ordnance Pattern Room, Nottingham.)

French model 1892 service revolver (below). Produced at the government arsenal of St Étienne, the model 1892 was a replacement for the hefty model 1873 which had been the first centre-fire revolver adopted by the French army. With a solid frame and a loading-gate at the rear of the cylinder, this pistol was reliable and was produced in huge numbers. It remained in common use until the Second World War. (The Smithsonian Institution, Washington DC.)

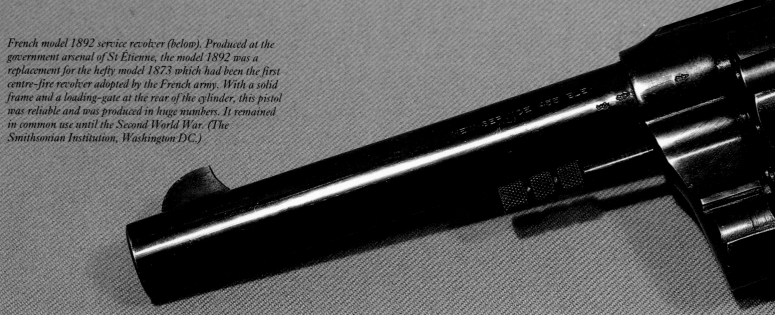

Borchardt patent semi-automatic or 'self-loading' pistol (top, far left) by the Deutsche Waffen und Munitionsfabriken, Berlin, c.1897. Hugo Borchardt (1845–1924) was a German citizen who spent much of his working life in America, being employed successively by the Pioneer Breech Loading Arms Company, the Singer Sewing Machine Company, Colt, Winchester and Sharps. With this tremendous manufacturing pedigree he returned to Europe, rising to works director of a royal armaments factory in Hungary by 1890. In 1893 he approached Ludwig Lowe of Berlin with a design for a new pistol, subsequently to become known as the 'C93'. The pistol was tested by several agencies, including the Swiss government and the US navy. It was found to be swift and surprisingly accurate; however, it did not sell in large numbers as it was thought too expensive and complex for a military arm and too big and powerful for the civilian market. (The Smithsonian Institution, Washington DC.)

Colt 'New Service' .455 inch revolver, USA, 1897 (centre). Designed in the last decade of the nineteenth century, the Colt 'New Service' was typical of the heavy, powerful revolvers then in use in many nations. It was manufactured in 'Target', 'Army and Navy' and 'Marine Corps' models, and was available in calibres from .38 inch to .476 inch. Solid and well made, it remained in service well into the twentieth century. (The Royal Ordnance Pattern Room, Nottingham.)

Webley–Fosbery .455 inch self-cocking revolver (left), British, c.1900. Colonel G. V. Fosbery, who designed this gun, was a highly unusual and inventive soldier. After winning the VC on the North West Frontier of India in 1863, he turned his mind to gun and cartridge design. Between 1866 and 1891 he took out thirteen patents relating to arms and devised an exploding bullet. The Webley–Fosbery's self-cocking mechanism operated on a recoil principle. Discharging the first round forced the whole top of the frame backwards, cocking the hammer and rotating the cylinder ready for the next shot. The new gun was first demonstrated on the ranges at Bisley in 1900, and production began soon after. (The Royal Ordnance Pattern Room, Nottingham.)

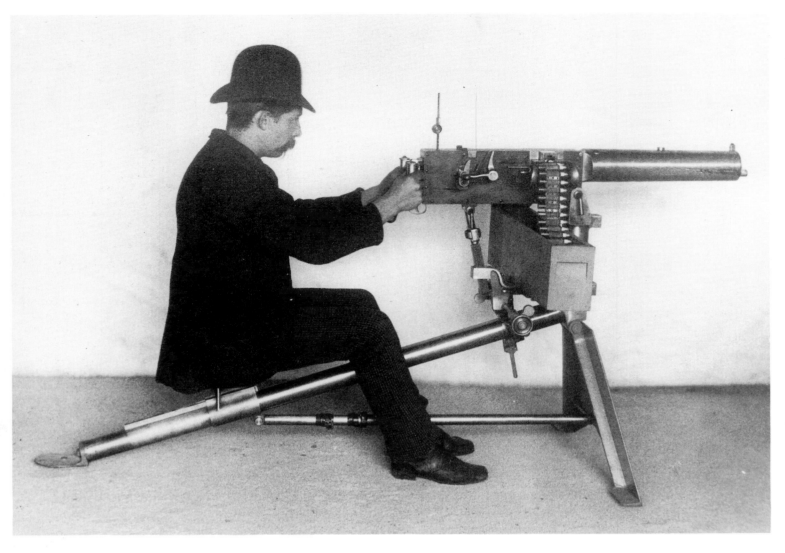

Hiram Maxim's assistant, Louis Silverman (above), demonstrates a transitional model Maxim machine gun, c.1886. This gun was a simplification of the first design which allowed easy removal of the breech block and feed block and, with the aid of a new extractor, perfected the belt feed system. The tripod shown includes a saddle for the firer and an armoured front for protection. (National Army Museum, London.)

American 1874 model Gatling gun. Richard Jordan Gatling was born in 1818 in Hertford County, North Carolina. With little formal education but an extremely agile mind, he set up his own business as a storekeeper and then turned his attention to inventions as diverse as propellers, agricultural equipment, bicycles and toilets. Although not the first gun of its type, the Gatling was one of the most practical. It was not a true 'machine' weapon because it required cranking to keep firing, but it was none the less capable of impressive and heavy bursts of fire. Gatling himself referred to his gun in his patents as a 'revolving battery gun' and claimed a rate of fire around two hundred rounds per minute. Adopted in several countries, the Gatling gun was available in different calibres including .42, .45, .50, .65, .70 and 1 inch. It was also manufactured under licence outside the USA. Its application varied: in some places it was used as a support to infantry; in others it was used as close defence for warships or as a substitute for artillery. One or two versions did make claims for man-portability. The 'Chinese' adaption, for example, involved mounting the Gatling in a wheelbarrow, and the miniature 'Police' model in the USA was intended for crowd-control use from the back of a cart! Neither seems to have been made in large numbers. (The Royal Armouries, London.)

The Maxim .30 calibre 'solid-action' machine-gun, after firing 15,000 rounds in the Rock Island Arsenal tests of November 1899. By the end of the nineteenth century, machine-guns were a necessity for any modern army. New models were being developed all the time, though the most successful were derivatives of the Maxim.

In this test, the US army pitted a 'solid-action' Maxim against The Vickers 'R.C.'. Both were taken to pieces, minutely examined and reassembled, then timed bursts of fire with set numbers of cartridges were fired. Then both guns faced the 'endurance test', firing continuously until they failed. Subsequently they were blasted with sand and fired again. The Vickers was eventually withdrawn from the test, but the 'solid-action' Maxim was fired until so hot that even the spare barrel bent and parts began to break. The testers concluded of the 'solid action Maxim':

'This gun is regular and reliable in its action and the great number of rounds fired show that its durability is excellent. It is not complicated in its construction, the parts generally strong and durable and all of the parts are readily accessible in case of breakage. It's accuracy is excellent. Comparing the endurance of this gun (18,000 rounds) with that of any other automatic gun not supplied with a water jacket, the value of the water jacket is at once apparent.'

The function of the water jacket which so impressed the testers was to cool the gun – very much in the manner of a car radiator. Water was put into the jacket and allowed to boil and escape as steam. (Rock Island Arsenal, Texas.)

Hiram Stevens Maxim (1840–1916), inventor of the Maxim gun; from the frontispiece to his autobiography My Life.

Maxim's ancestors were French by extraction but, being Huguenots, moved first to Kent, England, then to Massachusetts and finally to Maine, where Hiram was born. However, Maxim did much of his munitions work in Crayford in Kent. Guns were not the first subject of his attentions, and he spent some time working on projects as diverse as engines, lighting and sprinkler systems. In 1883 he managed to produce an elementary form of self-loading by using a system of levers to harness the recoil energy of a model 1866 Winchester rifle. The next year he experimented with the use of gases generated by a gun's burning charge to effect reloading, but it was the recoil system which was eventually to be perfected in the Maxim machine-gun. What really made this possible was a 'toggle' lock at the breech which broke upwards and backwards on firing. Similar locks were later applied to the Borchardt and Luger pistols. (The British Library, London.)

*Tripod-mounted .45 inch Maxim machine gun (above),
c.1900. Earlier Maxims are usually distinguished from later
Vicars' models by their smooth brass water-jackets. Notice also
the raised sight at the breech and the twin spade grips, the
trigger between the grips was actually depressed with the
thumbs. (The Royal Armouries, London.)*

*British troops with a .45 inch Maxim on wheeled carriage
(right), c.1887. Though useful for carrying ammunition and
transport, wheeled carriages hampered the tactical flexibility
which was later the mark of the man-portable machine gun.
This particular cart was capable of carrying 2,672 rounds of
ammunition in pre-packed belts. With the gun dismounted it
could be used as a limber and harnessed by means of the shafts
directly to a draught-horse. (National Army Museum,
London.)*

Colt machine-gun, .30 inch, USA, c.1895 (above). Designed by John Moses Browning (1855–1926), the Colt model 1895 was the first really successful gas-operated machine-weapon, using the explosive gases from the cartridge to operate the mechanism. Browning is much better known as the designer of the celebrated self-loading pistol of the same name, but his machine-guns are also of considerable importance. Known to American troops as the 'potato digger', the gun did not catch on quickly in its native country, a few only being sold to the navy. A number were also purchased by the British, but by the First World War it was relegated mainly to training. The 'potato digger' is air-cooled and fed from a rectangular box magazine by means of a fabric belt. It is seen here on a small tripod mounting. (The Royal Armouries, London.)

Colt model 1895 machine-gun in British service, South Africa, 1900. The 'potato digger' saw little action but was purchased in small numbers for Yeomanry use in the Boer War. It is seen here on its 'Dundonald' wheeled carriage, with an Imperial Yeomanry crew of three and an officer in charge. The 'bandoleers' carried by the crew contain .303 inch rifle ammunition for their personal arms. 'Slouch hats', foreign-service helmets and khaki uniforms suitable to the veld are worn. (The National Army Museum, London.)

CHAPTER 6

ORIENTAL AND TRIBAL ARMS AND ARMOUR

I n the past three hundred years, western European and American arms have come to dominate the battlefields and armouries of the world. Where Asiatic and Third World forces have triumphed, they have done so because they have adopted the European arsenal and adapted it to their own ends. It is therefore easy to forget that almost every culture has, or has had, its own distinctive styles of arms and armour and that these often show a considerable continuity over the centuries.

Within the vast range of different regional types, it is possible to identify two very different categories of oriental and tribal arms. On the one hand, India, China, Japan and the Arab world have a long tradition of metalworking and weapons technology which developed independently of Europe. All were familiar with sword blades, metal arrowheads, siege-engines, cavalry, pyrotechnics and written records before contact with Western colonizers and traders. Africa, Australasia and the American Indian worlds, however, were largely innocent of such devices. It is probably not coincidental that Western colonization has therefore achieved most lasting success in these areas.

Japan

The Far East has produced some of the world's most remarkable weapons, none more so than the fabled Japanese fighting-sword. The secret of the construction of the *daisho* or pair of swords carried by the samurai was that they were hard externally and softer internally. During manufacture, all of the blade except for the cutting edge was coated in clay, and the whole was placed in a furnace. When the smith judged its colour to be correct, the metal was removed and placed in water. The cutting edge thus acquired an incredible hardness whereas the body of the sword retained the correct degree of flexibility. Blows of great violence could now be struck with an extremely sharp sword without danger of breakage. The ancient way to test a highly polished first-rate blade was on a human body, such as that of a condemned man, for example. When the blade had passed this *tameshi'giri*, it could be marked.

Armour in flame and gold of an officer of the Daimyo of Sakai, Japanese, c.1550. The kabuto *or helmet is decorated with very tall horns or* kuwagata, *and long* sode *protect the shoulders and upper arm, while the* do *or cuirass is laced together and has a skirt of tassets protecting the thighs. (The Metropolitan Museum, New York.)*

Mounted Samurai (left) wiping his sword by Tosa Mitsuaki (1848–1875). Hanging scroll, coloured ink on silk. (British Museum, London.)

Japanese samurai armour, eighteenth century (below). On the head is worn a kabuto *or helmet: this has a small peak or* maizashi *and a wide neck-guard or* shikora. *In the middle of the brow is the* maidate, *the equivalent of a Euroepan crest. The face is covered by a grotesque mask or* menpo, *to which is attached a laminated neck-guard or* yodare-kake.

On the shoulders are large, square guards known as sode, *and the body is enclosed by a corselet or* do *made of plates of strips laced together. On the lower part of the* do *hang* kusazuri *or rectangular thigh-guards. The hands are protected by gauntlets and the feet by boots.*

A particular feature of many Japanese armours was the extensive use of lacquer, applied in many layers to achieve an even, translucent depth. The silk cords which were used to attach various parts could also have symbolic meanings – flame and gold cords, for example, originally denoted a princely family. (The Royal Armouries, London.)

Both the blade and the mounts of the Japanese sword were of ritual significance. The blade of a sword might well be handed down from father to son and be rehilted when necessary for different purposes. It was not unknown for officers in the Second World War to carry family swords which dated back four or five hundred years. The traditional way to mount them was in a wooden grip covered in fishskin and bound with black cord secured by a peg, with a guard or *tsuba* of rectangular or oval outline in front of the hand. These *tsuba* were often intricately decorated with pierced work or inlays – so much so that a few collectors specialize simply in this one beautiful item.

The two main types of sword were the *katana* or long fighting-sword and the shorter *wakizashi*. Before the medieval era, straight single-edged blades and even double-edged blades are known, but most *katana* since then have been essentially similar in style. They are usually two feet or more in length, slightly curved, hatchet-tipped and with a long grip allowing occasional two-handed use. Sixteen types of sword blow were recognized, (all requiring extreme skill), the most difficult of which was crosswise through the hips of an opponent.

In use, the swords were carried thrust through an *obi* or sash or fastened to a belt carrier or *koshiate*. When not in use, a sword was reverently laid up in the home on a *katana-kake* or lacquer stand. Blades were never touched with bare fingers, for fear of moisture causing blemishes or rust marks – a practice that modern collectors would do well to emulate.

The significance of the sword has often masked the fact that the Japanese were also great archers. The *yumi* or longbow was a single curve made of strips of seasoned bamboo and other woods. These were bound together with vegetable glues and fibres and lacquered.

Japanese armour was also highly distinctive. Both plate and mail were used, but the most unusual feature was the widespread use of lacquer. Good-quality lacquer work is extremely difficult to achieve and requires many many coats of lacquer applied expertly and evenly to achieve depth and a clear even sheen. Sunlight causes clouding and blemishes in the finished work, so Japanese armour requires particularly careful storage. The original body armour was the *yoroi*, and the cuirass was known as a *do*.

Composite Japanese kabuto *or helmet (opposite page). Like Japanese sword blades, some pieces of armour continued in use for long periods. In the case of this particular helmet, the skullpiece or* hoshi *dates from the early sixteenth century while the neck-guard or* agemaki *is from the mid eighteenth century. The decorated upswept and backswept plates on either side of the head are called* 'fukigayeshi'. *(The Royal Armouries, London.)*

Portrait of Sakakibara Yasumasa (1548–1606), Japanese seventeenth-century ink and paint drawing on a paper scroll. Yasumasa is seen wearing the armour given to him by Tokugawa Ieyasu and in his lap are a tachi *or single-edged sword slung from a belt and a* wakizachi *or short-sword. The stick-like object in his hand is a* saihai *or signalling-baton.*

Behind him, stuck into the ground, is a sashimono *or personal pennant. When on the move, this was often fixed to a bracket on the back of the armour, leaving the hands of the samurai free. The* mon *or sign upon the banner was the Japanese equivalent of a European heraldic device. (Agency for Cultural Affairs, Tokyo.)*

Pair of Japanese swords (right), katana *and* wakizashi, *by Nomura Masayuki, Edo period, eighteenth century. Both the long sword or* katana *and the short sword or* wakizashi *have scabbards of ray skin lacquered blue overall. The mounts are decorated in a style known as the Tanabata Festival theme. The* tsuba *or guards are covered with insects on a copper ground.*

Japanese sword-mounts of the Edo period (eighteenth century). The most important of the Japanese sword fittings is the tsuba or guard, seen here at the top. The fuchi and kashira are respectively the ornamental ring at the mouth of the hilt next to the guard and the pommel cap. This set is signed by the maker, Yokoya Soyo (1699–1779). Each element of the design has its own symbolic meaning: the mythical shishi seen here teaches its young to survive in a harsh world by dropping them over precipices. The flowers are peonies.

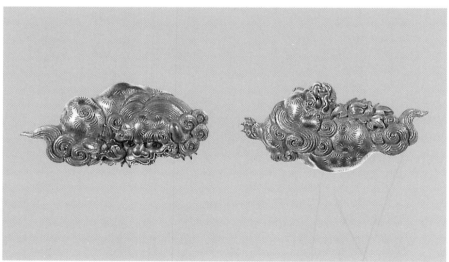

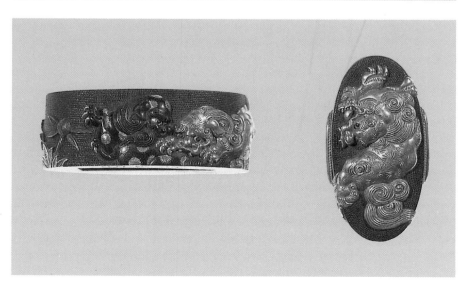

Page from a Japanese drill book (right) showing the use of matchlock muskets, early nineteenth century. Apart from demonstrating the long-continued use of both the matchlock and body armour in Japan, this illustration is interesting in terms of firing technique. Each musketeer has a rope attached to his musket, like a long sling, at the fore end and butt. Placing the left foot down on the rope and pulling up against it with the musket steadies the gun as firmly as though it were in a rest. The major drawback is that little or no sighting is possible. (The Royal Armouries, London.)

Japanese matchlock musket, eighteenth century. The matchlock musket continued in use in Japan longer than in Europe or America. Unlike European muskets, the 'serpentine' which holds the smouldering match is behind the pan of priming-powder. Two other obvious differences from European muskets are the truncated butt and the small button-like trigger. (The Royal Armouries, London.)

Japanese longbow, nineteenth century (opposite page, below). The Japanese developed their longbow independent of the Europeans, using bamboo in place of yew. Most Japanese war bows are actually a combination of materials, with a deciduous wood sandwiched between pieces of bamboo for durability and resilience. Japanese bows are often of extraordinary size, and can easily exceed seven feet in length. Some longbows have a ceremonial significance and are accordingly laid up in temples. The best are decorated with a coating of coloured lacquer. (The Royal Armouries, London.)

Detail from the Battle of Ozaki *(opposite page), a Japanese eighteenth-century handscroll depicting a sixteenth-century battle. Most of the Japanese martial weapons of the period 1600 to 1800 appear in this picture: the Japanese longbow, the matchlock musket, the spear or* yari, *and various types of sword. The cavalry are armoured, and some of the infantry wear* harumaki-*style corselets.*

The general term for a helmet was *kabuto*, different types being distinguished by a prefix. The *suji-kabuto*, used from the fourteenth century, was built up of vertical overlapping plates; the *tatami-kabuto* was laced together and designed to fold. Under the helmet was often worn a *hachimaki* or headcloth for shock absorption.

Widespread use was also made of pole arms. The generic term for a spear is *yari*. There were a multitude of different patterns, but by far the best known is a straight-bladed spear, mounted on the shaft by means of a long tang or socket.

The earliest Japanese firearms contrast awkwardly with the excellence of their edged weapons. The most widespread long-arm was the heavy matchlock musket; its barrel was rather like that of a small cannon, sometimes multifaceted and inscribed.

China

Chinese weapons bear a superficial resemblance to those of Japan, as, for example, in the frequent use of lacquer, but they are less well known and not usually accorded the same status. That Chinese body armour was well developed very early on cannot be doubted, especially since the unearthing of the impressive terracotta army at Xi'an. Bronze helmets have been found from the Shang dynasty of the eighteenth to twelfth century BC, and regulations exist for the court armourers of the Chou dynasty, which ended in the third century BC.

Leather was a favourite medium for the Chinese armourer – and not only the more common varieties but also exotic types such as rhino hide. *Kiai* or coats of scales were made from leather, copper, bronze or iron. Lamellar armour with the 'lames' laced together were also used and were known as *t'ie cha*.

Chinese swords were often large and two-handed or slightly curved. Crossbows were often used, and government agencies were producing officially marked bronze crossbow mechanisms for army use as early as AD 200. The contention that the Chinese invented firearms is not, however, really sustained by any evidence, even though fireworks and military pyrotechnics were extremely popular.

Archer of the Terracotta Army, Xi'an, China, c.210 BC (right). One of the best and earliest sources for the use of coats of plate, this life-size figure shows considerable detail. The 'corselet' consists of rectangular metal scales riveted to some form of backing garment. Each scale is held by from two to four fasteners. The shoulder-guards, reaching about midway down the upper arm, are secured and articulated by means of laces or cords, as are the plates below the waist. The padded neck of the garment may have a defensive function, but the head is unprotected. (Visual Arts, Xi'an.)

The Terracotta Army (below), Qin Shihuang Mausoleum, near Xi'an, China. Qin Shihuang, first Emperor of China, died in 210 BC and was buried in a massive tomb amid sacrifices and many objects. Most remarkable, however, was the burial of 8,000 life-size figures representing men and horses of his army. Pictured here is the number one vault, 250 yards wide and 68 yards long, discovered in 1974. Astonishingly, no two figures are completely identical – faces, hairstyles and expressions are all different. Both cavalry and infantry are featured, as well as charioteers. Among the foot-soldiers are crossbowmen and archers as well as some who once presumably held edged weapons or spears.

Armour for the rank and file consists mainly of padded garments and coats of scale or multiple plates, some of which protect the shoulders as well as the torso, others of which are more like waistcoats. Some figures which represent officers wear better-quality armours which have coats of a greater number of smaller plates with fancy lacing and shin-guards or greaves. (Visual Arts, Xi'an.)

Quilted Chinese armour of the Kienlung period, 1736–95 (left). Here quilted fabric is the main form of protection: plates appear only on the shoulder and in the helmet. The helmet itself has a quilted lining, and the metal parts are decorated with dragons soaring in clouds. (The Field Museum, Chicago.)

Chinese armour of copper scales from Sichuan (below). This type of armour is extremely difficult to date, as this traditional style continued in use from earliest times until at least the eighteenth century. The copper scales are fastened by means of brass wire to a hessian backing with leather shoulder-pieces. The coat fastens by means of a fold which is secured at the side by means of brass rings and cords. (The Field Museum, Chicago.)

Nepalese kora *or sword, eighteenth or nineteenth century (below). The national sword of Nepal has a very heavy single-edged blade, incurved and greatly widened at the end. This example ends in two concave curves, and the handgrip is protected by a disc-shaped guard and a pommel of metal. Also found in Tibet, the* kora *is usually quite short – often no more than two feet long. (The Royal Armouries, London.)*

Indian elephant armour, early seventeenth century (opposite page). Elephants have been used in war since classical times, with varied tactical application. In some instances a small castle or 'howdah' of wood was fitted, and archers and spearmen fought from the animal's back. In other cases the animal was itself the weapon, directed by its mahout to smash into and disorganize or panic enemy troops. Often the elephants would be screened and protected by skirmishers. This particular elephant armour was brought to England by Lord Clive of India and is believed to be a trophy of his victory at Plassey, north-west of Calcutta, in 1757. The rider wears a typical Indian armour of mail and plate and a helmet with a hanging screen of mail to protect the neck. (The Royal Armouries, London.)

India

The Indian subcontinent had a rich and varied heritage of arms and armour, and the diversity was reinforced not only by several different religious and cultural divisions but also by the fact that India consisted of many independent princedoms before British rule. The Sikhs, for example, had their own distinctive weapons in the *chakram* or steel throwing-quoit and in the tiny symbolic knives which adorned the turban.

The Mahratta cavalry favoured a long, straight gauntlet-sword or *pata* which slipped over the hand and was grasped by a transverse bar inside the handguard. In the Scind region (now part of Pakistan), elaborate mounted armours were popular and continued to be made until quite recent times. In their traditional form they were a mixture of mail and plate worn head to foot. The plates were rectangular and articulated one to the next by links of mail. The front of the coat of plates was laced together, and the head was completely enclosed with a shield-shaped facemask with stylized slots representing the eyes and nose, for vision and breathing.

Elephant goads or ankus *(right). A vital part of the equipment of the 'mahout' or elephant-rider in peace or war, the* ankus *was the main means of controlling the animal. Both these are nineteenth-century examples of very high quality. The lower one has a hollow haft enclosing bells which roll and jingle when it is raised. The* ankus *lying on top is decorated with gold koftgari work, rubies and diamonds. The upper part is in the form of an elephant's head with eyes of onyx. (The Wallace Collection, London.)*

Archer's thumb-ring of jade (below). Oriental archery technique varied from the normal European method in that the archer's thumb was normally hooked around the bowstring, rather than using a number of fingers. This brought tremendous pressure to bear on the thumb, and thus the thumb-ring was invented to protect it. The type of ring depicted, with one side much wider than the other, is normally associated with Turkey, Persia or India. There was also a distinct Chinese type which was either cylindrical or D-shaped. Thumb-rings were made of a bewildering variety of materials, including jade, agate, stag-horn, metal, pottery, wood, ivory, bone and glass. Some of the most ornate examples were not intended for practical use but were worn for decoration. (The Royal Armouries, London.)

Two types of Indian projectile weapon (below). In the centre is the composite bow or kaman, *with three different styles of arrow. The strength and suppleness of the oriental bow comes from composition rather than length: this late-eighteenth century example from Lucknow is built up of horn, whalebone and cane lacquered red. The circular objects are steel throwing-quoits or chackram. The outer edge was sharpened, and they could be thrown with considerable force and accuracy up to about thirty yards, but their effect was seldom fatal. Normally carried by Sikh warriors, they could be worn on a special painted turban or* dastar bungga. *(The Wallace Collection, London.)*

Many areas of India showed strong influences of Persia, the Middle East and Islam. The typical Indian helmet style of the seventeenth and eighteenth centuries – with steel dome, nasal bar and spiked top – was indeed common to Persia and much of the Arab world. The Indian *shamshir* or sharply curved sword was similarly influenced by Persian or Turkish designs, as was the *kilij* which was similar but sported a wider blade at the tip.

Indian shields or *dhal* were almost invariably round, but they varied considerably in size, style and material. The best-quality examples were of metal inlaid with gold, silver and jewels. More practical types were often of leather with four, or occasionally five, cast brass bosses. They were often held by means of two handles at the back, a cushion between which padded the hand and helped to absorb sudden blows. A few *dhal* are known which use the shell of a turtle as a body for the shield.

Like the *dhal*, a number of edged weapons are commonly found all over India. The *tulwar*, for example, is a curved sword with a knuckle-bow and often a disc hilt. The *firanji* was similar but usually straight-bladed and double-edged. The vicious *katar* – a thrust or punch dagger – was also widespread but especially associated with the Hindu peoples. Its grip was H-shaped, and the hand held the crossbar while it was used with a thrusting motion.

Perhaps the most extraordinary of Indian edged weapons was the 'tiger's claw' or *bagh-nakh*. This consisted of four or five hook-shaped blades on a bar. A ring at either end of the bar fitted over the index finger and smallest finger, turning the fist effectively into a claw. It was supposed to have been favoured particularly by the assassin and bandit.

Maces and axes found widespread use in India, and the latter were particularly decorative and varied in form. The best known was perhaps that with the crescent-shaped blade known as the *tabar*. Other types like the Mahratta 'crowbill' or *zaghnal* had tapering pick-like blades for maximum penetration. Occasionally axes became combination weapons by having a dagger concealed in the haft or were treated as ceremonial objects, in which case they might bear religious inscriptions or depictions of Krishna.

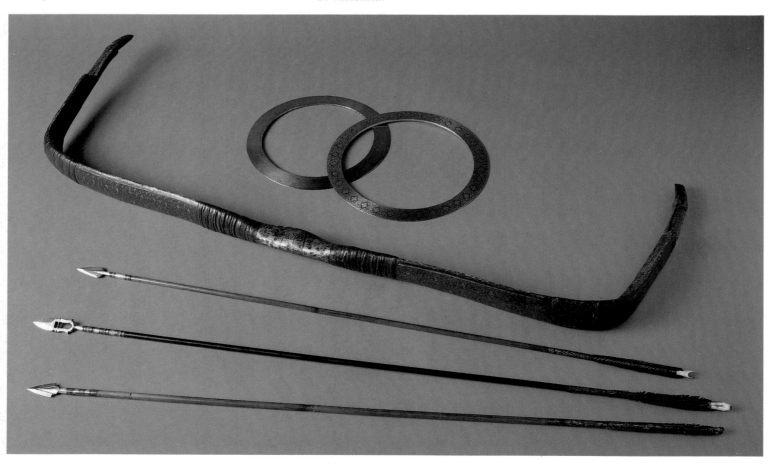

Persian processional axe (left). Formed with two crescent-shaped blades, the head is chiselled with figures and circular panels containing couplets of poetry. The decoration is completed with gilt and coloured stones. Concealed in the haft is a knife, a feature found on quite a number of Indian and Persian axes. It is dated AH 1276, which is AD 1859 in the Christian calendar. (The Wallace Collection, London.)

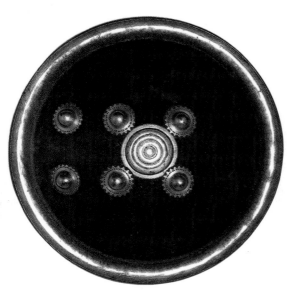

Indian dhal *or shield (above). The form of the* dhal *changed little over many centuries. This example is pronouncedly convex and has six brass bosses and a deeply rolled edge. Those shields with six bosses are often interpreted as being of the 'Persian' style and have three handles inside rather than two. The arm can be passed through one while the other two are held. (The Royal Armouries, London.)*

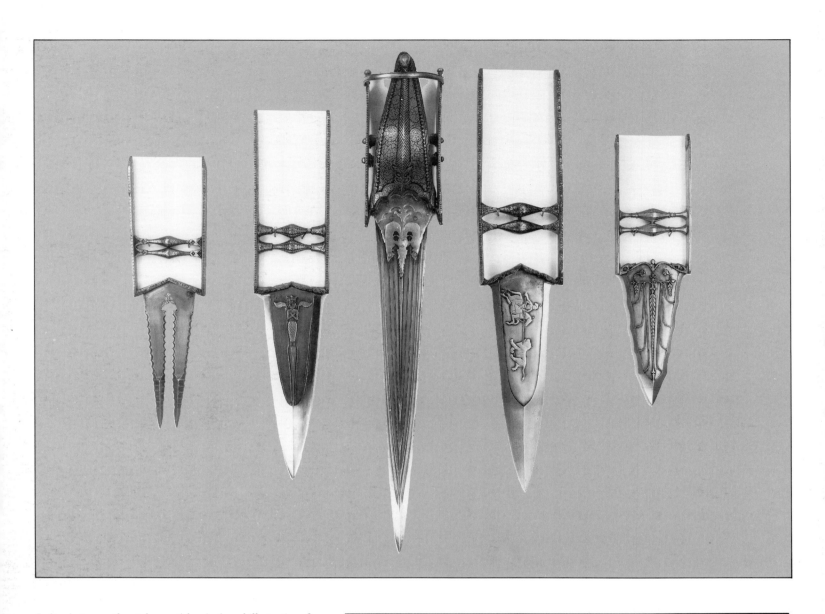

Indian katars or thrust daggers (above). A good illustration of how a native design can remain little changed over a period of centuries. Left, Double-bladed katar with russet iron hilt, serrated edges and gold floral decoration – Indian, late eighteenth century. Second from left, late-seventeenth-century katar with watered-steel blade and bird decoration; bears the maker's name 'Muntsins'. Centre, A turup, Hyderabad, late seventeenth century. A similar design to the katar, but in this case the back of the hand is protected by a curved plate. Second from right katar from Hyderabad, late eighteenth century. On the blade is an illustration of a horseman spearing a tiger. Right, Gold-plated katar with a leaf-shaped blade, Lahore, eighteenth century. (The Wallace Collection, London.)

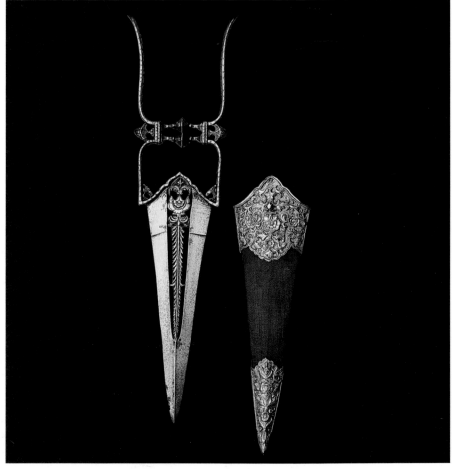

Highly decorated Indian katar or thrust dagger (right), eighteenth century. The scabbard is of red velvet with a golden chape and throat, and the blade has a central panel with a leaf-style decoration. (The Royal Armouries, London.)

Chilanum or Indian dagger with doubly curved double-edged blade. This style of knife is usually associated either with the Mahratta (or Maratha) or Nepal. This example is of outstanding richness and quality: the hilt is of pure gold with an exaggeratedly long pommel of diamond section, the blade socket forms two tiger's heads and the knuckle-guard finishes in the form of a duck's head. Set into the surface are rubies, emeralds and diamonds. (The Wallace Collection, London.)

Indian firanji *or sword (right), with flat pommel and broad knuckle-guard, eighteenth century. This particular example is decorated with bird designs and* koftgari *foliage. The double-grooved blade is inscribed 'Dimese Aterro' and may actually be of European manufacture. (The Wallace Collection, London.)*

Pair of Indian vambraces or arm defences (opposite page, below), otherwise known as dastana *or* bazubands, *Mogul, eighteenth century. These have hinged underplates and leaf-pattern borders and end in velvet open-ended mittens. (The Wallace Collection, London.)*

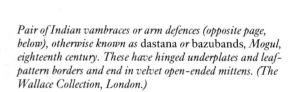

Complete north-Indian armour, eighteenth century (opposite page, above). This warrior is wearing a shirt and trousers of fine butted mail; the use of different metals creates a hatched pattern in the armour. The helmet is of a traditional hemispherical form with a hanging guard and a sliding nasal bar. Over the shirt is worn a small cuirass of four plates joined by straps and buckles and arm-guards or dastana. *Slung around his neck is a small metal* dhal *or shield decorated with gilt bosses in the shape of lotus flowers. The weapons are a* tulwar *in a wooden scabbard covered in crimson velvet and a matchlock gun or* toradar. *The wooden stock of the gun is lacquered all over and decorated with bands and panels of red and green flowers on a gold background. (The Royal Armouries, London.)*

Daggers were a universal weapon in the Indian arsenal, but again they were extremely varied. In the north the *choora* or 'Khyber knife' was popular. Straight-bladed, often with a broad rib at the back, it was of various lengths and directly related to the Persian *peshkabz* and *kard*. Another popular form was the *khanjar* (the term is again of Arabic or Persian extraction), which often has a curved blade and a pistol hilt.

Another unusual edged weapon was the *madu*, used for thrusting or parrying. This consisted of a pair of buck horns so joined that they faced in opposite directions. At the centre, where they were grasped or a handle was fitted, was a tiny shield for the hand.

Indian firearms were influenced both by European and by Middle Eastern designs but evolved a number of distinctly local styles. Best-known of these are the *jezail* and the *toradar*. The former was associated principally with Afghanistan and northern India. It has a crooked stock and a long barrel and may be either a matchlock or a flintlock. The best examples are well made and quite accurate, being sometimes rifled and fitted with English locks and a hinged bi-pod at the front. The *toradar* is more generally a straight-stocked matchlock weapon and occasionally exhibits a square-sectioned barrel. Both *jezail* and *torador* are often decorated with brasswork or studs.

One decorative technique which is common to much of the more valuable Indian arms and armour is *koftgari* work. This is like an inlay of gold or silver but is actually applied only to the surface in thin layers. First the blade, barrel or armour is scratched and picked and then a thin coat of the precious metal is applied to the roughened surface. In the best examples, realistic pictures or strictly geometric designs are combined with jade or precious stones.

Indian toradar *or matchlock gun, eighteenth century (below). The Indian peoples probably first obtained firearms through contact with the Muslim states to their north and west. Matchlocks remained popular for a long period and, like the Japanese versions the jaws of an Indian matchlock normally move forward to the pan, away from the eye of the firer. Stocks were of hardwood attached to a long barrel by means of bands of wire or leather. This straight-stocked form with trigger set well back is normally associated with northern India and is believed to be the oldest type. (The Royal Armouries, London.)*

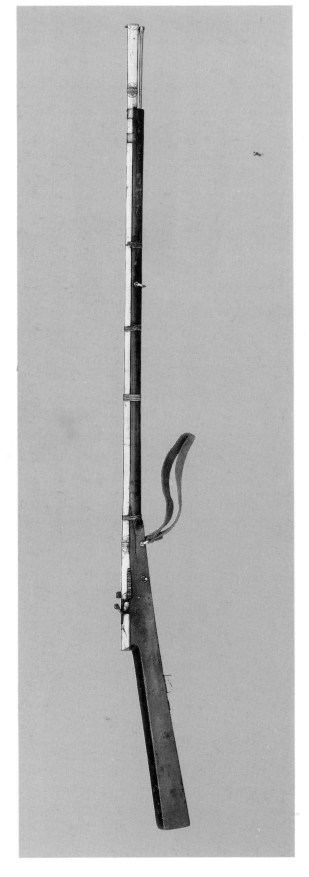

The charge of the 14th Light Dragoons at Ramnuggur, India, 1848 (left). At this action in the Second Sikh War, the 14th Light Dragoons and the 5th Native Cavalry charged a large body of Sikhs who threatened to capture some of the British artillery. In Colonel Havelock's wild charge he himself was killed along with fourteen men, and another 27 were wounded, but the Sikhs were repulsed. Like many other colonial actions in which a small unit achieved much, the defeat of the Sikhs at Ramnuggur (now Ramnagar) was not simply the product of superior firepower and courage but had a good deal to do with organization and the fact that a good number of Indians remained loyal to the British. The turbaned Sikh warriors shown here use a mixture of European and Indian-style weapons. The long-arms are mainly flintlock, but a number of men carry the tulwar or curved sword with a dhal or round shield. (The 14/20th Kings Hussars, The Lancashire County and Regimental Museum, Preston.)

Soldiers of the Bengal army, British Indian, c.1785 (opposite page, below). Contact with Westerners quickly began to influence oriental weapons and methods of warfare, particularly when colonial powers raised their own forces. From left to right the men shown here are a 'golandar' of the Bengal artillery, a 'sepoy' of the Bengal Native Infantry and a 'subahdar' of the Governor-General's bodyguard. Both the firearms shown are flintlock muskets similar to the 'land' pattern. In general, indigenous troops received new patterns of arm more slowly than British troops, but in some cases the East India Company and the later East India Government were able to order their own weapons of the latest type direct from the manufacturer. Such arms are marked with 'HEIC' or the 'bale' mark for East India Company pieces, or 'EIG' for East India Government. The sword is of Indian type and is contained in a typical scabbard. Indian scabbards were usually of wood with a leather covering. (The National Army Museum, London.)

Indian mace, eighteenth century (below). Oriental maces were of many varied forms; Indian types, for example, were often equipped with sword-type grips and flanged metal heads. This one has scalloped edges to the head, koftgari work around the base of the shaft and a disc pommel. (The Royal Armouries, London.)

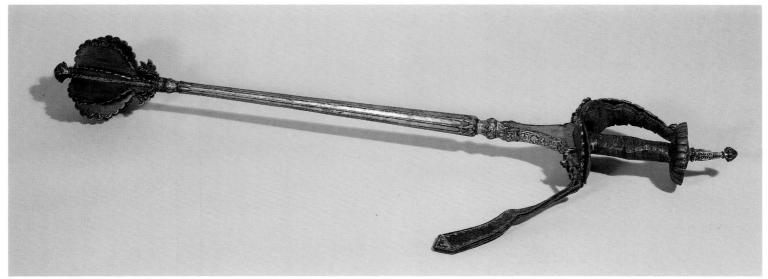

Persian dagger, late eighteenth century (right). An example of the best Persian workmanship, the grip is of agate inlaid with an arabesque design in gold, the method being known as 'tamashah' work. Round the base of the hilt is a silver band set with green paste stones. The blade is double-edged for part of its length and is encrusted with gold decorations depicting jackals and hares. This gold encrusting work was known as 'zarnashah'. (The Wallace Collection, London.)

Persian Kulah or helmet, nineteenth century (below). This shows many traditional Persian features like the sliding nose-guard and the plume-holders, which were often decorated with peacock feathers. The main material is bright steel, but there is a band of gold koftgari work. (The Wallace Collection, London.)

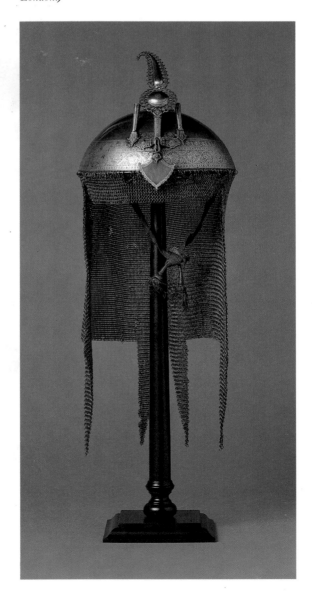

The battle between Bahram Chubina and Khusrau Parviz (left), from a manuscript by Nizami, Persian, c.1540. The gamut of Persian weapons in use in the sixteenth century appears in this one illustration. Most in evidence are many recurved composite short-bows with large quivers of arrows. Many figures also carry long lances or curved shamshir *swords. The elephant-rider carriers a goad or* ankus, *and some fighters are protected by round shields or distinctive conical helmets. The family resemblance between Persian and Indian arms and armour is unmistakable, for there is nothing here which does not have its Indian equivalent.*

Mameluke-hilted sabre or shamshir *(below), Persian or Turkish, eighteenth century. The blade is sharply curved and has inscriptions from the Koran on its watered surface. The hilt style, with pistol-shaped grip, straight quillons and no knuckle-bow, was common to north Africa and the Middle East. After the French campaign in Egypt in 1800, this style of sword gained popularity in western Europe. The grips of this example are of buffalo horn, but British or French examples often used ivory – either from the elephant or from the Russian mammoth, whose tusks were found frozen in Siberia. (The Wallace Collection, London.)*

185

The Turkish Patrol *(right)* by Alexander Decamps *(1803–60), French. Turkey may have been the 'sick man of Europe' in the later nineteenth century, but it had a rich Islamic heritage in art and arms and armour which belonged more to the Middle East. Practicality meant an ever greater assimilation of European methods in war and production, but this painting shows an interesting mixture of East and West – muskets and socket bayonets alongside traditional edged weapons. (The Wallace Collection, London.)*

Turkish armour with 'turban' helmet, sixteenth century *(below).* The use of conical helmets and of armours using mail and plate together has distinct parallels with European forms of the fourteenth century. The 'turban' helmet was forged from a single piece of steel and topped by a point finished with an inverted cone. Two arched openings allow easy vision, and there is a sliding nasal guard. Mail to protect the neck joins directly to the lower rim of the helmet. Decorative inscriptions are applied to the helmet in two bands around the top and brow. (The Royal Armouries, London.)

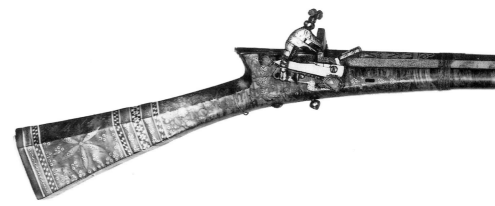

Turkish 'snaphance' musket, late eighteenth century (left). The 'snapping-cock' or 'snaphance' lock was an early form of flintlock which was generally out of use in Europe by the eighteenth century but continued for many years in Turkey and the Middle East. The shape of this musket is typically Turkish, with a very straight stock, a ball trigger and no trigger-guard. The elaborate decoration is achieved by inlaying ebony and ivory into the maplewood stock and applying brass, gold and coral to the breech, butt and lock. The barrel is octagonal, and the rear 'peep sight' is a solid, upright, arched plate. (The Wallace Collection, London.)

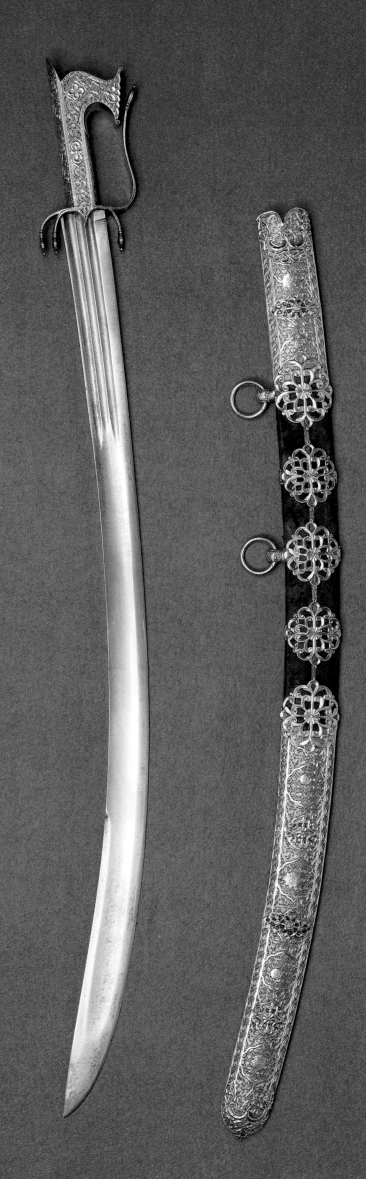

Arabian nimcha *or sword, late eighteenth century. The*
particular features of the nimcha *are the squarish knuckle-*
guard and the quillons which droop forward over the blade.
In this case there are three quillons and the blade is curved.
(The Wallace Collection, London.)

Highly decorated Persian shamshir *(left), eighteenth or nineteenth century. This highly curved sabre was a traditional weapon of the Middle East and India. The English 'scimitar' may be derived from* shamshir. *Rather than slashing or thrusting at his target, a warrior armed with the* shamshir *would normally deliver a 'draw cut', pulling the blade towards himself across the target. The hilt of a* shamshir *is normally of 'Mameluke' style – that is, with a single cross-guard, a pommel projecting to one side and no knuckle-guard. This example is particularly fine, being decorated with animal heads, metal inlays, and blue and green enamels. (The Royal Armouries, London.)*

Earthenware handgrenade (centre), Middle Eastern, probably Syrian, sixteenth century. Early handgrenades, European and oriental, were made in a variety of materials including glass and pottery. Some were intended to be merely incendiary in effect, while others were for blast or fragmentation. Especially useful in sieges, grenades could also be used in the field to break up troop formations or attack strong points. As Peter Whitehouse described them in 1562:

> *'They are evrye good to throwe over the walles into a towne or fortress, or into a campe, to hurte and give a terrour to those that are within; but these balles after they are fired . . . must be quickly throwen, least they hurt such as would hurle them.' (The Royal Armouries, London.)*

Russian sword or shashqua, *nineteenth century (below). This distinctive style of sword with a slightly curved blade but no knuckle-bow was native to the Caucasus but subsequently became fairly widely used throughout Russia. Used by Cossack troops, it was then adopted by the Imperial Russian Army and continued in use by the Soviets. The scabbard of the* shashqua *is unusual in that it was often made of two layers of Morocco leather and was long enough to come a good way up the handgrip when the sword was sheathed. Some of the more basic military examples have a fitting on the side of the scabbard which allows the bayonet of a service rifle to be carried as well. (The Royal Armouries, London.)*

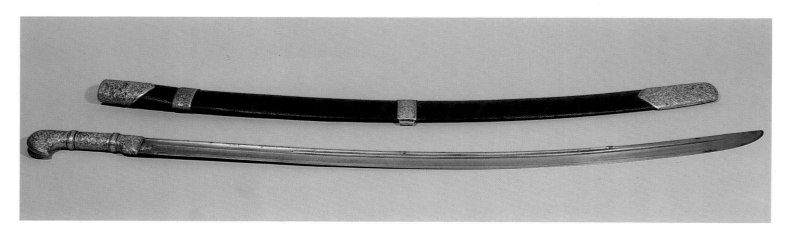

Knobkerrie (above) taken by British troops from the dervishes at Omdurman, Sudan, 1898. Most commonly associated with the Zulu, the knobkerrie is also found in other parts of Africa. Most knobkerries are of various sorts of hardwood, but bone or horn examples are not unknown. Omdurman, where General Kitchener led an Anglo-Egyptian force which defeated a force of 40,000 of the Madhi's dervishes, was the death knell of the Madhi's rebellion. Supported by no less than 44 field guns and 20 Maxims, Kitchener created a havoc that one war correspondent described as more like an execution than a battle. (The National Army Museum, London.)

The Battle of Isandhlwana, 1879, by C. E. Fripp (1854–1906). Native troops were at a disadvantage against the breech-loading rifles of the Europeans in the late nineteenth century. Many tribes therefore attempted to obtain their own firearms, either in the shape of flintlock 'trade guns' which were exchanged for local produce or by capturing weapons of the enemy.

The Zulu were more successful than most for they had fairly sophisticated organization and tactics. The Zulu 'impi' or battle horde advanced in a crescent-shaped formation, subjecting the enemy to a rain of throwing-spears and then rushing in to close quarters. Firearms were used to harry the enemy from vantage points. These methods had spectacular success at Isandhlwana, where an ill-prepared British square was overwhelmed and a battalion of the 24th Foot was all but annihilated. (The National Army Museum, London.)

Africa

The African continent is a rich field for the arms and armour specialist but a dark one, owing to the lack of written records. The Arabs penetrated north and north-east Africa early, and the culture of Egypt and the Sudan is particularly heavily stamped with their mark, but the Eastern-style 'Mameluke' swords of the north are a world away from the Stone Age bows and spears of the southern deserts.

The Sudanese have several weapons which set them apart from their neighbours: large leaf-shaped spears, round hippopotamus-hide shields and the remarkable *trombash*. This last is a form of throwing-stick of hard wood, the end of which turns sharply upwards. Perhaps best-known of all Sudanese arms is the *kaskara* – a long sword with a simple cross hilt which at first glance look like medieval European work. Often the blades were imported from either Europe or Arabia, and they are carried in a traditional leather scabbard with a large coffin- or lozenge-shaped chape or end.

Of perhaps all the African people, the Zulu have the reputation for being most warlike. In 1879 they came closer than most to an outright defeat of the British army, using, for the most part, their traditional tribal weapons. Chief among these was the 'assegai' or spear. This came in two distinct varieties: a longer, lighter version for throwing and a shorter, heavier type with a long head for thrusting.

Another close-action weapon, which could also be thrown, was the 'knobkerrie' – a wooden club with a round or faceted end. The 'knob' at the end of the stick varies a lot in size. Some giant versions are believed to be either for executions or ceremonial, and regarded as a mark of rank. Another piece of folklore suggests that the Zulus' colonial masters imposed a limit on the size of the club head, permitting only what could comfortably be fitted into the mouth!

The Zulu shield was large and oval, with pointed ends and a central stick to act as a grip. The hair was left on the cowhide, presenting a pleasing and colourful pattern on the exterior. Different areas and different 'regimental' groups specialized in different cattle, and so their shields varied accordingly and acted as a mark of distinction.

Over the rest of Africa there are other marked ethnic variations in weaponry, but the primary arms were shield, spear, bow, club and dagger. In central and east Africa, elongated shields of various types were popular. Basketwork was well known but, like the Zulu, the Masai favoured hide – in this case highly convex and painted for decoration.

The Masai also had a distinctive form of spear, in that the metal head was as long as the shaft to which it was attached. The vocation of spearmaker was especially respected, and spearmakers were often selected as chiefs. Among the Ashanti the shaft of the spear was sometimes covered in decorative leatherwork, and leaf-shaped knives were common, though latterly much of the metalwork has tended to be recycled European metal. In the Congo, spearheads were broad and sometimes waisted in shape, and the shafts were bound with metal. Ceremonial axes and clubs were also popular in this region.

Mounted Bornu warrior from northern Nigeria (above), late nineteenth century. Both man and horse are covered in quilted-cotton armour, and the saddle has a very high cantle and pommel in a style reminiscent of medieval Europe. The spear carried has an elongated leaf-shaped blade. Similar armour was last used by dervish cavalry at Omdurman in 1898. (The Liverpool Museum.)

Zulu shield or 'ishilunga' (above), together with a throwing-spear or assegai, c.1879. The shield is an oval of cowhide with the hair left on to colour the outer surface. It is reinforced by a weave of two further strips of hide through two lines of vertical slots which produce the characteristic pattern. The stick behind serves as a handle. Most warriors' shields are well over three feet in length, but smaller versions are sometimes encountered; these are variously interpreted as boy's or women's shields, but it is likely that some are made purely for the tourist market. The Zulu shield was very light and practical to parry a blow from an edged weapon but useless against firearms. Assegais have narrow metal heads and wooden shafts held together by means of a leather binding. The traditional binding is a cow's tail, used like a tube and shrunk into place. (The National Army Museum, London.)

Lieutenant John Caldwell (opposite page) of the 8th (Kings) Regiment of Foot in the dress of the war council of the Ojibwa Indians, USA, 1780 (artist unknown). Caldwell was commissioned as ensign in the 8th in 1774 and promoted to lieutenant in 1777. By 1780 he was acting as a liaison officer with the Indians and had been elected a chief and given the Indian name 'A Petto' or 'The Runner'. In Caldwell's left hand is a tomahawk with a slender haft and a hatchet-shaped head, on the back of which is mounted the steel pipe bowl. Around his neck are three silver-coloured discs of metal which are probably Indian, but over them he wears his gilt gorget – a mark of rank in the British army. (The Liverpool Museum.)

Indian tomahawk (right), probably of French manufacture, nineteenth century. This is a good example of one of the better made tomahawks complete with pipe bowl to the rear of the head. Many had no pipe, while others were equipped with a spike in its place. Pre-conquest tomahawks are stone with short wooden handles but replacement with metal commenced soon after the coming of the whites. Most tomahawks have narrow hatchet type blades, but a few are diamond or lozenge shapes coming to a vicious pick-like point. (Sotheby's, London.)
Below, Piped tomahawk, English, c.1800. (The Royal Armouries, London.)

The Americas

The Americas again show a vast number of different styles of weaponry which vary as much with climate and available materials as with ethnic group. The Inuit or North American Eskimo relied mainly upon animal products for their raw material, as for example harpoons of bone and coats and caps of leather. Wood was a rarity in the frozen north, and metalwork was unknown until contact with Europe.

Further south, wood began to play a more important role in weapons production. Many of the American Indian tribes were incredibly skilled archers, and wood was also used in clubs and the hafts of pole arms. Contrary to popular belief, however, the metal-bladed 'tomahawk' or axe was not really a purely native weapon. Axe heads were imported from England and France as early as the seventeenth century and were a useful unit of currency for trade with the American Indians: pre-conquest Indian axes usually have stone heads.

Similarly, the 'Green River' and 'Bowie' knives now so much associated with American European settlers were not usually produced in the USA in the early days. According to tradition, the broad, long-bladed hunting-knife now known as the 'Bowie' was designed by Rezin P. Bowie and was given to his more famous frontiersman brother James in 1827. This may be true, but many of the knives of this pattern which occur in America were originally made in Britain and exported.

The American Indians did, however, adapt rapidly to the white man's arms. 'Trade guns' were quickly acquired or captured and decorated to Indian tastes. Leather covers were highly practical, and coloured beaded decoration was for both aesthetic and ceremonial purposes. In the later-nineteenth-century 'Indian wars' or local risings, assimilated European weapons combined with fast-moving horses, which had also been

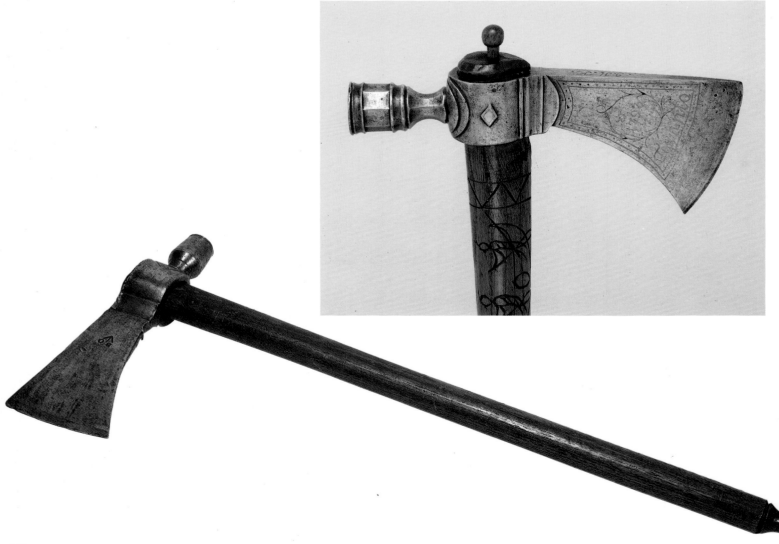

Eskimo hide armour (below) from the Chukots Peninsula, USSR, nineteenth century. This strange garment was actually a cuirass of wooden slats covered in two sealskins which the Eskimo, wrapped around his body. North American Indians and Inuit tended to favour armours of a 'rod and slat' construction, the design of which dated back to prehistory, but again the main materials for the cuirass were wood and leather. (The Field Museum, Chicago.)

Eighteenth-century American hide armour from Tlingit (right), Alaska, reinforced with Chinese coins. The traditional armour of the indigenous peoples of Alaska was of two layers of hard tanned moose skin, but this garment demonstrates the existence of trade links between the far north-west of America and the far north-east of Asia. Use of Chinese coins from the Shunchi, Kang-hi, Yung-cheng and Kienlung periods has turned the traditional leather cuirass into an effective scale armour. (The Field Museum, Chicago.)

Maori whale bone club or 'patu pounamou' (opposite, top). Most clubs of the natives of New Zealand are short and heavy. Wood, bone and stone are the most popular materials, usually of simple shape. (The Horniman Museum, London.)

Axe from the Congo (Zaire) (opposite, centre). Most axes from central Africa have the distinctive bulbous wooden handle, but this is one of the simplest and most practical forms. Ceremonial examples may have complex blades, copper sheet over the haft and be decorated with images of heads. (The Horniman Museum, London.)

introduced, were the mainstays of the warrior. Together with intimate knowledge of the country and tracking, these could make a small war-party very difficult to combat. In their last campaigns, Geronimo and his Apache braves numbered tens rather than hundreds.

South American Indians had much in common with their early North American counterparts but specialized in a number of distinctive weapons. Most characteristic was the blowpipe, still used by a few Amazonian tribes. This was often over eight feet in length and made of a single piece of wood.

The darts were also fashioned from wood, with their butt wrapped in cotton to obtain a tight fit in the bore of the pipe. Lightness and lack of power made it difficult to kill all but the smallest birds and animals without the use of poison. In the South American context, the most commonly used toxin was curare.

The 'bolas' was a favourite weapon of the Indians of the South American plains and consisted of two or three stone balls joined by cords. The balls were whirled around the head of the hunter to attain speed and were then hurled at the legs of an animal. The prey would be disabled by becoming entangled in the cords, giving the hunter the chance to catch it. In this context it is interesting to note that many primitive hunting-weapons were not designed to kill outright but were intended to hamstring, disable or panic the quarry into such a position that the hunter could get close enough to administer the *coup de grâce*.

South East Asia, Polynesia and Australasia

Outside the main continental contexts, many island peoples have developed distinctive weaponry. In Indonesia, for example, not only has the 'kris' or native knife developed on lines independent from other Asiatic weapons but there are different variations on different islands. Something that all krises have in common, however, is that the blade widens considerably towards the hilt, often forming a sort of pointed guard. Kris blades may either be straight or 'flamboyant' – that is, wavy. The handle may be either straight or bent like a pistol grip. Krises vary greatly in size – tiny examples being carried by women; huge, heavy ones being used as an executioner's arm.

Another distinctive edged weapon of the region is the *klewang* or 'Malay sabre'. Unlike the kris, this is usually large and has a single-edged, straight blade.

In Polynesia and the islands of New Zealand, the club was most notable in the native arsenal. Again, each tribe or district had its own shape or pattern. Maori clubs tended to be short and heavy, made of wood, stone or jade. Often known as *wahaika*, they could contain much elaborately carved work. The *patu* was a simpler fighting weapon. In Fiji, the club was often long and straight, or long with a picklike end usually of wood. One specialized Fijian variety was the *ulas* – much shorter, and with a bulbous head. This was designed for throwing.

Perhaps the ultimate in independent development lay with the Australian Aborigine. The throwing-stick was a common idea over much of the world and was used especially widely in Africa and India, but to take this idea a stage further to the returning 'boomerang' was a uniquely Australian development. It should be noted, however, that the returning boomerang is not particularly useful as a weapon, its hunting use being limited to killing small birds – war boomerangs are bigger, heavier, and do not return.

Armour was virtually unknown to the Aborigine, but one sort that was widely understood was the spiritual or symbolic protection – an idea that occurs in many cultures. In Australia, the 'Kurdaitcha shoe' was a particularly potent form. Woven of human hair and emu feathers, it protected an avenging warrior from the effects of witchcraft. Such beliefs were not unique to the Third World, for in Europe there had been long-held myths regarding weapons – lasting in some places to the eighteenth century. For example, some people carried charms or crucifixes, in the belief this would make them invulnerable; others thought that only silver or gold bullets could kill a prince.

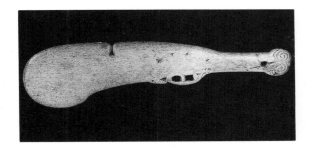

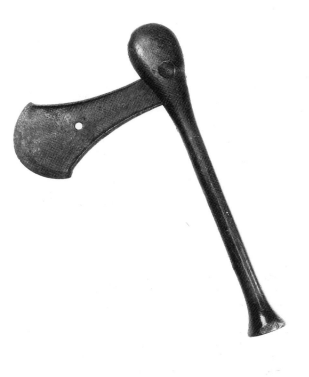

Maylay knife or kris *(bottom, left and centre). One nineteenth century authority suggested that there were over 100 varieties of* kris, *each associated with a different area and with more than 50 names used to describe them. This example with sharply bent handle and plain scabbard probably originates from Sumatra. The* kris *may vary in size from a small knife right through to a full size sword. Both plain and wavy blades are encountered. (The Horniman Museum, London.)*

Sudanese throwing knife (bottom, centre right). Throwing knives were especially popular in central Africa, but are sometimes found further north. This is one of the simpler forms, having only two branches; some from the Congo (Zaire) have three or four. Most of these large knives are thrown in a horizontal plain, and may inflict injury with any of the projections. (The Horniman Museum, London.)

Fijian war club (bottom right) with projecting point; sometimes known as the 'pineapple' type. (The Horniman Museum, London.)

CHAPTER 7

SPORTING ARMS AND ARMOUR

porting weapons are many and varied but divide into two major categories: those that men use on animals and those that men use on each other. We will look at these in turn.

Hunting-weapons have a long history – palaeolithic spearheads and arrowheads are not uncommon. Composite bows were in use by about 2000 BC for hunting purposes in ancient Egypt – sometimes from the chariot – and the fish-spear is of very great if indeterminate antiquity.

Many of the early weapons used by hunters were identical to those in use in war, but in the classical world and in early medieval Europe a number of distinctive hunting-weapons were developed. The 'barred spear' must have been among the first, and was certainly known by 600 BC. This simple device was very much like an ordinary spear with a crossbar behind the head which prevented it entering the animal too deeply. The Athenian soldier and commentator Xenophon (*c.* 428–354 BC) described hunting boar with this sort of weapon:

> The spears must have blades fifteen inches long and stout teeth at the middle of the socket, forged in one piece but standing out and their shafts must be of cornel wood as thick as a military spear . . . let him present the spear, taking care that the boar does not knock it out of his hand . . . and . . . thrust it inside the shoulder blade where the throat is and push with all his might. The enraged beast will come on and, but for the teeth of the blade, would shove himself forward along the shaft far enough to reach the man holding the spear.

The Sleeping Huntsman (*far left*) by Gabriel Metsu, Dutch, *mid seventeenth century. This was just the sort of painting that was well appreciated in the seventeenth century – full of well-observed details and possible hidden meanings.*

By this time, wildfowling with a long-barrelled flintlock sporting gun was an accepted pastime of the rich and a possible, if often illegal, means of support for the poor. It may be that this careless individual with loose stocking, broken tobacco pipes and pot of drink may be about to lose his wife as well as his prize game-bird. (The Wallace Collection, London.)

Chamois hunters, from The Triumph of Maximilian, *1526. The long, slender spears shown were particularly useful for poking chamois and ibexes from mountainous ledges. The wheel-like objects carried are snow-shoes. One of the hunters has dismounted the blade of his weapon for wear at the belt, while three others carry heavy woodknives. The best hunters were also capable of throwing the spear short distances with accuracy. (The British Library, London.)*

The Lion Hunt *by Horace Vernet, 1836. Depicted here is a hunt in north Africa with the hunters mounted on both camels and horses. The weapons used are an interesting mixture of traditional and modern. The prostrate figure is still clutching a pair of flintlock pistols, while the horsemen behind have flintlock long-arms. The rider in the foreground prepares to throw a javelin. (The Wallace Collection, London.)*

Hunting 'trousse' (right), of Georg Friedrich Carl Margrave of Brandenburg-Culmbach (1688–1735), dated 1732. This set consists of a heavy hunting-knife or chopper with a sheath and six smaller knives. The large knife has a handle of gilt bronze in the form of a stag being attacked by a greyhound, and the blade bears the crowned arms of Brandenburg. The smaller knives, decorated with scrollwork, a stag and a bird, were for the evisceration of animal carcasses.

It is believed that this hunting-set was given by Frederick the Great to Prince Charles Edward Stuart (Bonnie Prince Charlie), who had applied to him for aid to regain the throne of England. The splendid 'trousse' was a hint that Charles should confine himself to hunting. (The Wallace Collection, London.)

Whaling harpoon (below), nineteenth century. Unlike small, multi-bladed fish-spears, the harpoon has a single point and a massive, sharp head for deep penetration. Small barbs on the back of the head help prevent the harpoon from slipping out of the quarry. Whether hand-thrown or projected from a gun, the harpoon was normally attached to a rope or hawser so that the whale remained tethered to the whaling-float when hit. (The Royal Armouries, London.)

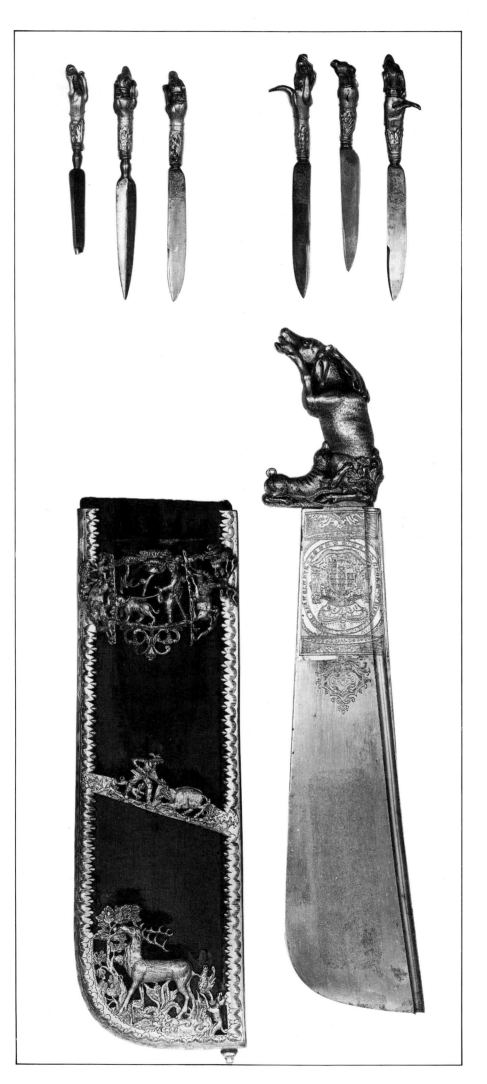

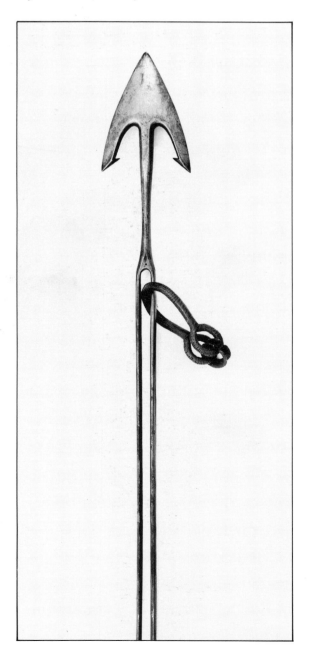

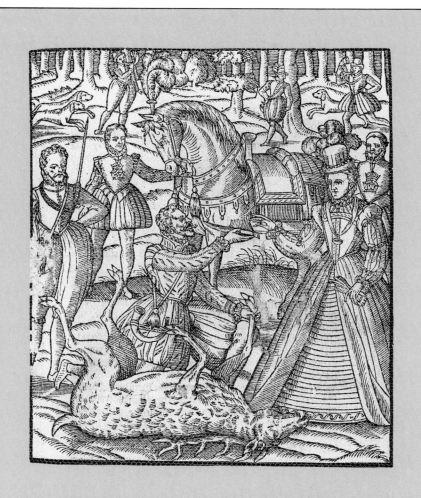

Elizabeth I of England (top) is handed a hunting knife to open a stag, from G. Turbervile's The Noble Arte of Venerie or Hunting, 1575. A good deal of ceremony often surrounded the removal of trophies from fresh kills and the division of the spoils. Until recent times participation in hunting has been the norm rather than the exception with the monarchy. Elizabeth's father, Henry VIII, was perhaps best known for the pursuit, but Elizabeth's femininity was no bar to her taking part. Many of the great forests of Europe survive today because they were once the preserve of royal and noble hunters of stag and boar. (The British Library, London.)

An otter hunt (bottom left), depicted by Richard Bloome in The Gentleman's Recreation, 1686. Hounds are used to flush out the prey while the hunters are armed with two-pronged spears or 'otter-grains'. These weapons usually had ash poles and barbed heads which prevented the escape of wounded animals. This plate was dedicated to Sir John Hobart, of Blickling, Norfolk. (The British Library, London.)

Detail of a French or Italian boar-spear (below), c.1600. The large leaf-shaped blade with a pronounced medial ridge and a toggle at the base of the socket mark out this spear as for hunting rather than war. The toggle acts in the same way as a fixed bar, preventing too deep a penetration of the prey. The decoration applied is silver and gold on a blackened ground. (The Royal Armouries, London.)

HUNTING ỹ OTTER

Edward Barnes the Woodman, aged 68 (far right), from Erdigg Hall, near Wrexham, painted 1830. Weapons of various sorts were common in both the sports and the daily work of the countryside, and edged weapons were no less significant than firearms on landed estates. This picture is especially interesting for it demonstrates that military arms were occasionally seen in more peaceful roles. The woodman's axe is self-explanatory, but the sword is actually a militia 'hanger' of the type used by the Denbighshire Militia and still used to decorate Erdigg. (The National Trust.)

Hunting-swords (below), 1540–1640. The typical hunting-sword of the period was a 'hanger' with a curved blade and a knuckle-bow to protect the hand, but there were many subtle variations.
Top, 'Hanger' with English hilt and German blade, c.1640. Perhaps the most typical of the three swords shown, this has a short curved blade, a knuckle-guard of flattened section and a shell guard. The blade is decorated with flowers, a bird on a twig and figures of Faith and Hope.
Bottom, Broad-bladed falchion, probably German or Dutch, c.1630. The falchion – heavy and broad-bladed – had existed since the medieval era for both war and hunting purposes. This example, with curved quillons and a boxwood pommel in the shape of a helmeted head, is inscribed 'Edwardus Prins Anglie'.
Centre, Sabre or hunting-sword by Gemlich of Munich, c.1540, with a later gilt copper hilt. The pommel is in the shape of an eagle's head and the quillons end in lion masks. The blade is etched along its entire length, showing the siege of a town on one side and a stag hunt on the other. (The Wallace Collection, London.)

Special fish-spears usually had multiple points or blades – the trident carried by Neptune is perhaps the best-known example in the ancient world. Harpoons with broad-bladed heavy heads intended for whales and large fish cannot be much more modern.

By the fourteenth century, new types of hunting-spear had been developed. One of the most distinctive was the 'ear-spoon' type, the broad wings of which prevented deep penetration. Barred spears of various designs remained in use, with bars of wood, metal or even boar tusk. By the sixteenth century the heads themselves were often triangular in section and could be highly decorated.

Swords for boar-hunting were also in existence by this time. The 'estoc' or 'tuck' with its heavy thrusting blade was also useful for war, but a new variant on the theme was introduced around 1500. This weapon had a distinctive spear-type tip to the blade and usually a crossbar or stop behind it. The rest of the blade or shaft was blunt, with a round, square or hexagonal section.

Shorter hunting-swords were similarly developed for other tasks. Hunt servants and beaters often carried a short, broad-bladed falchion which could equally well clear undergrowth as provide defence against animals. The 'hanger' was also a short sword or long knife often carried for hunting – the term, like 'woodknife', covered a wide range of types and designs.

Daggers and smaller knives have been part of the hunter's equipment for many centuries and were useful both for cutting up the kill and as a last-ditch defence. The *scramasax* (see Chapter 2), with its 'Bowie'-type blade, was used in this role in the Saxon era. The medieval *Hauswehr* for hunting and domestic purposes was similar in many respects and was descended from the *scramasax*. The *Hauswehr* was usually single-edged, slightly curved and with a flat tang to which could be riveted the plates of the handle. The earliest 'dirk' and 'skean-dhu' daggers and stocking-knifes were also doubtless used in hunting.

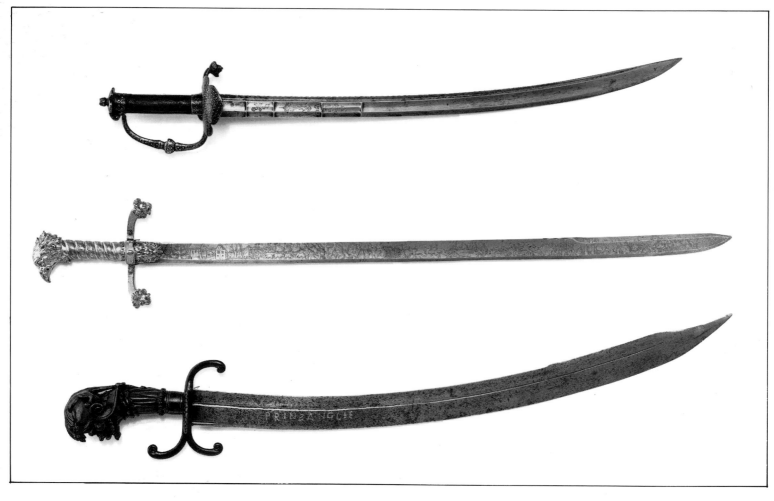

*Hilt detail (right) of short German hunting-sword or 'hanger',
c.1700. Often made without knuckle-bows, swords of this type
were generally broad-bladed and decorated with appropriate
themes – in this case a mass of animals on the scabbard mouth,
quillons and grip. (The Metropolitan Museum, New York.)*

*'Hanger' or sword (below) from the household of the Duke of
Montagu, English with a German blade, c.1720. John, Duke
of Montagu (1688–1749), Master General of the Ordnance
and Knight of the Garter, kept a set of these swords at
Boughton House for the use of his retainers. The design of this
weapon is typical of a good hunting-hanger of the period,
having a brass hilt and a stag-horn grip. The pommel bears the
crest of the Duke, and the blade is slightly curved and
single-edged. (The Royal Armouries, London.)*

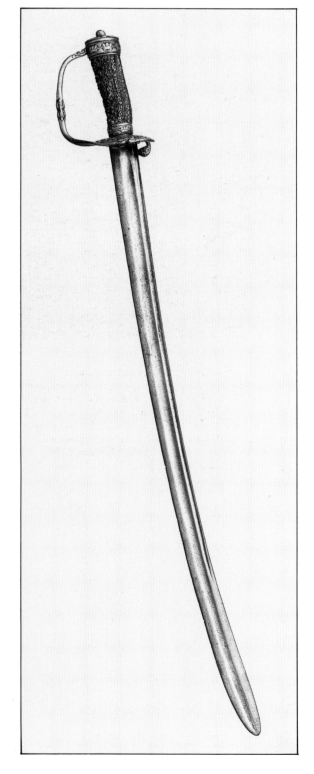

Another hunting-arm which was in vogue in the sixteenth and seventeenth centuries was the 'calendar sword'. This was usually broad-bladed, sometimes with a stag-horn grip, and showed a calendar for a year or a number of years with saints' days or phases of the moon engraved upon it. These may well have had an astrological as well as a practical significance. Not only was the season of the year relevant to the hunt but it was believed by some that days under certain conjunctions of the planets or signs of the zodiac were more propitious than others.

Crossbows were certainly in use for hunting purposes from the late classical era. In the Middle Ages, new varieties were developed with specialized functions. The 'stone-bow' or 'prodd' was one of these: it fired a small stone or pellet and was particularly useful for small game. Special 'quarrels' or 'bolts' were also used for hunting. Some were flat-headed and blunt, so as not to damage the fur or feathers of the quarry; others were broad-headed, to avoid deep penetration and to transfer the shock to the animal's body rather than pass straight through. In one extraordinary Scandinavian variant – the *ravknivar* – a bolt with a crescent-shaped head wider than the span of a man's hand was used in fox-traps.

By the fifteenth century there was a fashion for highly decorated sporting crossbows, and these became more intricate and more general as time progressed. There are a good number of examples from the sixteenth and seventeenth centuries where almost the whole surface of the bow is covered in bone or ivory showing hunting-scenes and animals. Sometimes other materials such as parchment, wood, brass and even leather were used in the embellishment.

For the first hundred years of their existence, firearms were not used for hunting. Unwieldiness, lack of accuracy and the mess the projectile would have made of a carcass in the unlikely event of a hit all made them unsuitable. By the sixteenth century, however, the refinement of the matchlock and the new wheel-lock began to make hunting with firearms an exciting possibility.

Any long-arm loaded with scatter-shot could hope to have an effect against small game, but it was not long before more specialized types were evolved. The expensive but comparatively accurate wheel-lock rifle was soon a favourite hunting-arm of the rich. Held up to the cheek for a better aim, and with a heavy barrel to absorb recoil, there are still many exquisitely decorated late-sixteenth- and seventeenth-century examples of this rifle in existence.

As sportsmen with firearms became more successful, more rules were laid on them by the authorities. Hunting deer – the chief sport of medieval kings – was especially restricted. In some countries, deer-shooting could incur the most extreme penalties: in Scotland, for example, the mid-sixteenth-century punishment was not only death but the confiscation of all property. Birds were perhaps the least restricted quarry, but, given the slow ignition systems of the contemporary firearm, most wildfowl were shot 'sitting' rather than in the air. In fact virtually anything that could be shot was killed – from cats and dogs to otters and bears.

Early in the seventeenth century, flintlocks were also put to use for hunting, and from then on firearms began to attain precedence in the field. Flintlocks generally were easier to carry and use, and the pan cover was slightly more weather-resistant than that of the matchlock. With the flintlock it even became possible to attempt shots at birds on the wing.

One of the best ways to obtain more rapid fire without pauses for reloading was to use a multi-barrelled weapon. Sporting firearms with more than one barrel were not common until the later seventeenth century, when light, 'side-by-side' double-barrelled weapons were introduced. In some models there was only one lock, and barrels turned or revolved to marry up with it for the second shot. In France the double-barrelled flintlock sporting gun caught on quickly. Acceptance was rather slower in England, but, even so, it was the norm there by the late eighteenth century.

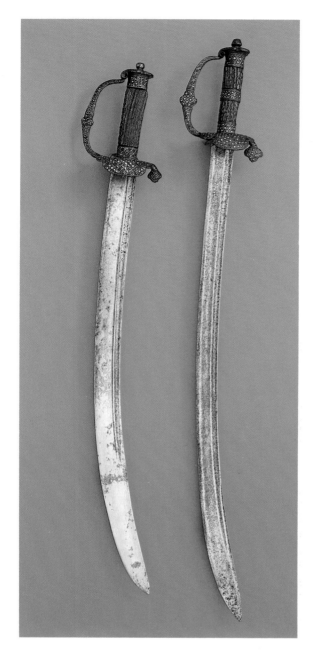

Mid-seventeenth-century hunting-swords or 'hangers', probably English. The horn grips and shell guards which bend over towards the blade are typical of the period, as are the silver decoration and the wide, curved blades. The practicality of such 'hangers' certainly declined with time, and the increasing use of materials such as tortoiseshell, gold, porcelain and ormolu in the eighteenth century was solely for the enhancement of appearance. (The Victoria and Albert Museum, London.)

By now, decoration of such arms was becoming usual rather than exceptional, and designs were circulated and published by artists for gunmakers and engravers to copy.

Shooting small game with firearms was now accepted as a suitable pursuit for royalty, and some of the most incredible 'bag' totals were now recorded by European princes. In 1753 the Emperor Francis I of Austria with a party of 23 guns went on an eighteen-day shooting trip. They fired 116,209 shots and a total of 47,950 animals were killed, most of them partridges, hares and pheasant. In many ways this was more a triumph of the gamekeepers and beaters whose job it was to ensure a plentiful supply of game and drive it endlessly under the muzzles of the shooters. With massed driven game and scatter-shot, it was quite possible to bring down more than one animal at a time.

Perhaps the most successful killers of large numbers of game with a single shot were the punt-guns – wide-bored with long and heavy barrels sometimes fired from a rest. As with smaller shotguns, a large 'pattern' of shot was achieved at the right ranges, and a good shot with a punt-gun into the centre of a large flock could bring down a dozen or more birds. With charges of shot weighting over 2 lb, this was hardly surprising, but it left the problem of a rain of injured birds. Many hunters therefore kept one or more smaller weapons handy for 'cripple shooting'.

In the nineteenth century, some punt-guns were made which were little short of naval artillery, having anything up to seven barrels and a permanent swivel mounting on the punt. It was because of weapons like this that punt-gunning was prohibited in the USA in 1916.

By the middle of the nineteenth century, hunting-firearms had essentially divided into two major classes: the sporting rifle with its single and usually solid projectile for larger game at longer ranges and the shotgun with its multiple charge for smaller game. The shotgun was now usually percussion ignition and double-barrelled – 'side by side' rather than 'over and under' – and still usually muzzle-loaded. An exception to this rifle/shotgun divide was the German *Dreiling* – a three-barrelled weapon with two shotgun barrels and a rifle barrel below.

Lady 'toxophilites', England, 1876. In Europe the bow had ceased to be a practical weapon of war at the close of the sixteenth century; in 1595 the Privy Council of England decided that it was not even useful for the militia. Its hunting use also declined as rifled weapons achieved greater accuracy and flintlocks became cheaper and more reliable. The last serious attempts to resurrect the bow for practical purposes were in the late eighteenth century.

In the nineteenth century, antiquarian and sporting interest led to a significant revival of archery. It was considered a healthy pastime for both sexes; but bows, particularly those for youths and ladies, were made with lighter 'pulls' than those of the original war bow. Shooting was usually conducted against circular straw targets at close ranges. Sporting use was further encouraged by the re-publication of Roger Ascham's Toxophilus *or* Boke of the Schole of Shoting, *first printed in 1545. (The Mary Evans Picture Library.)*

Engraving by Hans Burgkmair from Der Weiss Kunig, *1516, showing Maximilian I, Holy Roman Emperor, hunting with a crossbow on horseback. Apparent in this illustration is the forked-headed bolt, which would be less likely to glance off the hide of an animal and could also hamstring if it hit a leg. Other bolts were made with blunt wooden heads, 'chisel' heads and broad barbs, depending on the game and whether or not it was intended to preserve the skin. (The British Library, London.)*

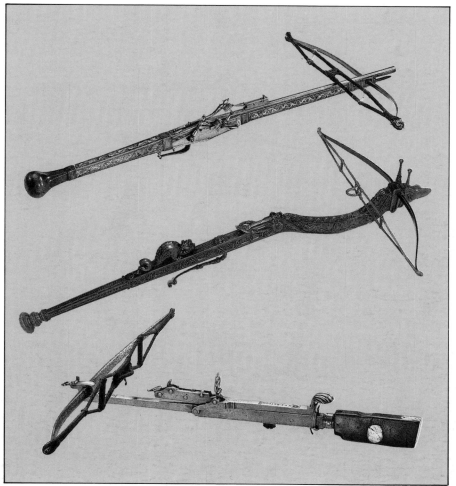

Combined stone-bow and snaphance gun (top left), north Italian, c.1630. Combined guns and crossbows date back to the early sixteenth century and remained popular for hunting for over a century. This example has a box-lock release mechanism for the bow on top and a snaphance lock for the gun set into the right-hand side of the stock. The bow trigger is on top and the gun trigger underneath. The wooden stock is decorated with bone veneer and includes the arms of the original owner, Prince Galeatto Pico Della Mirandola, and his wife. (The Royal Armouries, London.)

Stone-bow or prodd (centre) of Baron Wratislaw II von Pernstein, Grand Chancellor of Bohemia (1530–82). The prodd was designed to project small bullets of lead or stone against small game or targets. This excellent example, made in about 1580, probably in Italy, is of steel with a stock of yew and a double string. It is decorated with monsters and the heads of a wolf and a bull. (The Wallace Collection, London.)

German stone-bow or prodd (bottom), by Moritz Sam, c.1600. This weapon has the double string typical of stone-bows together with a combined bending-lever and box lock. The backsight is quite sophisticated, consisting of a large pierced plate. The shooter looks through different holes in the sight to achieve different ranges. The bow itself is of steel, but the rear part of the butt or 'tiller' is wood inlaid with plaques of bone and mother-of-pearl. (The Royal Armouries, London.)

207

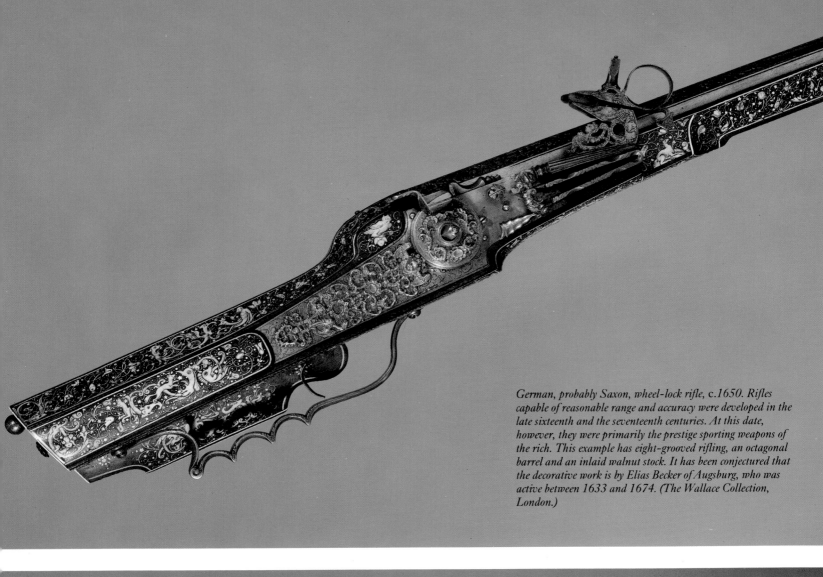

German, probably Saxon, wheel-lock rifle, c.1650. Rifles capable of reasonable range and accuracy were developed in the late sixteenth and the seventeenth centuries. At this date, however, they were primarily the prestige sporting weapons of the rich. This example has eight-grooved rifling, an octagonal barrel and an inlaid walnut stock. It has been conjectured that the decorative work is by Elias Becker of Augsburg, who was active between 1633 and 1674. (The Wallace Collection, London.)

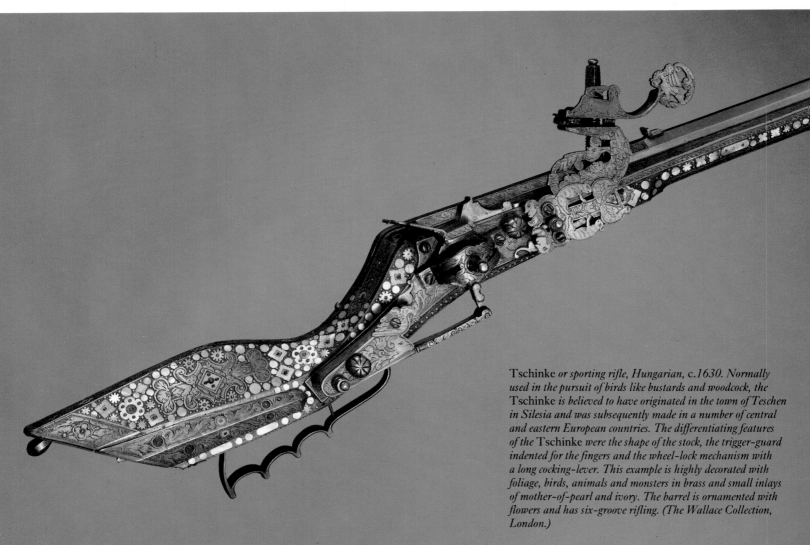

Tschinke or sporting rifle, Hungarian, c.1630. Normally used in the pursuit of birds like bustards and woodcock, the Tschinke is believed to have originated in the town of Teschen in Silesia and was subsequently made in a number of central and eastern European countries. The differentiating features of the Tschinke were the shape of the stock, the trigger-guard indented for the fingers and the wheel-lock mechanism with a long cocking-lever. This example is highly decorated with foliage, birds, animals and monsters in brass and small inlays of mother-of-pearl and ivory. The barrel is ornamented with flowers and has six-groove rifling. (The Wallace Collection, London.)

The great age of English sporting gunmakers undoubtedly coincides with the reign of Queen Victoria. Purdey – most famous of the shotgun-makers – already existed in the early nineteenth century and was soon followed by a host of other London craftsmen, including Holland & Holland, Churchill and Rigby, Birmingham probably had the bulk of the trade and certainly was dominant in barrel-making. Among the most famous Birmingham makers were the Greeners. William Greener was author of *The Gun* in 1835 and winner of a prize medal at the 1851 Great Exhibition. His son, William Wellington Greener, was the author of *The Gun and its Development* and also an inventor. His best-known contributions were a system for 'choke' boring, which helped to determine the spread of pellets from a shotgun, and the 'wedge-fast' crossbolt breech-locking mechanism. Other Birmingham makers included Bonehill, Hollis, Pryse, Westley, Richards, Riley, Scott, Swinburn, Tooley and Webley, and also Joseph Bentley, known principally for his pepperboxes and other revolvers. In the second half of the nineteenth century the application of many breech-loading mechanisms to both shotguns and rifles added considerably to the efficiency of the hunter's arsenal. Ultimately the standard cartridge for the shotgun became the centre-fire 12 bore. The term '12 bore' is familiar to many people, but few know its exact meaning. In fact the gauge or bore of a shotgun is given in terms of the number of spherical balls of diameter equal to the bore that go into a pound weight.

Except for police duties, shotguns were seldom used with solid shot; instead, a number of different cartridges were selected to match the intended game. Small birds demanded many small balls in the load; larger vermin demanded a lesser number of heavier shot.

The 'Simpson gun' (top); English mid-eighteenth-century flintlock sporting gun. Finely decorated with rococo silver inlay, this was made by William Simpson of York and was the most important piece in the collection of the Yorkshire landowner William Constable (1721–91).

The lock has a couple of individual features: a safety-catch operated by a two-pin tool and screws turned by a strangely modern square key rather than a screwdriver. One of the finest of its type, this weapon has recently been acquired by the Royal Armouries at a cost of £235,000. (The Royal Armouries, London.)

Russian flintlock sporting gun (bottom) made at Tula arsenal, c.1752. This fine gun is part of a garniture which also included a pair of pistols, a pair of stirrups and a powder-flask. All the firearms bear the monogram of the Empress Elizabeth of Russia (reigned 1741–62).

The French-style decoration of the shotgun is chiselled on a gilt ground on the barrel and laid into the stock in silver wire. An unusual feature of the lock is an extra safety-catch which can be engaged to keep the pan covered and prevent accidental discharge. (The Royal Armouries, London.)

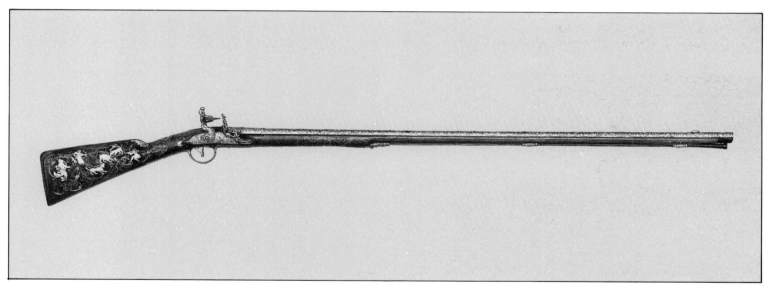

Double-barrelled sporting rifle (top) by Clarke of London, c.1850. Before the advent of magazines and brass cartridges, the surest way to achieve repeating fire was multiple barrels. It is not commonly appreciated that this was applied to percussion rifled arms as well as to the ubiquitous shotgun. This weapon is particularly lucky to have survived, since it was one of those handed in to the police during the 1988 firearms amnesty. Spotted by a sharp-eyed member of the armouries staff, it was then saved for the nation. (The Royal Armouries, London.)

Cased presentation percussion target rifle (right) presented to Edward Ross, 1861. In the 1850s a 'Rifle Volunteer' movement began in Britain – motivated partly by a desire for entertaining sport and partly by patriotism and fear of war with France. This rifle, though rather similar to the contemporary military patterns, was made for target-shooting. It is shown here in its case with its barrel removed and surrounded by stripping tools, lubricants and a powder-flask.

Edward Ross, later Lord Ross, was winner of the first 'Queen's Prize Shoot' at the National Rifle Association meeting on Wimbledon Common in 1860. Queen Victoria herself opened this meeting by firing a shot from a Whitworth rifle fixed in a stand. (The Royal Armouries, London.)

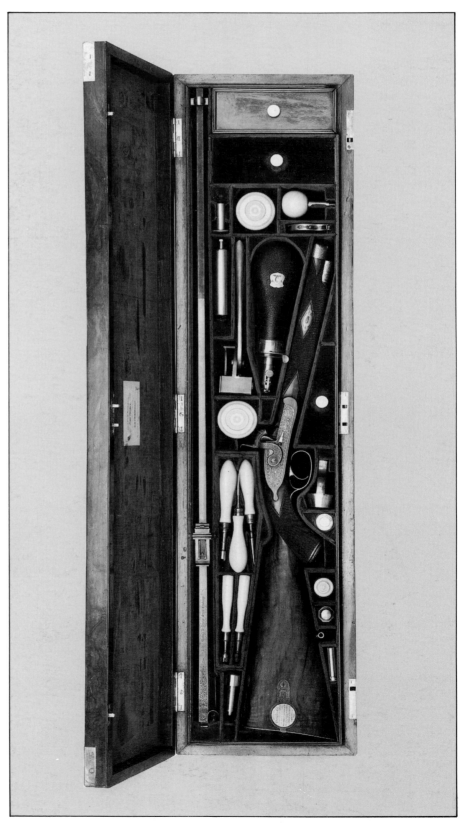

Webley 'Junior' air pistol (above), .177 inch, early twentieth century. With time and tightening gun laws, the arms collector's net spreads ever wider. Air weapons have existed since the seventeenth century but, with one or two notable exceptions, have seen little use in war.

Cheapness and quietness, however, make air weapons useful for both game and target shooting. This pistol was made by the great Birmingham gunmaking firm of Webley. Like Birmingham Small Arms' production of bicycles and motor cycles, it is an excellent example of product diversification. The slender tube along the top is the barrel; lifting this up and forward charges the larger cylinder with air. The tiny pellet is then inserted and the gun is closed ready for use. (The Royal Armouries, London.)

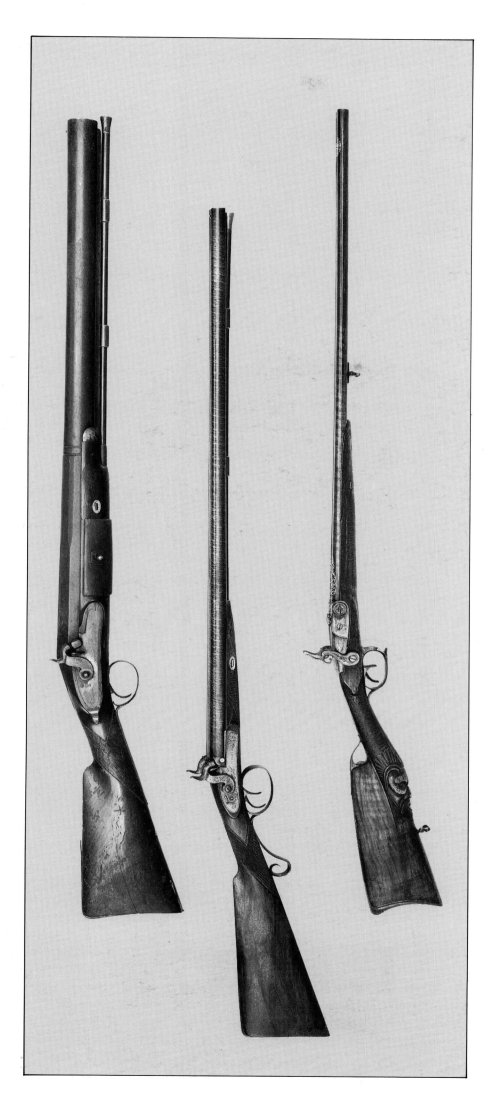

'Elephant' or big-game percussion gun (left) by Pether of Oxford, English, c.1830. Weighing 15 lb and with a bore of 1.5 inches, early big-game weapons such as this relied on the sheer mass of the projectile rather than high velocity. As the gun was twice as heavy as a military musket, it was fitted with a mounting for a swivel, visible as a square section in front of the lockplate. It was not unknown to mount really heavy pieces on small carriages, screened at the front to hide the hunter. (The Royal Armouries, London.)

Copy of a double-barrelled hammer gun (centre) by Purdey of London, mid nineteenth century. Now synonymous with quality and craftsmanship, the firm of Purdey was started by James Purdey (1784–1863), who had already worked for Joseph Manton and the Forsyth Patent Gun Company. His son, James the younger (1828–1909), entered the business in 1843 and took control in 1857, by which time the premises had been moved from Harrow Road to 314½ Oxford Street, London. Purdey's are now, by appointment, gunmakers to HM The Queen and HRH The Duke of Edinburgh. (The Royal Armouries, London.)

Double-barrelled, centre-fire (right), breech-loading sporting gun by Samuel Johannes Pauly (1766–1819), French, c.1815. Pauly was Swiss by birth and both an engineer and a balloonist; his remarkable weapon is generally regarded as a forerunner of the modern gun. Operating a lever in the butt opens the breech-block for the insertion of reloadable metal-base cartridges. On the base of each cartridge is a small depression filled by a priming-compound. When fired, the external hammer drives a firing-pin into the primer, which in turn sets off the main charge.

Pauly pistols were commoner than his rifles or shotguns, but a number of other makers in France, Denmark and England copied his system. Interestingly, one of Pauly's workers in Paris was a lockmaker called von Dreyse, who subsequently invented the needle-gun. (The Royal Armouries, London.)

English 'great helm', c.1515. Formed of two pieces with a low, slightly domed skullpiece, this tilt helmet weighs a mighty 16 lb 10 oz. What is not apparent at first glance is that the helm's smith has skilfully formed the metal so that the most vulnerable areas are thickest, and that the top and back are all a single piece. The 'frog mouth' allows the jouster to protect his face and eyes by raising his head slightly at the last moment. The hole at the very top of the helmet was not there originally but may indicate that a crest was fitted at a later date when the helmet was used as a funerary decoration in a church. (The Wallace Collection, London.)

Medieval triple-pronged lance head for the 'joust of peace' or 'joust à plaisance' (below). From the early thirteenth century there were an increasing number of non-lethal weapons for use in jousts and tournaments. Foremost among these was the lance with a blunt end known as the 'rebated' or 'coronel' head, depending on shape. The shaft of the lance was often partially hollow or jointed, so as to break on impact. In some contests, extra points were awarded for the shattering of lances or hits on the head or body. (The Royal Armouries, London.)

Sporting rifles also varied in size and calibre according to the intended quarry. Rook and rabbit rifles were at the lightest end of the spectrum, often with a cartridge as small as .22 inch. For these sorts of target a very light rifle was perfectly adequate; sights were usually kept simple; and stocks could be folding, skeleton or dismountable. Deer-shooting required a somewhat larger cartridge, and a .300 or so was deemed perfectly adequate. For really big game something special was required – a bullet with either exceptional mass or exceptional velocity, and preferably both.

In the American West, 'buffalo' guns of about half an inch calibre and a heavy barrel were adopted. With these weapons the vast herds of buffalo were slaughtered far more efficiently than could be managed by the Indians with bows. Particular favourites of the professional hunter were the Sharps, Ballard and Winchester single-shot rifles, but there were eccentrics who preferred a more sporting or dangerous approach. These were men like H. A. Leveson, Colonel G. W. Schofield or Walter Winans, who preferred to 'run' the buffalo on horseback and shoot it at close range with a heavy-calibre revolver! Among the pistols chosen for this task were the Colt 'Frontier' and the .44 Smith & Wesson revolver. The British firm of webley took the 'game pistol' idea a stage further, marketing its .410 'Game and Vermin' pistol with detachable shoulder-stock just after the turn of the century – but novelties such as this were strictly for smaller animals.

Real 'big-game' weapons such as the 8-bore flintlock 'elephant gun' had existed as early as the beginning of the nineteenth century, but the combination of really good range, accuracy and stopping-power did not really emerge for another fifty years. By 1860, really powerful weapons were being likened to express trains – an allusion to their speed and impact – and the term 'express rifle' soon gained currency for any powerful sporting arm. In the 1890s, smokeless powders and brass cartridges combined with nitrocellulose propellants aided the emergence of really modern bolt-action big-game rifles.

Probably the best cartridge for delivering a smashing short-range blow against pachyderms or tiger was the .600 nitro express, but an alternative was to deliver a solid shot from a shotgun. One way to do this was to rifle a part of the shotgun barrel – preferably the part near the muzzle – with a 'choke' or narrower section. Such weapons were often known as 'paradox guns'. The idea probably came from the British inventor G. V. Fosbery, who subsequently devised the Webley–Fosbery revolver.

Optical or 'telescopic' sights had been devised as early as 1800, and experiments in their application had taken place in many areas with different weapons. One of the most successful was that of the British Colonel Davidson, who, in India in the 1830s and 1840s, applied his telescope to a rifled percussion pistol with shoulder-stock. A few snipers had made use of such sights on rifles in the American Civil War, but it was late in the century before there was any widespread sporting application. Even so, there was a sufficient body of sporting knowledge to allow the telescopic sight to transfer from the civil to the military sphere in the Boer War in South Africa (1899–1902) and again in 1914. Many of the best sniping shots in these conflicts had indeed served their apprenticeship in hunting in Canada, India or the forests of Germany.

The tournament at St Anglevert, 1390, from Froissart's Chronicles. *This slightly later manuscript illustration shows all the important elements of the high-medieval joust as run in the fifteenth century. The protagonists face each other with their left sides to the central tilt barrier and charge with their lances held across the body.*

They wear 'frog-mouthed' jousting helms with decorative crests, carry stylized small, squarish shields and stand in their stirrups supported by high saddles for maximum impact. The horses are caparisoned with cloths and wear defences on the head and neck. The privileged onlookers are provided with a platform from which to watch the combat. (The British Library, London.)

The sporting weapons which men devised for use against other men were as diverse as those which were intended for use on animals. Staged combats had existed in the classical era. The Roman 'gladiator' used not only the normal arms and armour of war against other men and animals but also a number of special adaptions. The *retiarius*, for example, was armed with a trident and net but usually went unarmoured. The *mirillo* wore a jointed metal guard on the sword arm, a helmet and a greave on the left leg. In other cases, prisoners, slaves or criminals who had been taken outside Rome fought with their own national weapons, spears or projectile weapons. In the most spectacular bouts of all, an amphitheatre could be filled with water and the combat could take the form of a sea battle.

This tradition of man-to-man combat continued in early medieval Europe, often as part of the judicial process, as in 'trial by combat'. The two aggrieved parties would be provided with identical weapons and allowed to fight out what could otherwise have become a feud. This was the essential basis of the later duels, which were eventually to become illegal. The eighteenth- and early-nineteenth-century duel was in fact highly stylized, and duels could be fought over comparatively small slights or points of honour.

The preferred weapons of the later duellists were the rapier and the pistol. Contrary to popular belief, very few weapons were made specifically for duelling – most pistols now commonly identified as duelling weapons are simply good pairs of flintlock or percussion pistols intended for the officer or aristocratic market or given as presentations.

French knights jousting, from a fifteenth-century manuscript illustration. In this illustration the combat is taking place not across a barrier but in a fenced enclosure. Rules for jousts and tournaments varied considerably. The earliest were often unruly bouts between groups of men and involved a good deal of bloodshed; only later did the idea of capturing your opponent for ransom or the price of his armour evolve. Similarly late inventions were the methods of scoring by unhorsing or breaking lances. In this depiction, one of the knights wears the 'frog-mouthed' helm, while the other has a 'close' helmet with a moving visor. Both horses are caparisoned with coloured-cloths. (Bibliothèque Nationale, Paris.)

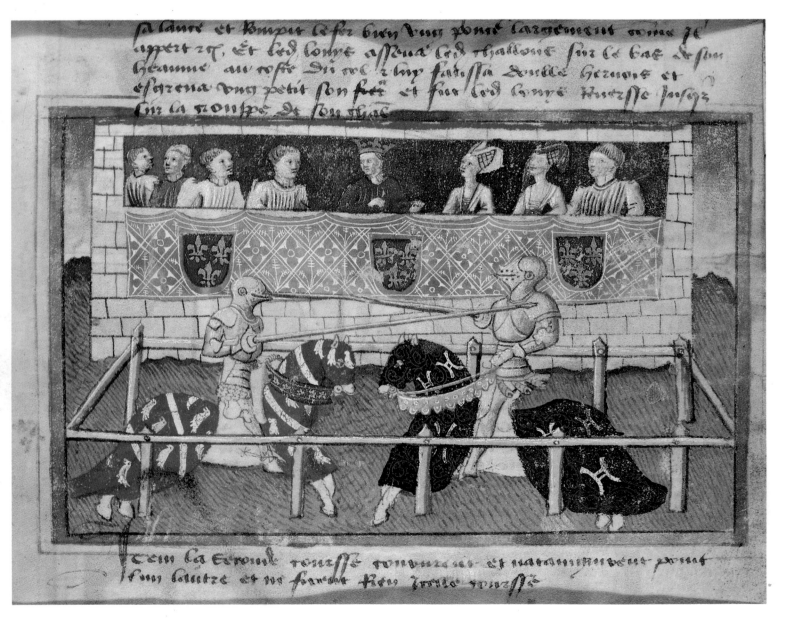

German armour for the Stechzeug *or joust, c.1510 (left). The* Stechzeug *was a German variation of the joust, fought in an open field without a tilt barrier. The object of the combat was to unhorse the opponent and splinter lances. This harness is one of the heaviest in existence, weighing just over 90 lb. Such a great weight would have precluded uses other than jousting and made it difficult to walk any significant distance.*

The helm is of three parts – skull, back and front – and is 'frog-mouthed' to protect the eyes. The breastplate is fitted with a lance rest and a small wooden shield or Stechtarsche *of oak over an inch thick coated with gesso and painted in oils. The bridle hand is protected by a 'manifer' or solid plate. (The Wallace Collection, London.)*

Tournament armour or Rennzeug *of the Emperor Maximilian I (1459–1519) (below). Originally at the Imperial Armoury in Vienna, this armour was subsequently in the collection of the American newspaper owner William Randolph Hearst before being presented to the Royal Armouries in 1952. It is actually made up from the parts of more than one armour, but it appears predominantly German and the sallet is probably from Augsburg.*

Most notable is the very large 'vamplate' or handguard, composed of an inner plate and three outer plates attached by bolts. The upper two plates fly off dramatically if struck in the right place by an opponent's lance. A leather-covered 'grand guard' protects most of the rest of the body. A pair of large shield-like Dilgen *were hung loosely over the saddle on either side, to protect the thighs. (The Royal Armouries, London.)*

One specialist duelling weapon which does turn up occasionally is the German *Schlager* or sabre. This has a large basket to protect the hand and a long slender blade; most date from the later nineteenth century. The *Schlager* was not intended to inflict a mortal wound, however: the combatants often wore goggles, and the duels were between students and fought to definite rules. The principal objective was to inflict cuts upon the opponent's cheek – hence the number of duelling-scarred German officers at the turn of the century. In one or two places the practice may even continue.

The joust and the tournament spawned specialist weapons – partly because many of these contests were intended to be non-lethal, partly because the nature of the combat became so stylized. Tournaments had existed as early as 1100, but at that stage normal fighting weapons were employed and the whole thing was regarded as a realistic training for war. In the words of Roger de Hovenden, 'A youth must have seen his blood flow and felt his teeth crack under the blow of his adversary, and have been thrown to the ground twenty times' before he was ready to see a real war!

Despite initial Church disapproval, the tournament flourished and a special emphasis was put on individual prowess. Often the losers were not killed but 'captured' by the victor, who might demand the loser's horse and armour or a money payment as 'ransom'. Many such events were therefore the medieval equivalent of the later prizefight. Towards the end of the twelfth century, Richard I legalized tournaments in England and introduced new controls: they were held by permission of the King and were subject to a special tax.

*Armour for the tilt of Robert Dudley, Earl of Leicester;
Greenwich armoury, c.1575. Leicester was both England's
senior commander in the Netherlands against the Spanish and
a favourite of Elizabeth I. Although only the parts for the tilt
now remain, this garniture was probably also intended for field
use. Among the embellishments are the initials of the owner,
'R.D.'; the bear and ragged staff of Warwick; and two of
Leicester's decorations – the Order of the Garter and the
French Order of St Michael.*

*At the tilt, the contestants rode either side of a 'tilt' or
barrier, exposing mainly their left sides to the adversary. Tilt
armours are therefore generally thicker or specially adapted on
this side. This armour has provision for additional plates or
'reinforces' on the left. (The Royal Armouries, London.)*

*German tilt armour, probably by Anton Peffenhauser, c.1590.
This was one of the last specialized jousting armours made for
the sport, which went into decline in the seventeenth century.
Peffenhauser (1525–1603) worked at Augsburg, and it is
quite possible that this armour was made for one of the
Bavarian nobility. On the left of the breastplate is a steel shield
or 'targetta', and on the right is a lance rest. The helmet and
breastplate are immensely strong, weighing between them 31 lb
or almost half the weight of the complete harness. (The Wallace
Collection, London.)*

Charles K. Sheridan (far right) dressed for the Eglinton tournament, 1839. An excellent reminder that in the world of arms and armour, as in other fields of antiques, all is often not what it seems. During the early nineteenth century, inspired by the novels of Sir Walter Scott and other Romantic literature, there was a major Gothic revival. The 13th Earl of Eglinton, in Ayrshire, Scotland, went so far as to recreate a whole tournament with the participants clad in reproduction armours. Heavy rain made a fiasco of the day which had to be repeated. The armour in this painting has every appearance of fifteenth-century plate, but it is most certainly one of the reproductions. Replica of high medieval armour continued throughout the nineteenth century alongside gothic churches and domestic architecture, and one was often used to decorate the other. (The Royal Armouries, London.)

German Schlager or duelling sabre, nineteenth century. This example shows several features typical of the type. Most obvious is the very large, round basket formed by narrow bars, offering good protection to the hand. In some variants the bars run both horizontally and vertically, making the guard like a cage. Also typical are the narrow blade and the slightly inclined handgrip. (The Royal Armouries, London.)

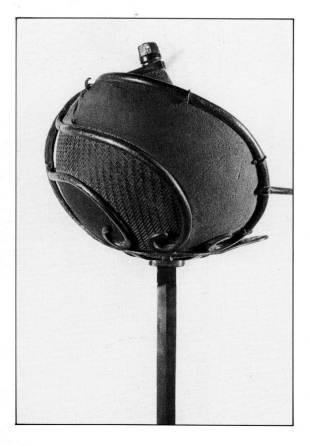

By about 1250 it had become established practice for two knights to run at each other with blunted lances in a 'joust of peace', and special swords were made of whalebone so as not to inflict serious injury. Probably the first piece of armour to be designed for the joust was the 'frog-mouthed' helm of the fourteenth century. The vital design feature of the 'frog-mouth' was that vision was through a narrow slit in the upper surface. The knight could thus take aim through the slit while riding towards his opponent in the 'list' and then raise his head slightly at the last moment, preventing his opponent's lance from reaching his eyes or face.

A proper 'tilt barrier' or fence between two equestrian opponents appears to have been introduced in Italy early in the fourteenth century. This led to further specialist development of the tilt armour, in that it meant that it was the upper left-hand side of the knight which was exposed to the opponent and therefore was more heavily armoured. Helmets similarly tended to have their breathing-holes only on the right, in the least vulnerable area.

With death and disablement now comparatively rare, new scoring methods had to be devised. Unhorsing an opponent was one way of achieving a victory; another was to shatter your lance against the opponent's armour as evidence of a strong, accurate hit. Armours were now often provided with a lance rest on the breastplate, to allow a good aim and to take some of the shock from the arm and shoulder.

From the fifteenth century, the joust became an increasingly organized spectator sport. Special stands were erected for the viewers – royalty and nobility having first claim to the best seats and special boxes. The participants were identified not only by crests on their helmets and 'coats of arms' bearing their symbols but also by small highly painted wooden shields known originally as *Stechtarsche*.

In the German-speaking world, jousts were now divided into the ordinary joust and the *Scharfrenen* ('sharp tilt') or joust of war, in which pointed weapons were used. A new novelty was introduced into the combat in the late fifteenth century, in the form of armours which were designed to shed parts or drop the shield in the event of being hit. The Holy Roman Emperor Maximilian I was one of the most famous practitioners of this form of joust, and he used a special form of mechanical breastplate which flew apart when hit by a lance.

Foot combat or mêlées often followed mounted jousting, and these too evolved their own special arms and armour. In a fifteenth-century German version – the *Kolbenturnier* – the knights fought with clubs and wore large globular helmets. In England, Henry VIII was a keen aficionado of both mounted and dismounted fights, ordering several suits, which still survive, from the royal workshop at Greenwich. For his famous meeting with Francis I of France in 1520, on the Field of the Cloth of Gold, a special 'tonlet' harness for foot combat was assembled. The tonlet was a wide skirt of armour protecting the legs and torso when dismounted.

To have many specialist armours for mounted and dismounted use for war and for parade was the privilege of only the very rich. Partly for this reason, 'garnitures' were evolved in which many pieces of similar styles could be mixed and matched depending on the function for which the armour was to be worn. There might, for example, be only one breastplate but this could be worn with reinforcing plates which could be taken off at will and a number of different helmets.

The tournament continued right through into the early seventeenth century, but by now it was essentially a pageant and a spectacular social gathering. In this spirit, the whole idea was revived in nineteenth-century Britain – as for example in 1839 at Eglinton, in Ayrshire, where the day's festivities were marred by heavy rain. The Victorians similarly made many copies of medieval armours during the 'Gothic revival'. Such pieces are cheaper and easier to collect than their medieval counterparts but still form a significant trap for the unwary.

Lancer of Skinner's Horse 'Tent-pegging' in India, by *John Reynolds Gwatkin (1807–77)*, c.1840. *Probably the most popular sport of skill devised for the lance was tent-pegging. Lancers would ride at speed and attempt to score points by skewering pegs set in the ground. Skinner's Horse was one of many light-cavalry units raised by the British in India, with Indian troops and European officers. Their yellow coats made them most distinctive.*

Most lances of the nineteenth century were of wood, with a metal head and a 'shoe' at the rear end for balance. A short leather strap at the centre often provided a firm grip, and regimental pennons were sometimes flown. Oriental lances were generally light, and often of bamboo, whereas European examples are normally of a more solid wood. 'Langets' or 'cheeks' of metal running down from its head made the lance less vulnerable to breakage or enemy weapons. (The National Army Museum, London.)

INDEX

BIBLIOGRAPHY

Anderson, A.S. *Roman Military Tombstones*, Princes Risborough, 1984.

Arms and Armour *Journal of the Arms and Armour Society*, Society London, (continuing).

Aylward, J.D. *The Small Sword in England*, London, 1945.

Bailey, D.W. *British Military Longarms, 1715–1865*, London, 1986.

Blackmore, D. *Arms and Armour of the English Civil Wars*, London, 1990.

Blackmore, H.L. *British Military Firearms*, London, 1963.

Blackmore, H.L. *Hunting Weapons*, London, 1971.

Blair, C. (Ed). *Pollard's History of Firearms*, Revised Edn., New York, 1985.

Clayton, M. *Victoria and Albert Museum Catalogue of Rubbings of Brasses and Incised Slabs*, London, 1968.

Clepham, R.C. *History and Development of Hand Firearms*, Newcastle, 1906.

Connolly, P. *Greece and Rome at War*, London, 1981.

de Cosson, Baron, and Burgess, W. *Catalogue of the Exhibition of Ancient Helmets and, Examples of Mail*, Chertsey, 1881.

Dowell, W.C. *The Webley Story*, Leeds, 1962.

Durdik, J.,Mudra, M., and Sada, M. *Firearms*, Prague, 1981.

Escritt, L.B. *Rifle and Gun*, London, 1953.

Evans, A.C. *The Sutton Hoo Ship Burial*, London, 1986.

ffoulkes, C. *Arms and Armament*, London, 1945.

Flayderman, N. *Flayderman's Guide to Antique American Firearms*, many editions, Northfield, Illinois, 1978 onwards.

Fournier, F.A. *Museo de Armeria*, Vittoria, 1983.

George, J.N. *English Pistols and Revolvers*, London, 1938.

Goldsmith, D.L. *The Devil's Paintbrush*, Toronto, 1989.

Hayes-McCoy, G.A. *Sixteenth Century Irish Swords*, Dublin, not dated.

Heath, E.G. (Ed) *Bow Versus Gun*, Wakefield, 1973.

Hicks, J. *French Military Weapons*, Connecticut, 1964.

Holmes, M.R. *Arms and Armour in Tudor and Stuart London*, London, 1957.

Grant, M. *Gladiators*, London, 1971.

Kaestlin, J.P. *Museum of Artillery Catalogue of Personal Arms*, London, 1963.

Kennard, A.N. *French Pistols and Sporting Guns*, London, not dated.

Laking, G.F. *Wallace Collection Catalogue: Oriental Arms and Armour*, London, 1914.

May, W.E., and Annis, P.G.W. *Swords for Sea Service*, two vols., National Maritime Museum, 1970.

Meyrick, S.R. *Observations upon the History of Hand Firearms*, London, 1829.

Military Illustrated Magazine, London, 1986 (continuing).

Myatt, F. *Pistols and Revolvers*, London, 1980.

Ncumann, G.C. *Weapons of the American Revolution*, New York, 1967.

Newman, P.R. *A Catalogue of the Sword Collection at York Castle Museum*, York, 1985.

Norman, A.V.B. *The Rapier and Small Sword 1460–1820*, London, 1980.

Norman, A.V.B. *Wallace Collection Catalogue: European Arms and Armour Supplement*, London, 1986.

Norman, A.V.B., and Wilson, G.M. *Treasures from the Tower of London*, University of East Anglia, 1982.

Oakeshott, R.E. *The Sword in the Age of Chivalry*, London, 1964.

Parker, G. *The Military Revolution 1500–1800*, Cambridge University, 1989.

Payne-Gallway, Sir R. *The Crossbow*, London, 1903.

Ritchie, W. F. and J.N.G. *Celtic Warriors*, Princes Risborough, 1985.

Roads, C.H. *The British Soldier's Firearm 1850–1864*, London, 1964.

Roads, C.H. *The Gun*, London, 1978.

Robson, B.E. *Swords of the British Army*, London, 1975.

Rodriguez-Salgado, M.J. *Armada: The Official Catalogue*, National Maritime Museum, 1988.

Russell Robinson, H. *The Armour of Imperial Rome*, London, 1975.

Russell Robinson, H. *Oriental Armour*, London, 1967.

Rule, M. *The Mary Rose*, Leicester, 1983.

Scoffern, J. *Projectile Weapons of War*, London, 1858.

Skennerton I.D., and Richardson R. *British and Commonwealth Bayonets*, Margate, Australia, 1984.

Snodgrass, A.M. *Arms and Armour of the Greeks*, London, 1967.

Stone, G.C. *A Glossary of the Construction, Decoration and Use of Arms and Armour*, New York, 1934.

Tarassuk, L. and Blair, C. *The Complete Encyclopedia of Arms and Weapons*, Milan, 1979.

Temple, B.A., and Skennerton, I.D. *A Treatise on the British Military Martini*, Burbank, I D, Australia, 1983.

Tojhusmuseet, *Billedkatalog for den Permanente Udstilling*, Copenhagen, 1979.

Tweddle, D. *The Coppergate Helmet*, York, 1984.

Wagner, E. *European Weapons and Warfare 1618–1648*, Prague, 1979.

Wahl, P. and Toppel, D. *The Gatling Gun*, London, 1966.

Wallace, J. *Scottish Swords and Dirks*, London, 1970.

Walter, J. *The German Rifle*, London, 1979.

Watson, G.R. *The Roman Soldier*, London, 1969.

Whitelaw, C.E. *Scottish Arms Makers*, London, 1977.

Wilkinson, F. *Arms and Armour*, London, 1978.

Wilkinson-Latham, J. *British Military Swords*, London, 1966.

Winteringham, T., Blashford Snell, J. *Weapons and Tactics*, Baltimore, 1973.

ACKNOWLEDGMENTS

Thanks are due to the following collectors and museums for permission to reproduce photographs:

The Board of Trustees of The Royal Armouries, London: 8 (bottom), 16, 53, 62, 63, 66, 71 (top), 72 (bottom), 78, 79, 80, 82, 86, 88 (bottom), 89, 90, 98 (top), 100 (left), 102 (left), 104, 105, 106, 109, 110, 112, 115, 118, 119, 120, 122, 123, 124, 125 (bottom), 128, 129, 130 (bottom), 135, 138, 142, 144, 145, 150, 152, 160 (bottom), 162 (top), 163 (top), 166, 167, 170, 173 (bottom), 175, 176 (top), 177, 178, 181, 182, 183, 186, 189, 192, 199, 200, 201 (bottom), 204 (left), 207, 209, 210, 211, 212, 215, 216, 218; *The Wallace Collection, London*: 49, 73, 75, 77, 81, 82, 83, 88, 92, 96 (top), 97, 99, 100, 101, 102, 103, 104 (top), 107, 108, 111, 121, 122 (top), 139, 141, 174, 176, 177 (left), 178 (top), 179, 180, 181 (bottom), 184, 185, 186 (right), 187, 188, 196, 200 (right), 202, 207, 208, 212 (top), 215 (top), 217; *The Victoria and Albert Museum, London*: 6, 8 (top), 9, 10, 11, 13, 17, 35, 57, 93, 110, 123 (left), 125, 127, 145 (bottom), 146 (bottom), 156 (top), 205; *The British Museum, London (by courtesy of the Trustees)*: 19, 20, 24, 25, 26, 27, 30, 31, 34, 38, 40, 71, 73, 164, 167, 168, 169, 171; *The British Library, London*: 51, 84, 109, 114, 116, 161 (bottom), 197, 201, 207 (top), 213; *National Army Museum, London*: 130, 131 (top), 136, 148, 160, 162, 163, 182, 190, 191, 219; *The Royal Ordnance Pattern Room, Nottingham*: 145, 147 (top), 152, 154, 155 (top), 157, 159; *The Lancashire County and Regimental Museum, Preston (photography: Mike Seed)*: 140, 142 (top), 143, 151, 155, 183; *By Courtesy of Sotheby's, London*: 17, 61, 192; *By Courtesy of Christie's, London*: 7; *The Museum of London*: 43, 70; *The National Maritime Museum, London*: 134; *The Horniman Museum, London*: 195; *The Museum of Artillery, Woolwich (photography: Cloudy and Bright, London)*: 103 (top); *The National Gallery, London*: 74 (bottom); *Bridgeman Art Library/National Gallery, London*: 94; *The Mary Evans Picture Library, London*: 206; *Lambeth Palace Library, London*: 69;

The Liverpool Museum: 22, 191 (top), 193; *The Corinium Museum, Cirencester*: 31 (bottom), 33; *Museum of Antiquities of the University and Society of Antiquaries of Newcastle-upon-Tyne*: 32 (top), 33; *The National Museum of Antiquities, Edinburgh*: 67 (top), 74; *The National Museums of Scotland, Edinburgh*: 131, 150; *The Colchester Museum*: 34 (left); *Courtesy of York Castle Museum, Dept. of Leisure Services, York City Council*: 41; *The Ashmolean Museum, Oxford*: 25 (top); *The Bodleian Library, Oxford/Woodmansterne Picture Library, Watford*: 61; *Wells Cathedral/Woodmansterne Picture Library*: 60; *Canterbury Cathedral*: 64; *The Master and Fellows of Corpus Christi College, Cambridge*: 49; *Tewkesbury Abbey/Woodmansterne Picture Library*: 56, 58; *The Mary Rose Trust, Portsmouth*: 68; *The National Trust, North Wales*: 130 (top), 203; *Metropolitan Museum, New York*: 23, 70, 76, 83 (top), 96, 98, 121 (top), 165, 204; *Pierpont Morgan Library, New York*: 14, 54, 55; *Library of Congress, Washington D.C.*: 126, 147, 150 (right), 153; *The Smithsonian Institution, Washington D.C.*: 146, 156, 158; *Field Museum of Natural History, Chicago*: 173, 194; *Rock Island Arsenal, Texas*: 161; *Wadsworth Atheneum, Hartford, Connecticut*: 21; *Bayeux Abbey/The Bayeux Tapestry, with special authorisation from the Town of Bayeux*: 44, 46, 47; *Bibliothèque Nationale, Paris*: 52; *Musée de l'Armée, Paris*: 76 (top-left), 132, 133; *The Louvre, Paris*: 28, 45; *Swiss National Museum, Zurich*: 67; *Romisch Germanisches Zentralmuseum, Mainz*: 32; *The National Museum of Denmark, Copenhagen*: 36; *Livrustkammaren, Stockholm*: 108 (right); *The Museum of Nordic Antiquities at Uppsala University (photography: O. Lindman)*: 39; *Universitets Oldsaksamling, Oslo*: 45; *Baghdad Museum, Iraq*: 10 (top); *Archaeological Museum, Nauplia*: 20 (top).

The publishers would like to thank the following photographers for their contribution to this work: Rodney Todd-White & Son, London; Declan Williams, London.